# THE AFRICAN CALIPHATE 2

# The African Caliphate 2

## Ideals, Policies and Operation of the Sokoto Caliphate

### Ibraheem Sulaiman

DIWAN ⊕ PRESS

*Classical and Contemporary Books on Islam and Sufism*

Copyright © Diwan Press Ltd., 2021 CE/1443AH

The African Caliphate 2

Published by:                    Diwan Press Ltd.
                                 311 Allerton Road
                                 Bradford
                                 BD15 7HA
                                 UK
Website:                         www.diwanpress.com
E-mail:                          info@diwanpress.com

Author:                          Ibraheem Sulaiman
Edited by:                       Abdalhaqq Bewley


A catalogue record of this book is available from the British Library.

ISBN-13:                         978-1-914397-13-4 Casebound
                                 978-1-914397-14-1 Paperback
                                 978-1-914397-15-8 Epub and Kindle

# Contents

**Chapter One – A Home for Islam**                       1
The Ideological Divide                                   2
The Directive Principles                                 6

**Chapter Two – A New Dispensation**                     12
Muhammad Bello: *Amir Al-Muminin*                        12
The Constitutional Issues: Abdullahi vs. Bello           15
Reintegrating a Crumbling Edifice                        19
Unity and Rapprochement                                  22

**Chapter Three – The Winds of Change**                  25
The Change in Borno                                      26
The Revolution of Seku Ahmadu                            34
The Revolution of Umar Al-Futi                           36
The Revolution in Yorubaland                             40
Why This Phenomenon?                                     43

**Chapter Four – The Theory of Government**              44
The Imamate                                              44
The *Shura*                                              52
Key Political Institutions                               54
Establishment of Justice                                 57
Preservation of Social Morality                          63
Public Welfare                                           66
The Defence of Islam                                     73

**Chapter Five – The Conception of Law**                 80
A New Legal Process Advocated                            80
The *Shari'a* in a Changing World                        84
*Siyasat al-Shar'iyya*                                   88
*Shari'a* in the Political Process                       93

**Chapter Six – The Encounter with the West**            97
Mungo Park's Mission to the Niger                        98
The Mission to Borno                                     103

Clapperton in Sokoto Caliphate                          110
The Wall had been Breached                              113

**Chapter Seven – Abdullahi Bade His Farewell**         117
Abdullahi on Foundation of Life                         117
Abdullahi on Ethical Values                             122
Abdullahi on Morality                                   128
Abdullahi on *Uswatun Hasana*                           132
Abdullahi on Sufism                                     136
The Man, Abdullahi                                      139

**Chapter Eight – The Policies**                        143
On Principles of Statecraft                             143
Socio-Economic Development                              145
Human Mobilization                                      150
Foreign Policy                                          155

**Chapter Nine – The Imam**                             161
Commitment to Allah                                     161
Family Obligations                                      167
Obligation to Society                                   169
Women as the *Umma's* Conscience                        171
Unity of the *Umma*                                     175
The Epilogue to a Life                                  178

**Chapter Ten – A Sense of History**                    182
Conception of History                                   182
The Vicissitudes of Time                                187
And Behold, Darkness Fell                               192
A Ray of Light in the Darkness                          195

**Glossary**                                            198

# Chapter One

# A Home for Islam

The Sokoto Caliphate emerged from the *tajdid* process which was led by Shehu Usman Dan Fodio (1754-1817). The process of the revolution itself started in 1774, when Shehu Usman was about twenty years old, and culminated in the establishment of *dar al-Islam*, generally known as the Sokoto Caliphate, around 1803. Shehu Usman's death in 1817 brought to an end what we may call the revolutionary phase in the history of the Caliphate, heralding a new phase which covered a period of just over twenty years, from 1817 to 1837. It is that phase, in which the Caliphate was nurtured, with care, anxiety and pain, into the Islamic state and a centre of gravity for Islam in West Africa that is the subject of this study. We are concerned here mainly with the ideals that nourished the Caliphate, enabling it to grow from the city-state of Gobir into a West African super-state, as well as with the architect of it all, *Amir al-Muminin*, Muhammad Bello.

Our first task in this study is to reflect on the ideological basis of this *dar al-Islam*, as espoused by its founding father, Shehu Usman Dan Fodio. It must be said from the outset that the Shehu – as the father of the revolution is generally known – remained the symbol of the Caliphate, its central focus and final arbiter in moments of crisis, for as long as the Islamic dispensation lasted. Even to this day, he remains the veritable symbol of the Muslim *umma* in a considerable part of West Africa. The works of his which we shall be examining presently are as follows: *Kitab al-Farq, Siraj al-Ikhwan; Najm al-Ikhwan; Ta'lim al-Ikhwan; Tanbih al-ikhwan; Tamyiz Ahl al-Sunna; Tamyiz al-Muslimin min al-Kafirin* and *Nasihat Ahl al-Zaman*.

## The Ideological Divide

Mankind is divided, in its beliefs and ideologies, into two distinct categories – the unbelievers and the believers. This is the truth attested to in the Qur'an, where it is said: *'It is He who created you. Yet among you are unbelievers and among you are believers.'* (64:2) This divide, which transcends race and social and economic differences, lies at the very root of most, if not all, historical struggles. The believer struggles to make Islam supreme, the unbeliever struggles to make his faith supreme. The difference that exists between a believer and an unbeliever is not merely one of opinion: it is a profound difference, embracing at once ideals, morality, politics, culture and attitudes. No society exists in an ideological vacuum: all societies subscribe to a set of beliefs and assumptions which dictate their conduct, law and attitudes, as well as their goals. This is what creates the difference, and, in most cases the conflict, between one society and another, between one political and social persuasion and another, between one civilization and another.

The *tajdid* process was no different from this historical imperative: it was essentially a struggle between believers and unbelievers; and, in a political context, a struggle between tyrants and the advocates of justice. In short, the Sokoto dispensation was a repetition of the ever-recurrent drama involving the conflict between David and Goliath. In a struggle of this kind, you start first by cultivating your ideals and rebuilding the human mind according to them; you challenge the forces of decadence and oppression, who then strike back. As unbelief or tyranny feels more and more threatened, it resorts to coercion, bringing into being the phases of *hijra* and *jihad*. The latter is the most intensive stage in the process of *tajdid*: it serves, on the one hand, to purge the revolution of its wayward elements and graces some of its sincere elements with martyrdom; and on the other hand, *jihad* serves as a cleansing exercise, to rid the world of tyranny, together with its institutions and the men who symbolise it. To that extent, such a revolution, despite the bloodshed and destruction associated with it, can be seen as a blessing in its elimination of oppression and its creation of a new world with definite moral values and social commitment. People are given a new lease of life and a sense of direction after a long period of decay and aimlessness.

In the specific situation of Hausaland, this struggle was carried out on two levels – one intellectual and the other political. The first level involved an understanding of who was a Muslim – a believer – on the one hand and who was a non-Muslim – an unbeliever – on the other. This is the theme of many works of the Shehu, particularly those written during the *hijra-jihad* phase. In both *Tamyiz al-Muslimin* and *Siraj al-Ikhwan*[i] a Muslim is defined as a person who affirms his belief in Allah and in Muhammad as His Messenger, who keeps his faith pure and safeguards it against corruption, and practises Islam as laid down in the *shari'a* to the best of his ability. Moreover, he does not mingle Islamic belief or practices with those of *kufr*, nor mock or deny any of the essential elements of Islamic faith and practice. An unbeliever, on the other hand, is a person who does not affirm sound belief in Allah and His Messenger; he worships idols of all sorts; he mingles the practices of Islam with those of *kufr* – such as prostrating to trees and venerating pagan places of worship – even though he might claim to be a Muslim; and he speaks lightly of Islam and ridicules its sacred institutions.

Even though the distinction was sharp enough, the Shehu felt it necessary, in *Tamyiz Ahl al-Sunna*, to distinguish between those who desired the victory of Islam over *kufr* and those who did not mind where the victory went. A Muslim, in those circumstances, was not merely a person who believed *per se*, but rather a person who both believed and practised Islam and, in addition, hated unbelief, its symbols and men. An outright association with Islam and solidarity with fellow Muslims was demanded as an additional mark of belief. A person who, in spite of being a Muslim, fraternised with unbelievers and innovators and sought worldly benefits from them was, to all intents and purposes, a hypocrite but nevertheless remained a member of the *umma*, however tenuous his membership might appear to be.

All this was an attempt, on the part of the *tajdid* movement, to unite the Muslims on a clear-cut ideological basis and to consolidate their ranks. It was also an effort to instil in them the consciousness

i    Published in 1960s by Northern Nigerian Government but now apparently out of print. Its full title is *Siraj al-Ikhwan fi Ahamm ma Ahtaj ilayhi fi hadha Zaman.* It was written as an apology for the revolution.

of being a distinct and separate community, socially, morally, and ideologically. This fraternal solidarity of believers was meant to cover not only the pursuit of a common cause – the victory of Islam – but also the social relationships between the believers in a way that would identify them as an *umma* distinct from the rest of the people – as prestigious members of the family of Allah. 'I urge you, O people of the Sunna,' the Shehu declared in *Tamyiz Ahl al-Sunna*, 'to seek out your fellow believers whenever you travel; to associate with them, stay with them on your journeys; eat with them and offer them gifts, your assistance and help. Whoever does this will die a believer, and Allah will answer his prayer whenever he supplicates to Him.' At the same time, the people of the Sunna had to keep their distance from those who were the declared enemies of Allah. 'How,' the Shehu asked, 'could anyone claim to be a lover of Allah if he fraternised with His enemies?' Here the Shehu seemed to be saying that the notion of *ahl al-sunna* is not merely a question of doctrine; it is in a fundamental sense a question of ideological and moral commitment. Whoever genuinely strives to make Islam victorious belongs to the *ahl al-sunna*, and is a member of the family of Allah. And whoever fraternises with the un-Islamic forces and does not care about the progress of Islam cannot claim to belong to that noble fraternity.

On the political front, the process of integrating the Muslims into one large and loving family of Allah naturally led to a desire on their part to look for the 'home of Islam', the home of justice, as opposed to the home of the tyranny to whose rule they had been subjected. There was no doubt about the intellectual and moral superiority, which Muslims have over the unbelievers, and Shehu Usman's intensive educational, spiritual and moral programmes helped to sharpen the social consciousness of those who were being mobilized for change. It was this consciousness, which permeated all corners of society, that alarmed the ruling class – the oppressors. Muslims gained awareness of the fact that idol-worshippers, corrupt and inept rulers and tyrants had no moral right to rule over them and be their masters. It was beneath their dignity as believers to subordinate themselves to such tyrants. They had a duty, they were told, to seek the means to live as Muslims, to secure their own dignity and the integrity of Islam – in short, to overthrow the unbelieving power and establish the *dar al-Islam*.

In both *Ta'lim al-Ikhwan*[i] and *Tanbih al-Ikhwan*[ii] the Shehu justified his rising in arms against the Sudanese kings. Four broad reasons were given. Firstly, most of the rulers were idol-worshippers. The Hausa rulers in particular, the Shehu stated in *Ta'lim al-Ikhwan*, paid homage to trees and stones, made animal sacrifices to them and turned to them for the fulfilment of their needs. Thus they were unbelievers, even if they prayed and fasted and performed other rites of Islam. Secondly, the Sudanese kings consciously obstructed the path of Islam: they prevented people from becoming Muslim, persecuted those who had already joined its fold and organised their policies to favour pagan customs and institutions. They therefore, in Shehu's eyes, behaved in the manner of Pharaoh, and rising against them was perfectly justified. Thirdly, the kings were secular rulers: while pretending outward respect for Islam and its institutions and values, they, nevertheless, subordinated Islam to secular considerations and policies. They never, for example, fought in the name of Islam in their numerous wars, nor undertook the spread and consolidation of Islam. Instead they devoted themselves wholly to this world, acquiring its glory as avidly as they could.

Finally, in spite of all these considerations, it was not the Muslims who started the fight; it was the unbelieving powers that tried to crush them and annihilate Islam, as we are told in *Tanbih al-Ikwan*. The revolution was, therefore, provoked by the need of the Muslims to defend their faith, their lives, their family and their possessions. In other words, the *jihad* was forced on the Shehu and his movement, the *Jama'a*. The final stages before the revolution exploded were described by Abdullahi Dan Fodio whom the Shehu quoted in *Tanbih*:

i    BG. Martin's translation has been used here. See his 'Unbelief in the Western Sudan: Uthman dan Fodio's *Ta'lim al-Ikhwan*' in Middle Eastern Studies, 4, 1967-8, pp. 50-97.
ii    Palmer's translation is referred to here. See his 'An Early Fulani Conception of Islam'. Journal of African Studies, 13, 14, 1914-15.

So we fled from their land in the year 1218 A.H. [1803]... to a place outside Gobir territory. The Muslims all fled, following us. Many of them joined us with their people and property; some brought nothing but their people; some came with no following at all. The Sultan of Gobir ordered his chiefs to seize the goods of all who fled or prevent them leaving. Then he ordered those of the chiefs nearest to us on the East to keep on killing our people, and plundering and imprisoning. The people suffered sorely.

And Hausaland, in consequence, exploded. The Hausa establishment, by seeking to crush Islam, brought about its own end.

On the whole, the revolution was effected, as in all other Islamic revolutions, not in order for one set of people to annihilate another, or gain political ascendancy and land. It was principally aimed to achieve four things: to make the word of Allah supreme; to bring unbelief, corruption and tyranny to naught; to bring dignity and honour to Muslims and save them from the humiliation of having to live under an un-Islamic power; and finally to give people – Muslims and non-Muslims alike – the opportunity to enjoy a life in a territory ennobled by faith, permeated by morality and justice.

**The Directive Principles**

It may be worthwhile here to attempt to piece together some of the principles which the Shehu himself, especially in the last days of his life, put forward as a guide for state policy for all time. One could see in the Shehu an ardent desire to ensure the survival of the Caliphate, for which he had fought so hard. One need only go through the account of the *jihad* and what it reveals of the long and arduous trek – covering hundreds of miles – that Muslims had to undergo, enduring starvation, epidemics, deprivation, insecurity and death, to see how much they had invested to attain their *dar al-Islam*. 'Our country was ruined,' lamented Muhammad Bello in *Infaq al-Maysur*,[i] when assessing the effects of the struggle. It was now his responsibility to rebuild it, this time on Islamic principles.

i    Cairo edition.

The first principle nurtured by Shehu Usman is the absolute sanctity of the institution of the caliph. Four points, in particular, are worth considering from Shehu's elaboration of this principle in *Misbah ahl al-Zaman*[i] and *Najm al-Ikhwan*[ii]:

(i)     The caliphal office is an institution of the *shari'a* unanimously accepted by *ahl al-sunna* as valid and imperative.

(ii)    Giving *bay'ah* to the holder of this office is therefore obligatory; so also is showing loyalty to him both inwardly and outwardly, if only for the purpose of ensuring the unity and cohesion of the *umma*. 'Preserving the proper order of the *umma* is obligatory and promoting the well-being of the people is obligatory'; these two obligations cannot be met unless the *bay'ah* itself is secure.

(iii)   The need to preserve the caliphal institution is explicated by the purposes which it serves: it upholds the law and applies the *hudud*; it safeguards the territorial integrity of the Islamic state; it forestalls general disorder and bloodshed. In addition, the institution serves as a channel through which Allah spreads his bounty to the people; the earth and its people are nourished, and nations built and made to flourish by it; the economy thrives and people's wealth is made safe through it; above all, it is the caliphal institution that ensures the glory and supremacy of Islam, eliminates injustice and subdues corrupt people.

(iv)    Therefore, Muslims must think carefully before they throw off their *bay'ah* to this office. They must base their actions on two considerations: firstly, that the injustice of a given caliph may not be in any way comparable to the benefits which the institution itself provides for the *umma*, as a means through which people's welfare is maintained; and secondly, that it is the moral standards of the populace that determine the quality of its rulers. In short, patience rather than rebellion should be the the attitude of the people

---

i     MS in author's possession.
ii    Published privately by Alhaji Abdullahi Magayaki.

towards their caliphs. For, if the institution is destroyed, 'Allah will never again cast even a glance on the world.'

It is this principle, above all, that made the Sokoto Caliphate a going concern for a whole century. Certainly there were rebellions and, at times, upheavals of almost catastrophic proportion; but loyalty to the institution of the caliphate, rather than individual caliphs, always prevailed. Moreover, the caliphs never maintained a standing army; they relied on people's loyalty for the defence of the realm against both external and internal enemies. Prof. Last sums up the application of this principle in *The Sokoto Caliphate*:[i] 'Collectively, the Caliphate, in moral authority if not in armed force, was too strong to be broken.'

The supremacy of the law as the basis of all actions and policies further strengthened the Caliphate. It was created purposely to uphold the *shari'a* and apply the *hudud*. This principle, Prof. Abdullahi Smith[ii] has pointed out, remained in force throughout the entire life of the Sokoto Caliphate, where rulers had to justify their actions and policies on the basis of the sacred law. As he puts it:

Why must emirs consult their subjects before taking decisions? Because God said so. Why must emirs not take bribes? Because the last of the Prophets of God said so. Throughout the *jihad* literature it is the authority of the Qur'an and the accepted traditions that was invariably quoted to justify the ideals of government which emirs must continually have in mind. No other authority was adequate.

In the final analysis it was the absolute commitment to the application of the *shari'a* in almost all its ramifications – and clearly to a greater degree than can be found in Islamic history outside the *rashidun* period – that upheld the unity of the Caliphate. The *shari'a*, in effect, preserved the Caliphate, and not the other way round. As Prof. Last puts it: 'Respect for the Law and Islam was the source of authority for the Sokoto Caliphate. So long as the Caliph upheld the *shari'a*, he was unimpeachable, and those who denied his authority were unbelievers... The universal nature of the Law, having an existence and validity separate from the Sokoto Caliphate, gave

i    Longman (London), 1977.
ii   'The Ideal of Development Administration: an historical perspective', Journal of Public Affairs, Ahmadu Bello University, Zaria, Vol. 1 May, 1971.

Sokoto the power it did not have militarily. The emirs outside Sokoto ... respected this Law, and obeyed Sokoto as established under it... [The Law] gave to their position the same universal legality which the Caliphate possessed.'

The third principle emphasised the necessity for the Caliphate to pursue vigorously the integration of the Muslim *umma*. This entailed first of all the internal organisation of the society to ensure social harmony based on justice and brotherhood. If this required the subduing of venal scholars, rebels and all those who would seek to destroy the harmony of the *umma* by military means, so be it. On the other hand, the policy of integration entailed the absorption of weak and fragmented Muslim communities into the *dar al-Islam*, by peaceful means if possible, or by force of arms if need be. What was required was for the *umma* to remain strong and impregnable: this was a priority. 'It is not lawful,' Shehu stated in *Siraj al-Ikhwan*,[i] quoting al-Maghili, 'for a group of Muslims to remain without a ruler' or an effective government. 'So strive against them with the sword until they all enter into [the bond of] obedience to God and His Messenger. This is one of the worthiest and most important *jihad*s.' Oppressive rulers in Muslim countries should be fought 'as long as your fighting them is for the victory of the truth over falsehood, and the victory of the oppressed over the oppressor'. But all viable and just Islamic nations must be treated with absolute deference as sister nations belonging to the universal Islamic community. Integration, as conceived in the Caliphate, rests on two pillars: the need to establish Islam as a power above all powers, dictating trends rather than being dictated to; and the imperative for Muslims to resist oppression with the purpose of eliminating it, even if the perpetrators claim to be Muslims.

Then there is the principle that one of the fundamental functions of the Caliphate is to promote the welfare of Muslims and ensure maximum social justice. The Shehu, says Prof. Abdullahi Smith, 'continually cries out against bribery and corruption in government and the general immorality of officials, and emphasises the need

i    John Hunwick's translation has been used here. See his 'Al-Maghili's replies to the questions of Askia Al-Hajj Muhammad.' PhD. dissertation, University of London, 1974, pp. 279-47, for positive action by government to promote the welfare of the people. The chief official of the Sokoto Caliphs held the title *amir al-masalih* which could, I suppose, be translated ... as officer in charge of public welfare.' After noting in *Kitab al-Farq*[i] that the system of government which the Caliphate had displaced was characterised by arbitrary rule without respect for the *shari'a*, decadent luxury and universal corruption, as well as dispossession of the poor, the Shehu pledged that the Islamic government would in all respects create a society in which there would be justice and moral rectitude. The Caliphate would effect, as Abdullahi Smith puts it, 'spiritual reform aimed at raising the moral tone of society and providing a, social ideology in accordance with Islamic ideas'.

Then there would be universal dissemination of knowledge under a system of education based fundamentally on the Qur'an. There would be a reformed economic system which emphasised improvement of markets, the development of communication and the provision of social services to the poor and needy. The Shehu also promised to safeguard the economic well-being of the state by the strictest judicial control over the financial transactions of government and to promote the moral good of society.

The last principle for our consideration relates to the relationship between Muslims and non-Muslims. Here the Shehu established five guidelines aimed at covering the various possibilities in the relationship.

(i)    There is a relationship between Muslims and non-Muslims which is dictated purely by natural human sentiments, such as loving a neighbour, or a beautiful woman or a person from whom one has experienced an act of goodness or kindness. Since this love is inherent, it is outside the sphere of human responsibility, and can be considered to be without blame.

(ii)    A relationship dictated by force of circumstances, where Muslims must necessarily show open deference to non-Muslim powers, is permissible provided the regard shown is 'with the tongue, not the heart'.

i    Hiskett's translation, see his '*Kitab al-Farq*: a work on the Habe Kingdoms attributed to Uthman Dan Fodio' in Bulletin of the School of Oriental and African Studies, 25, 1960.

(iii) Any relationship which involves a severe compromise of Islam's vital interests, such as the surrendering of sovereignty, or of economic independence, and which makes Muslims dependent on non-Muslims, is prohibited.

(iv) A relationship whose purpose is to help non-Muslims repel oppression, obtain justice or rights due to them and which, in general, is intended to promote noble causes, is obligatory. 'It is permissible,' the Shehu said, 'to walk hand in hand with a Christian in order to fight oppression, or intercede in a good cause.' Moreover, it is necessary for Muslims to treat non-Muslims justly, equitably and compassionately in order to attract them to Islam.

(v) A relationship where Muslims support non-Muslims in causes contrary to the *shari'a*, such as those intended to weaken Islam or annihilate it or to raise unbelief above Islam is forbidden, as it borders on unbelief,

The Shehu did not leave anyone in doubt as to the kind of state he wanted the Sokoto Caliphate to be: a *dar al-Islam* that would approximate, as far as the exigencies of time could allow, the *Khilafa al-Rashida*, run by the upright caliphs.

# Chapter Two

# A New Dispensation

## Muhammad Bello: *Amir Al-Muminin*

The election of Muhammad Bello as the *Amir al-Muminin* on 3 *Jumada al-Akhir* 1232/20 April 1817 by the electoral college, comprising leaders, scholars and military commanders, can be said to mark the beginning of a new dispensation. For what emerged subsequently, be it political strategies, institutions, policies or even the ultimate shape of the Caliphate itself, bore the mark of Muhammad Bello. It may be said in passing that the electoral college elected Bello on the same day that Shehu Usman died, thus complying with the view held by the Shehu, in *Bayan Wujub al-Hijra*, that a new caliph should be elected before the incumbent's burial – a view based on the events leading to the appointment of Abu Bakr after the death of the Prophet Muhammad ﷺ.

There were two main candidates for the office of the caliph. The first was Shehu Abdullahi – although it has yet to be proved that he bid for the office – universally acclaimed as the champion of justice, the finest scholar in the Caliphate, and, above all, the veritable conscience of the revolution. The other was Muhammad Bello, the hero of Alkalawa, who led the battle that brought the old order to an irrevocable end. In the event, Muhammad Bello emerged as the choice of *ahl al-ikhtiyar*, the electoral college, and the community duly paid the mandatory *bay'ah* to him. Some scholars, separated from the momentous event by well over a century and a half, have sought to read motives into the decision of the electoral college. Prof. Sani Zahradeen,[i] for example, has suggested that some of the electors were apprehensive that, if Abdullahi became caliph, 'they

---

i    Zahradeen, "Abd Allah ibn Fodio's Contribution to the Fulani *Jihad* in Nineteenth century Hausaland.' Ph.D. dissertation, McGill University, 1976, pp. 181-2.

would have to change their lifestyles and some of them might even be killed'. This younger generation 'who favoured moderate luxury within the bounds of *shari'a*' pressed for the appointment of Bello. Dr. Balogun[i] saw the reason for appointing Bello as hinging mainly on the fact that he was 'realistic and flexible' in his interpretation of the *shari'a*, in contrast to Shehu Abdullahi who was supposed to be 'strict and inflexible'. These motives have not been substantiated. Even though the two candidates differed on many points of law, they maintained the greatest respect for each other, Abdullahi describing his nephew and student in *Tazyin* as 'a raging lion, leading other lions.' And Bello described his mentor as 'our blessed Shaykh ... the sword of God against the innovators, a mine of sincerity and knowledge'.[ii] Indeed, the two had played complementary roles in the *jihad*: Abdullahi started it all with his remarkable victory at Tabkin Kwatto, and Bello completed the victory five years later at Alkalawa.

Muhammad Bello[iii] was born in 1195/1781 as the third son of Shehu Usman Dan Fodio. It was a time when the father was already busy calling people to Islam. He was largely educated by his father and his uncle, Abdullahi. He studied the fundamental sources of Islam, Qur'an and hadith, with his father; he read in this regard some of the major *tafsir* work: al-Baydawi, al-Baghawi and *Lubab al-Tawil*, then in hadith, Bukhari, Muslim, al-Tirmidhi, Ibn Majah, al-Nasa'i and Abu Dawud. His father also taught him much *fiqh* – Islamic jurisprudence. He studied Arabic, some aspects of jurisprudence and Sufism with his uncle. Philosophy, *tawhid*, science of divination, medicine and other subjects, like other students in the western Sudanese scholarly tradition, he learned from as many scholars as were available to him.

i    Balogun, 'The position of Gwandu in the Sokoto Caliphate', in *Studies in the History of the Sokoto Caliphate*, ed. Yusuf B. Usman (1979), pp. 282-3.
ii    Zahradeen, *'Abd Allah ibn Fodio's Contribution*, p. 201.
iii    This profile draws fundamentally from Mahmud Minna's doctoral thesis: *Sultan Muhammad Bello and his intellectual contribution to the Sokoto Caliphate*, University of London, 1982, chapter one; and Omar Bello's doctoral thesis to the same university, *The Political Thought of Muhammad Bello (1781-1837) as revealed in his Arabic writing more especially al-Ghayth al-Wabi fi Sirat al-Imam al-Adl*, 1983, chapter three.

Bello grew up in an atmosphere which was immensely favourable to the shaping of his character. The first and foremost aspect was the influence of a father absolutely dedicated to knowledge and deeply involved in the building of an Islamic order. The influence of the Shehu was the most profound inspiration in Bello's life. 'From the time I grew up and read the Qur'an and the books of knowledge,' he said, 'I have been with the Shehu, observing his character and listening to his words.' The result is predictable. 'I have acquired, as a result of the Shehu's blessing, such knowledge and fame, that riders carry it about and night chatterers talk about it daily.'

Secondly, Bello was himself blessed by Allah with intelligence, love for learning and boundless energy. 'I became well-known,' he himself recounted, 'among other students for being indefatigable and untiring, and acquired tremendous knowledge within a very short time.' He was thus able to read widely and tirelessly; he reckoned that he had read over twenty thousand titles.

In the third place, he grew up in an entirely revolutionary atmosphere so that at the age of ten he had acquired enough social consciousness to talk about the impending *jihad*. Gidado Dan Laima wrote in *al-Kashf wal Bayan*:[i]

Among what he [Bello] heard from his father was in the following manner: The Sheikh gathered together his children and said to them, 'I have seen that the custom in this country is that anyone who is favoured by a worldly ruler would gather his children and take them to the ruler so that he might know them. Bear you witness that I would only take you to the presence of the Merciful (i.e. Allah). So promise me that none of you will ever go to the rulers of the world throughout your lives.' They promised him this.

When the Muslims swore allegiance to Bello as the Imam, his character had already been formed, he had a firm grounding intellectually and morally, and he had acquired political and military skill out of all proportion to his age. Gidado summed up his personality in these words:

---

i   Quotations from *al-Kashf wal Bayan* are taken from Malumfashi's *The Life and ideas of Sheikh Uthman, being an edited translation of Rawd al-Jirian and Kashf wal Bayan*, 6. M.A. dissertation, Ahmadu Bello University, 1971, Part Two.

He, may Allah be pleased with him, lived a good life in a praiseworthy situation in seeking knowledge, serving it and striving after it. He was endowed with intelligence, insight ... and wisdom ... He distinguished between all sciences and had a firm grasp over the meanings and mystical knowledge and has penetrated into secret and subtle matters. He was favoured by Divine happiness and was singled out for Divine care. The illumination of his father, the Sheikh, pervaded him and the Sheikh's blessing and goodness encompassed him. Through the praise of Allah, he became God's sign in His land: an army, the wonder of which ceases not, like the ocean.

## The Constitutional Issues: Abdullahi vs. Bello

Three weeks after the appointment of Muhammad Bello as *Amir al-Muminin*, Shehu Abdullahi published his controversial treatise, *Sabil al-Salama fil lmama*.[i] His purpose in writing it, he said, was to throw some light on what constitutes an Islamic government so that people could guard against adopting un-Islamic ways in government. It appears, from the content of the work, that Abdullahi, and perhaps several other scholars, were not altogether comfortable with the trend that the appointment of Muhammad Bello had set in motion. The Caliphate, Shehu Abdullahi feared, was moving rather too closely towards the pre-Islamic system of government: monarchy. The small treatise generates a constitutional debate between him and the Caliph, which we will presently examine.

Abdullahi noted the necessity for the *Shura*, or the Constituent Assembly, to elect the Imam, rather than his being appointed by an incumbent imam, or worse, coming to power by hereditary succession. It is improper for an incumbent imam to designate his son or his father as his successor – for this, Abdullahi felt, is monarchical, even if acceptable to some prominent jurists. Once he has been properly elected and people have duly offered their *bay'ah* to him, the Imam should be obeyed and no one should be allowed to contest his leadership. Loyalty, however, is conditional upon his being upright and just; if he is unjust, oppressive or immoral, then a

---

i    MS in author's possession.

contender could be supported against him '*until the religion of Allah becomes supreme*', in other words, until justice and the rule of law prevail. Abdullahi was in effect saying that two things are essential to establish the legitimacy of a government: firstly, its acceptance by the people resulting from their participation in the appointment of the Imam; and secondly, the government's commitment to justice and the rule of law.

Abdullahi proceeded to discuss the characteristics of Islamic government, contrasting it, by implication, with those of un-Islamic government – using the history of the early caliphate as his frame of reference.[i] As far as he was concerned, an Islamic government has the following fundamental characteristics.

1.  Leadership is based on merit. The office of the Imam goes to the person with the greatest merit in society – piety being the barometer by which to measure merit. The *umma* can be trusted to possess the inherent ability and sense of self-preservation to entrust its affairs to the best of its number. It is therefore safer and more appropriate to let the *umma* choose its leaders by itself.

2.  *Shari'a* is supreme. An Islamic government is subject to the rule of law in absolute terms and it thus operates as a nomocracy. The law here is the *shari'a* – the Qur'an, Sunna and the consensus of the *umma*. Abu Bakr, we are told by Abdullahi, would first consult the Qur'an when faced with a problem, then the hadith, and then the opinion of his council, abiding by its majority decision. He never ruled arbitrarily, but kept himself within the bounds of law. It was his view that Islam does not permit a government to exceed its limits, especially on issues involving the fundamental rights of its people.

3.  Wealth belongs to Allah. All wealth and state resources belong to Allah. This implies that the state has the prerogative, and indeed the obligation, to hold those resources on behalf of society – as a trust from Allah. State wealth does not belong to the ruler, nor to his government, much less to certain individuals or families, it belongs to the entire *umma*, symbolized by Allah.

4.  Protection for the weak. Islamic government has an abiding obligation to protect the weak and poor. State policies should be

i    Abdullah's sole reference here is Jalal al-din al-Suyuti's *Tarikh al-Khulafa*. The English translation of the work by Major H.S. Jarrett is referred to in the present work. It comes under the title *History of the Caliphs*, Karachi, 1977.

geared towards protecting their social and economic interests, and curbing the excesses of the strong and the wealthy, until economic and social balance is established in society.

5. Justice made to prevail. The establishment of justice is of paramount concern. What distinguishes the Imam or caliph from a monarch is that the former is known for being just and latter for being unjust. A caliph generates revenues from lawful sources and disburses them as required by law; a monarch, on the other hand, generates revenues by illegal methods and distributes them arbitrarily – especially as largesse to his relatives.

6. Evil is combated. Islamic government fights evil and corruption with all the force at its disposal. Abdullahi indicated that once a state compromises on justice and allows nepotism and misuse of public property to take place, it is bound to fail.

An un-Islamic government is symbolized by monarchy. It is based on a family relationship, by which a person accedes to power by inheritance; it operates without the proper institution of *Shura* – whereby people participate in the decision-making process as of right – and rules arbitrarily, without being accountable to the people.

In an 'instant rejoinder', to use the words of Mahmud Minna in *Al-Insaf fi Dhikr mafi Masail fil Khilafa*,[i] Muhammad Bello forwarded his own views about legitimate government. There is nothing wrong, he said, in an incumbent ruler designating his son to succeed him if the latter has the necessary qualifications, nor in *ahl al-ikhtiyar*, the Constituent Assembly, electing the son of an incumbent. The qualifications which the electoral college should look for in a candidate for the caliphal office include knowledge of the law, courage and firmness in uprooting corruption and injustice and implementing the *hudud*, uprightness in conduct as well as *adala*, an impeccable moral record and demonstrable inclination to justice. He agreed with Abdullahi that the ruler must be elected, not imposed.

i   MS in author's possession. Also, Mahmud Minna's 'Succession and legitimacy: the leadership crisis and intellectual dispute between Abdullahi and Bello.' Paper presented to Seminar on Sultan Muhammed Bello, University of Sokoto, April, 1985.

A state could be blessed with several people possessing the necessary qualifications for leadership. Other factors have therefore, according to Bello, to be considered. The most important is the political climate prevailing at the time of the election. Thus, if the pressing issue of the day is how to integrate the Muslim *umma* in the face of rebellion and general disorder, then a candidate who has the ability to integrate society must be elected rather than a more learned one. Or if there is a fear that the more qualified candidate might not be acceptable to the people, then the more acceptable candidate should be chosen. To ensure that the right candidate is chosen, given the circumstances of the time, the members of the electoral college must be men of *adala*, possessing the political sense and wisdom to make the right choice.

Muhammad Bello postulated a third option: that of the Imamate being taken by force. If, in a climate of general dissension and disorder, this happens, the issue that the *umma* has to grapple with, as he saw it, is not so much as who the *de jure* leader is as who the *de facto* one is. In that situation, he said, quoting al-Qurtubi, 'its rightful owners should not contend with the new ruler because the question is he who rules, not he who is the rightful person. Obedience is necessary from everybody and patience in such a situation is better than working towards impairing relationship.'

Our discussion so far suggests that there was a fundamental conceptual disagreement between Shehu Abdullahi and Muhammad Bello. Abdullahi did not question Bello's qualifications; his fear lay probably in the fact that the trend towards monarchy might yet prove unstoppable and the Muslims in the Caliphate might subsequently lose their right to choose their caliph. Muhammad Bello, on the other hand, did not feel that his election amounted to a compromise of the Islamic principles: he was, after all, qualified, and absolutely dedicated to the objectives of Islam; and he possessed the necessary ability as well as the broad appeal which were needed in the immediate circumstances to integrate the restive community. Mahmud Tukur sums up the two standpoints:[i]

i    Tukur, *Values and Public Affairs: The relevance of the Sokoto Caliphal experience to the transformation of the Nigerian polity.* Ph.D. dissertation, Ahmadu Bello University, 1977, pp. 249-53,

While Abdullahi ... remains faithfully wedded to the tenets which he and the Shehu developed and taught initially, Caliph Bello built on the accommodationist ideas which his father began to introduce in 1812 ... Moreover, while Abdullahi has assumed freedom of action for the *ahl al-ikhtiyar,* Bello allows the incumbent leader to nominate, or even pre-empt the selectors, by making the appointment himself ... Bello had not uttered a word on hereditary succession and it seems justifiable to assume that the studied silence is not accidental. His appointments not long after his assumption of office indicate that he found it impossible to avoid hereditary succession.

Moreover, as Mahmud Tukur observes further, Bello's argument seems to have carried the day – the Caliphate had veered almost irrevocably in the direction of monarchy. 'Whichever selection system ultimately prevails,' says Tukur in support of Bello's stand, 'beliefs and political values have to contend with the tendency for dynasties to form and perpetuate themselves in politics, business or the professions because of man's process of socialisation. It is, after all, in groups that mankind is initially raised. To the extent that this observation encapsulates the facts of human condition, to that extent Bello's understanding of the idea of succession carries the day.' But Abdullahi's objections, and the principles he espoused so forcefully, proved, in the final analysis, to be far-sighted, indeed, impressively prophetic.

### Reintegrating a Crumbling Edifice

The Shehu, on his death bed, told his son who was then in charge of the eastern parts of the Caliphate and destined to succeed him: 'When I am gone, the whole country will go back to paganism. Those who have seen the light, have seen it because of me. You will find yourself in difficulty and there will be no one to help you.' The Shehu's dying words, Prof. Abdullahi Smith has observed, came true.

'The people of Sokoto swore allegiance to his son, and on the same day the whole land of Zamfara abandoned the faith.

This was perhaps to be expected, for pagans like Zamfarawa could not be converted to Islam overnight, and the death of the Shehu followed by the installation of his warlike son was the signal for revolt. At the same time the reaction to Bello's installation by his brother Ariku was in doubt, and uncle Abdullahi held aloof in Gwandu. Reports of revolt in Katsina and among Gwari were also coming in. And then only a few miles to the north of Sokoto one of the oldest supporters of the Shehu, the Hausa *muallam* Abd al-Salam dan Ibrahim, turned against his new masters.'[i]

This was in addition to the revolt of other states, notably Kebbi and Gobir. The situation was indeed precarious, for it seemed as if the entire structure of the Caliphate was on the brink of total collapse. The social order was, it appeared, disintegrating. This, nevertheless, was not unexpected as far as Muhammad Bello was concerned, for he knew that the Arabs apostatized in the wake of the death of the Prophet 👼.

It was his responsibility, now, to hasten to administer medicine before the disease took hold: that is, to crush the revolts and hold back the mad rush towards apostasy, as Abu Bakr had done in the early days of Islam, with the decisiveness which the situation demanded. At first Muslim forces faced defeat after defeat, but eventually, thanks to their perseverance, they regained the initiative, enabling them to put down most of the revolts. The most serious of the revolts was that of Abdus Salam who was not only a scholar in his own right, but a companion of the Shehu and a prominent figure in the *jihad*.[ii] It was the attack on his followers by the Gobir forces that had sparked off the *jihad* initially. His revolt was not like that of Zamfara or Kebbi or Gobir, which could easily be explained as apostasy, it was a crack in the structure of the *Jama'a* and, if sustained, could cause a serious rent in the political and social cohesion of the Caliphate. The Caliph was thus put in a moral dilemma: on the one hand, he had to give Abdus Salam the respect and deference he commanded

---

i    Smith, 'Muhammad Bello, *Amir al-Muminin'* in *Ibadan* No. 9, June, 1960. See generally, pp. 16-19.

ii   This section draws heavily from Mahmud Minna's discussion of the revolt of Abd al-Salam. See especially pp. 68-90 of his work, *Sultan Muhammad Bello.*

as a scholar, a companion of the Shehu and a prominent fighter in the cause of Allah; and on the other, he had to preserve the cohesion of the Caliphate and retrieve its integrity no matter whose interests were affected as a result.

Abdus Salam's tendency to revolt had been longstanding. Even when the Shehu was alive he had attempted a revolt. He was brought to the Shehu who rebuked him and threatened to disown him if he continued with his recalcitrant attitude. And when Bello assumed office as caliph, Abdus Salam at first refused to pay him the *bay'ah* and saw in the initial setbacks suffered by Muslims a chance to revolt himself. Muhammad Bello summoned him to Sokoto, under threat, where he renounced his pretensions and asked for Caliph's pardon. But Abdus Salam's worldly ambitions blinded him to the extent that he neither kept his words nor considered the consequences of his actions on the ultimate well-being of the Muslims and the cohesion of the Caliphate, which he had helped to create. So at last he raised the standard of rebellion and proclaimed himself as caliph. He rallied unbelievers to his support and rekindled the fire of pre-Islamic tribal solidarity in his effort to subvert the Islamic order. He gathered a considerable following which he used to harass Muslims and disturb the order of the *umma*. He went into alliance with the rebellious states and proved a real threat to the young Islamic power. In a letter to the Caliph he explained why he had raised the flag of revolt:

> This is the diagram of the world which God gave to all Muslims through His benefaction.... Where is my own share, I, Abdussalam? I have not owned, during the days of Islam, more than what I had during the days of unbelievers, and that is a house and farm land. By God, the Most Gracious, this is the most unjust division of the time, we all belong to God and to Him we all shall return.

He thus pointed to the crux of the matter: his efforts to break up the *umma* and destroy the Caliphate was based on the desire to acquire wealth.

The Caliph wrote a letter to Abdus Salam virtually entreating him to renounce his rebellion, impressing upon him the consequences of his actions in fragmenting the *umma*. Further, the Caliph promised to give him the worldly reward he wanted for his role in the *jihad* but insisted that responsibilities in the Caliphate were allotted on the basis of competence. 'Know that your importance is not hidden from us,' the Caliph told Abdus Salam, 'nor is your right to the increase in share that you mentioned. But remember ability is a pre-condition in law as well as in administration of affairs. We will, therefore, and God-willing, give you a good share.' Abdus Salam apparently was not convinced: who can get us any land, he said, while Bello controls everything?

In his pursuit of land and wealth Abdus Salam resorted to confiscating goods from traders in the Caliphate and hindering agricultural produce from reaching the Muslims thus virtually blockading them. He stepped up his harassment of Muslim villages. The Caliph, as a consequence, declared him an apostate and ordered retaliatory attacks on him and his followers, but was hesitant to use full-scale military operations to resolve the issue, preferring a peaceful solution. So Muhammad Bello wrote again to him, followed by two further letters – a personal letter to Abdus Salam's family, urging them to prevail on him to renounce his rebellion and assuring them he had nothing but goodwill towards him; and another to the community under Abdus Salam asking them to embark upon *hijra*, since the area they now lived in had become a land of war on account of Abdus Salam's activities. He involved rulers and scholars in reasoning with Abdus Salam. All these methods failed to yield desirable results.

The Caliph finally decided on a full-scale military solution. After initial setbacks he sent a full force, under his Commander-in-Chief, Ali Jedo, to crush the revolt. In a full-day battle, Abdus Salam's forces were defeated, he himself escaped to Bakura in Zamfara territory, where he died three days later from the wound he had sustained in the battle. That was in 1233/1818, the rebellion having lasted for about four months.

## Unity and Rapprochement

In the first few years the Caliph had to divide his attention between two concerns – putting down the various revolts and apostasy on the one hand, and administering the caliphate on the other. But a serious moral problem persisted – the aloofness which Abdullahi had maintained since the Caliph's appointment. Abdullahi had been in charge of the western parts of the Caliphate since the days of the Shehu, an assignment he continued to carry out after his death. Because of Abdullahi's enormous prestige as the greatest living scholar in the Caliphate – and perhaps next only to the Shehu in moral authority – the Caliph restrained himself from tampering with his authority, and to that extent, he remained a co-ruler with Muhammad Bello.

Even so, the gulf that existed between these two principal pillars of the Caliphate had to be bridged to allow for a healthy development and consolidation of the Caliphate. Abdullahi, to his credit, had not sought in any way to weaken the authority of the Caliph: in fact, he continued to write books for the guidance of the *umma*, and to feed the Caliphate with scholars. Whatever friction that had arisen between him and the caliph was considered by Abdullahi as an unfortunate development and an unnecessary diversion – these are the sentiments he expressed in a poem, contained in his *Diya Ahl ar-Rashad*: 'I seek refuge with the Lord of Men,' he said, 'from every harmful object ... from the dissensions that are taking place between loved ones. May God protect me from the caprices of my soul and from my negligence, and from my ignorance, by giving me intelligence and by endowing me with patience and perseverance.'

The opportunity for rapprochement came in 1234/1819 when the remnants of the forces loyal to Abdus Salam regrouped and revolted against Abdullahi's authority in Gwandu. At a certain point the rebels proved a real threat to Abdullahi and as a result Bello decided to act quickly and decisively. An army was raised with the Caliph himself in command, which included most of the elders and statesmen of Sokoto and some of the Caliph's own relatives. The composition of the army would suggest the Caliph's desire to revive the memories of the days when the *umma* was solidly united under the Shehu and to emphasize the ties of kinship that bound them together. And it worked. After defeating the rebels at Kalambaina the Caliph and Abdullahi came face to face for the first time in several years. There and then Abdullahi formally recognized Muhammad

Bello as caliph, and confirmed Bello's *wazir*, Gidado, by investing him with his own *alkyebba* – indicating a transfer to Gidado of the office of the *wazir*, which he had held since the days of the Shehu. It was time for all to put aside differences and personal grievances and to renew the original commitments which had brought greatness to Islam – the struggle in the cause of Allah and the attainment of martyrdom. Abdullahi wrote to the Caliph:

Let us stand for *jihad* and pray for our martyrdom
That, in my view, is purity — indeed purity at its best.
Certainly sins are a filth which nothing can remove,
Except the swords held firmly by the infidels.[i]

i    The translation was kindly made for me by Sambo Waziri Junaidu.

# Chapter Three

# The Winds of Change

The impact of the Sokoto Revolution throughout Bilad al-Sudan was profound and far-reaching. The spectacular rise of the Caliphate was in itself a historic phenomenon, the like of which had not occurred before. 'The process of its emergence,' Yusufu Usman[i] has observed, 'involved the supersession, in various ways, of over a dozen sovereign polities many of which had developed, over several centuries, a great degree of coherence... A nucleus covering about 50,000 square miles was established within five years of the formation of its governments.' Within three decades the Caliphate comprised about thirty emirates and numerous sub-emirates, and extended over an area of approximately one hundred and fifty thousand square miles. The Caliphate's strategy of political and cultural integration of the various communities and nations into the *dar al-Islam* helped to shift the balance of power in the region in favour of Islam for the first time in several centuries. 'This transformation,' says Yusuf Usman, 'was on such a scale, with an intensity and coherence equal, if not greater, than any that had, produced by internal forces, occurred in the recent history of the African continent.' The Sokoto Revolution had the effect of releasing the social energy latent in Muslim communities, creating in the process a tidal wave of revolutions which swept across the whole of Bilad al-Sudan and which transformed irrevocably its political and social landscapes. In this chapter we shall examine some aspects of the impact of the Sokoto Revolution on Bilad al-Sudan.

i    Y.B. Usman, "The Transformation of Political Communities', in *Studies in the History of the Sokoto Caliphate*, pp. 35-36.

## The Change in Borno

Let us start with what happened to the Caliphate's powerful neighbour to the north, Borno, in the wake of the *jihad* in Hausaland. Borno served in terms of geography and culture, Abubakar Mustapha[i] has said, as 'the centre of Africa', strategically placed at the crossroads of African trade, as well as cultural transfusion, linked to Libya, Egypt, Kordofan, Darfur, and to the larger world of Islam. No wonder then that it was the first state in western Sudan to come into contact with Islam. The effects of the expeditions of Amr b. al-As and Uqba b. Nafi which led to the Islamization of Egypt in the first century of Islam, reached the borders of Borno, providing, Prof. Nur Alkali[ii] has suggested, a suitable background for the penetration of Islam into Kanem-Borno.

Little is known of how Islam first made its appearance in Borno, but by 1096 it had become an Islamic state under Hume Jilmi. Throughout its recorded history it was ruled by the Seyfawa dynasty, belonging to the Kanuri-speaking people, who claimed descent from Yemen. Mai Hume was succeeded by his son, Mai Dunoma, whose reign, according to Nur Alkali, 'seemed to have strengthened the Kingdom of Kanem and, for the first time, the existence of Kanem as a strong Islamic state was made known to the Islamic world of the time'. By the end of the twelfth century the *shari'a* had become the supreme law of the land. The consolidation of Islam ensured a full-scale economic and political expansion, ushering in, in the middle of thirteenth century, the peak period in the first phase of Borno history.

Soon after that, the forces of decline made their inevitable appearance. Prof. Alkali has suggested that the causative factors in Kanem-Borno's deterioration include the incessant power struggle among the princes, resulting in the emergence of factions within the ruling family; a weak administrative structure; and the

---

i    A. Mustapha, 'A new interpretation of the history of Islam in Kanem-Borno', *Dirasat Islamiyya*, (1981/82 session), Department of Islamic Studies, Bayero University, Kano.

ii    Nur Alkali, *Kanem-Borno under the Sayfawa – a study of origin, growth and collapse of a dynasty*. Ph_D. dissertation, Ahmadu Bello Universiry, 1978, Except otherwise stated, all other references to Prof. Alkali relate to this work.

'continuous sedenterisation process ... which was to give rise to a further situation of political instability and the struggle for the meagre resources.' Moreover, in spite of its economic hardships, the state over-stretched itself militarily. 'Their King, despite the weakness of his authority and poverty of his soil, shows an inconceivable arrogance,' al-Umari, quoted by Alkali, wrote: 'Despite the weakness of his troops ... he touches with his banner heaven itself.' A period of prolonged crisis followed. In the next two centuries the history of Borno was one of continuous decline. Mai Dabalemi's successor was assassinated, becoming the first ruler of Kanem to meet that fate. This encouraged rebellions, the most important and longest of which was the Bulala Rebellion (1376-1396), which saw all the succeeding Mais dying on the battlefield. The rebellion, according to Nur Alkali, was a decisive factor in the collapse of the Sayfawa in Kanem. The Arabs added to the distress by invading Kanem and plundering its resources and taking captive Muslim men, women and children. Kanem, under these unbearable strains, disintegrated.

But the Sayfawa Dynasty survived. In the dying days of Kanem, Mai Umar ibn Idris, after due consultation with the *'ulama*, evacuated his people, his army and his treasures from Kanem and moved to the land of Kaga, between 1392 and 1400. There, a new Borno emerged, with a renewed and more vigorous commitment to Islam than ever before. With the emergence of Mai Ali Gaji — the real builder of the new Borno in 1470 — the *shari'a* was firmly entrenched as the supreme law of the land, Birnin Gazargamu was established as the capital, and an Islamization drive based on education was launched on a massive scale.

This indeed was a period of expansion for Borno, followed in the course of another century by a period of consolidation, in which Borno extended its political, military and economic influence across Bilad al-Sudan. This did not mean that there were no worries for Borno: in the second half of the sixteenth century, the Sau and other tribes were in constant rebellion, fiercely resisting being integrated into the *dar al-Islam*. It required the power, dedication end courage of Idris Alamma, one of Borno's greatest rulers, to crush the revolts and lay the foundation for a sustained integration of the state. The Mai mobilized the entire state in the *jihad* against the Sau and after one and a half years of war the backbone of the Sau was broken, forcing them to migrate *en masse* to Mandara. Then came the revolts of Bulala which started in 1575 barely two years or so after the defeat of the Sau. The Mai preferred a peaceful settlement of the conflict, but the enemy refused; so he launched a full-scale war which ended in the defeat of the Bulala.

The process of state integration Idris Alamma had initiated continued after him, thanks to a strong military power, which helped Borno to check any possible invasion from its neighbours – the Tuaregs, Wadai and Konna – and bring other people under its control. Its economy prospered, 'Thus with the increased economic growth at home,' in the words of Prof. Alkali, 'conditioned by good harvests, developed crafts and industries … the availability of gold to attract foreign markets and the control of external trade, Borno was placed in a favourable position to exert its influence over a wider range of territory.'[i] This strength had already been displayed when Borno successfully destroyed the awesome power of Kwararafa – a pagan kingdom dreaded by almost all the Muslim states in those days. Integration continued and Borno reached its golden age both in strength and scholarship by the middle of the seventeenth century.

Three things may be noted as fundamental elements in the shaping of Borno. The first was the predominant role of Islam as the basis of state formation and integration, and *the* ideology of the state. 'The second element was that Borno maintained a revolutionary fervour, never hesitating to take on the enemies of Islam, or to take to the field to advance the frontiers of *dar al-Islam*. Its commitment to Islam gave Borno its impressive dynamism and revolutionary potential. Thirdly, Borno had always given a predominant role to the *'ulama* and considered the cultivation and spread of Islamic learning as one of its paramount duties. In fact, it was a deliberate state policy to incorporate the *'ulama* community into the royal family through marriage. The capital of the Caliphate, Birni Gazargamu, was seen

i    Kyari Tijani, *'Al-Idara fi Nizam al-Mamlaka wal-Idara by Muhammed Yanbu – a critical analysis'* in Nigerian Administration Research Project, second interim report, pp. 78-96, 1975.

first and foremost as the centre of learning, 'the focal point (as Kyrari Tijani puts it) of national and international commerce and therefore the fountain-head of cultural florescence from whence cultural elements radiated to areas far and wide.'[i] This, of course, was a feature shared by several other cities in Africa, such as Timbuktu, Gao, Katsina, Jenne and Kano, where the cities derived their prestige and sanctity largely from their role as centres of learning and piety.

It may be relevant here to say a word or two about the political structure of Borno. As a dynasty the Mai, as one would expect in all monarchies if not in all political cultures, was the main focus of attention, the supreme pillar of the state. He was required to be a man of 'sterling character', gentle, just, refined and above all, 'having the Book of God by heart, and knowledgeable in the Sunna'. He was also required to cater for the material needs of his people, for failure in this respect 'shows a preference for (self-)destruction and the break up of society'.[ii] He was regarded as the upholder of Islam and ultimate guardian of the *shari'a*, for which his throne was hailed as Degal Lisalambe – the cradle of Islam. Any form of departure from the *shari'a* on the part of the Mai would almost automatically have cost him his popularity among his people, who were bound to see him as a ruler who had left the path of Allah, as Prof. Alkali has observed. Thus the Mai had to rely largely on his Islamic advisors to secure his position.

In the course of centuries, however, the political and administrative structure of Borno became extremely complex, resulting in 'a stage of extreme decay'[iii] towards the end of the eighteenth century. Muhammad Yanbu shows how Borno in latter days was almost entirely obsessed with the protection of the person of the Mai and the magnification of his status. Various factors – economic, moral, demographic and ecological – combined to create serious

i   Kyari Tijani, *Political and Administrative Development in Pre-Colonial Borno*. PhD. dissertation, Ahmadu Bello University, 1980. All references to Kyari Tijani in this chapter, except otherwise stated, relate to this work. In fact, this section of Borno derives fundamentally from the works of Nur Alkali and Kyari Tijani.
ii  Kyari Tijani, *'Al-Idara fi Nizam al-Mamlaka wal-Idara by Muhammed Yanbu – a critical analysis'* in Nigerian Administration Research Project, second interim report, pp. 78-96, 1975.
iii ibid

hardships for Borno. Of particular significance was the prolonged drought (1704-1772) that ravaged the kingdom. The *'ulama*, who in fact had started to express their concern over the moral drift in the state much earlier, now became more active in their campaign for a better society. At the same time, the state proved increasingly incapable of devising what Nur Alkali calls a 'positive strategy' to tackle the mounting economic and social problems. Instead, ruler after ruler took refuge in scholarship, cutting themselves almost completely off from the affairs of the state.

Then, in 1781, Mai Ali Dunoma conceived the idea of attacking the neighbouring Muslim state of Mandara in a senseless show of strength. In a letter to the Sultan, Mai Ali Dunoma, who referred to himself as the 'burning embers whose empire will stretch from dusk to dawn', made his intentions known. The Sultan pleaded with his powerful neighbour, offering to pay tributes, stating that "we cannot give up this country and this land where we were born, for we have no other place, good or bad, where to fall back on'. Mai Ali Dunoma was unmoved by Mandara's pleas. 'If you have wings,' he wrote to the Sultan, 'you had better fly away and land on the top of the mountains which you use as a hide-out. Or else dig a hole and bury yourself underground... The way I will act in your country and the war I will wage will forever serve as an example and will re-echo throughout history.' Ironically, the reverse occurred as Kyari Tijan aptly says: 'it was in fact the resounding defeat which Mai Ali's forces suffered at the hands of the agile Mandara forces that re-echoed throughout history, for it seems to have decisively rung the death-knell of the aging Sayfawa dynasty'. At about this time Shehu Usman Dan Fodio was already deep in the building of a revolutionary force to the west, in Hausaland, requiring less than three decades to take on the forces of Borno.

In 1808, Birnin Gazargamu fell to the forces loyal to Shehu Usman, albeit temporarily, in a conflict whose origin is far from clear. The result is, however, an unequivocal fact of history. This temporary loss of its seat of power shattered irreversibly Sayfawa's power and, what is more, the myth of its invincibility. There was a more profound dimension to the victory of the Shehu's men over Borno suggests Tijani:

It is particularly damaging and paradoxical that the Sayfawa suffered this fate at the hands of adversaries who rode on the crest of Islamic religious revivalism. It was in this sense, even much more than the military sense, that the Fulata defeats of 1808 were devastating. They constituted defeats not only of the military might of the Sayfawa, which could have been reconstituted, but also defeats of the whole ideological basis of the Sayfawa power and authority, and the motive energy that had carried the Sayfawa through centuries of travail. In this sense, the Fulata revolts ... constituted the most radical challenge the Sayfawa faced in their centuries-long tenure as Mai's of Borno.

The Sayfawa Dynasty – the most venerated dynasty in western Sudan – made its exit, having endured for one thousand years.

A new era, ushering in a new dynasty, emerged. The leader of this emergent order was Sheikh Muhammad al-Amin al-Kanemi, to all intents and purposes a creature of circumstances. As a scholar in his own right and as a man fundamentally concerned with the establishment of the Sunna and having a genuine mass base, he was well qualified to save Borno. Al-Kanemi launched a two-pronged counter-offensive against Sokoto – military and ideological. He mobilized and led the army that recaptured Birni Gazargamu from the Fulata forces and brought back Mai Dunama to his seat of power, a feat he continued to repeat until he himself became the absolute ruler of Borno, establishing a dynasty of his own, to replace that of the Sayfawa.[i] It was however al-Kanemi's ideological assault on Sokoto, more than the military challenge, that was to prove more decisive and potent: it caused, as Muhammad Bello conceded in *Infaq al-Maysur*, a not inconsiderable consternation in the core of Sokoto leadership. For the first time, Sokoto was put on the defensive, of all things, ideologically. The challenge had one positive result, however; it gave rise to an upsurge of literature articulating the ideological and moral basis of the Sokoto

---

i    See generally, Louis Brenner, 'Muhammad al-Amin al-Kamemi and Religion and Politics in Borno', Studies in West African History, (Vol. One), ed. J.R. Willis, chap. V.

Revolution, not least Shehu Usman's *Ikhwan* series. We shall briefly examine the intellectual encounter between Sokoto and Borno.

In his first letter[i] to Shehu Usman, al-Kanemi demanded to know the reasons for the occurrence of the 'fire of war' and discord between Borno and Sokoto. If the reason was unbelief, al-Kanemi contended, then it was indeed an untenable one, for the people of Borno were Muslims to the core, living in *dar al-Islam*. Al-Kanemi asked pointedly: 'If the establishment of *salat*, payment of *zakat*, knowledge of Allah, fasting in Ramadan and tending of mosques amount to unbelief, what then is Islam?' If the reason was that certain evils were perpetrated in Borno, this too, in al-Kanemi's view, was untenable. He conceded that some of the rulers engaged in certain practices that offended the Islamic faith; that some women went about in public without observing the rules of *hijab* strictly, that is, not displaying modesty in their dress; that bribery, corruption and misappropriation of the property of orphans was rampant; and that there were incidents of oppression and misrule in government. But while all these constituted serious crimes in Islam, they did not, in al-Kanemi's view, amount to unbelief, and did not warrant the waging of war. The main thrust of al-Kanemi's argument, however, was that every period in Muslim history and every Muslim country had its own share of shortcomings and evils, but this did not imply that the people of those countries were unbelievers.

Abdullahi replied on behalf of the Shehu stating generally the reasons for the *jihad* in Hausaland. In his own reply Bello conceded that Sokoto knew very little about the circumstances in Borno and that they did not know exactly how the war had started. Even so, Bello went on, the war against Borno was justified on three broad counts: Borno rulers were aiding the hostile Hausa states against Sokoto; Borno had started to oppress the followers of the Shehu; and above all, some of the rulers were polytheists, who must be fought by Muslims. The Shehu urged al-Kanemi to order the people of Borno 'to return to Allah, abandon all the customs which are contrary to the *shari'a*, and establish a relationship of peaceful co-existence

---

i    All correspondence referred to in this chapter is to be found in *Infaq al-Maysur* by Muhammad Bello. See also Hodgkin, *Nigerian Perspectives*, (1960), Oxford University Press, pp. 198-205.

between them and the *Jama'a*, based on definite undertakings and written agreements'. Failing that, the Shehu added, it was obligatory on al-Kanemi himself to make a *hijra* from Borno to the *dar al-Islam*, which obviously meant the Sokoto Caliphate. In his reply, al-Kanemi reiterated his charges against Shehu's followers, that they persisted in causing bloodshed, confiscating property, destroying homes and enslaving Muslims. He agreed that the Shehu was following the way of *ahl al-sunna*, but insisted that his followers in Borno could not make the same claim, because if they were true Muslims there would have been no conflict whatsoever between them and Borno since, as he put it, 'we too are *ahl al-sunna*'. He complained further of the *Jama'a*'s lack of manners: 'each time I put off one fire of war, they kindled another'.

Despite the tough stance taken by both parties, the underlying trend in their arguments and attitudes pointed towards a desire for peace and mutual co-existence. Al-Kanemi, who always referred to the Shehu as 'our Master', even offered to pay a visit to the Shehu, not knowing then of the latter's death, adding: 'My regard for him is high, and my belief in him is sincere.' But even so, peace eluded these two powerful Muslim nations and the fire of war continued to rage between them, even as the correspondence went on.

In 1827, the end of the first decade of Muhammad Bello's rule, al-Kanemi prepared a formidable force with the object of recapturing Borno's territories held by Sokoto. 'The conquered Sultans joined with him,' Hajji Said, then in Sokoto, wrote in his *Tarikh Sokoto*,[i] 'and he promised to return all their kingdoms to them if he overcame the Commander of the Faithful. He collected numerous multitudes and a powerful army from the furthermost territories – Wadai, the Arabs of the Baghirmi country, and the indigenous folk of that land. The fear felt of him was great and his power became mighty. He set out against Kano with armies like mountains.' The Caliph immediately ordered his *wazir*, Gidado Dan Laima, to assume the overall command of Sokoto forces, and despatched letters to his emirs nearest to Borno to mobilize their forces to meet al-Kanemi's challenge. The Emir of Bauchi, Yakubu, not without considerable risk to his emirate, took to the field in obedience to the Caliph's order in an extraordinary

---

i   See Journal of the Royal African Society, no. 47 (1948), p. 162.

act of courage. 'I know not how to defeat al-Kanemi,' the Emir told his advisors, 'neither do I know how to slay him; but one thing I do know. I know that he has no power to raise the dead; that he has no power, if rain be lacking, to make it fall; that he has no power, if the grass does not spring up, to cause it grow.' Al-Kanemi lost the ensuing battle at Fake, in Kano emirate, The defeat was so complete that al-Kanemi abandoned all hope of recovering the territories lost to Sokoto Caliphate. Henceforth there were no major conflicts, other than border raids, between the two Islamic forces.[i]

Whatever the arguments on both sides, the conflict between Borno and Sokoto Caliphate was a conflict between two Muslim powers. The difference between Muhammad Bello and al-Kanemi was one of approach and not necessarily of ideology for both were committed to establishing a society in accordance with the Qur'an and Sunna. The Sayfawa dynasty had aged, and it duly gave way to the revolutionary waves that swept across the whole region. It was fitting that it was a Sheikh, not a despot, that rose to save Borno in its most difficult days. The *mujaddid*, Sheikh Umar al-Futi, who visited both Sokoto and Borno at the time of the conflicts, put the blame squarely on both Muhammad Bello and al-Kanemi for the bloodshed that occurred among Muslims, and for the hatred which one Muslim nation harboured against the other. The stubbornness and pride which made one Muslim group denounce the other as unbelievers were, to him, unnecessary and pointless.[ii]

### The Revolution of Seku Ahmadu

In 1818, a year after the death of the Shehu, one of his distant disciples, Sheikh Ahmadu Labbo,[iii] established a caliphate of his own in Masina, astride the Upper Niger and Bani rivers, with its capital at Hamdullah. Seku Ahmadu, as he was more commonly

---

i    Johnston, *The Fulani Empire of Sokoto*, Oxford University Press, 1967, p. 120.
ii   *Studies in West African History*, p. 182.
iii  This section on the revolution of Seku Ahmadu is based fundamentally on two sources: (1) Pref, Abdullahi Smith's article, 'A neglected theme of West African history: the Islamic revolutions of the 19th century', Journal of Historical Society of Nigeria, II, 1961, pp. 169-185; and (2) *The Caliphate of Hamdullah (1818-1864): A Study in African History*, WA. Brown, Ph.D. dissertation, Wisconsin University, 1969.

known, was born in 1775 to a family distinguished for piety and learning. Three forces seemed to have influenced Seku Ahmadu in his learning as well as his career as a *mujaddid*: the first was the training he had obtained in Jenne, a city almost as venerated as Timbuktu, with which it shared the same philosophy and tradition of scholarship; second, the sufic influence of Sidi Mukhtar al-Kunti, the influential and revered head of the Qadiriya order in western Sudan; and third, and perhaps the most far-reaching, the influence of Shehu Usman Dan Fodio, from whom it is said Ahmadu Labbo obtained the flag to undertake the *jihad* in Masina.

As a scholar, Seku Ahmadu maintained at first a peripatetic academy but later established his headquarters at a camp site near Jenne, where he taught and raised a community. He tried to operate in the manner of Shehu Usman, criticizing the un-Islamic practices prevalent in society, challenging the *'ulama al-su'* and raising his voice against injustice, while at the same time avoiding a direct confrontation with the authorities until his movement had grown strong. Seku Ahmadu grew steadily popular as his ideas about reform of society spread far and wide. The ever-increasing number of students and followers who flocked to his camp greatly annoyed the scholars of Jenne. Seku Ahmadu soon became the object of hostility and opposition both from the aristocracy – the ruling class dominated by the Dikko elite – as well as from the *'ulama* in Jenne, who had discerned in his activities and popularity a growing tendency towards a revolution.

Direct confrontation between Seku Ahmadu's *jama'a* and the ruling elite proved unavoidable, especially in the face of persistent attempts to destroy the movement. So in 1818, at Koubay, the Seku proclaimed the birth of his community – Dina as it was called – which, in turn, paid its allegiance to him. With the establishment of the Dina, a new state had thus come into existence with Seku Ahmadu as the *Amir al-Muminin*. Soon after this symbolic break with the old order *jihad* broke out, and within a few months, the Dikko supremacy was broken, to be followed by the destruction of Bambara power. Then Seku Abmadu summoned the generality of the people of Niger bend to his cause, urging them to accept the supremacy of the *shari'a*, and be integrated into the Dina. Many communities answered his call, others rejected it. The *jihad* for the consolidation of his Dina continued for a period of ten years.

Seku Ahmadu's *jihad* covered just over fifty-six thousand square miles and had less intellectual depth and profundity than the Sokoto revolution. The dearth of scholars in the movement proved to be a disadvantage to the Dina, making it impossible for the revolution to assert itself on the more scholarly communities of Jenne and Timbuktu. However, as Prof. Abdullahi Smith observes, Seku Ahmadu's achievement lay in the Islamization of some of the important tribes in the Niger bend, particularly the pagan Fulani, and in the fact that his revolution conditioned the activities of another *mujaddid*, Sheikh Umar al-Futi, to whom we shall presently turn our attention.

## The Revolution of Umar Al-Futi

The revolution in Masina was to be followed by an even more extensive one, directed by Sheikh Umar al-Futi, generally known as Hajj Umar. Born in Futa Toro, Senegal, Umar grew up in learned circles. 'Under his father's careful eye the young Umar began to hone those religious instincts that later brought him an international reputation for piety and scholarship. A precocious child, he is said to have committed the Qur'an to memory by the age of eleven, and subsequently the two *Sahih* of al-Bukhari and Muslim. At fifteen or sixteen he embarked on the traditional peripatetic shaykh-seeking, having already exhausted his father's rich quarry of knowledge.' After studying under several scholars, he found his mentor, Sheikh Abd al-Karim al-Naqili, who introduced the young student to the new sufi order, the Tijaniyya. The Sheikh died, but even before his death Umar had already decided to seek a higher authority in the sufi hierarchy in order to fulfil his own spiritual aims.[i]

He set out on a journey that was to mark the turning point in his life, and indeed in the history of a substantial part of western Sudan – the journey to Makka, for the hajj. On his way he stayed for seven

i   See generally Ralph Willis's impressive work, *Al-Hajj Umar b. Said al-Futi al-Turi (c.1794-1884) and the Doctrinal Basis of his Islamic Reformist Movement in Western Sudan*. Ph.D. dissertation, University of London, 1970. This section on the Umarian revolution draws fundamentally from this work.

months with Muhammad Bello and two with Abdullahi. He then proceeded from Sokoto to al-Kanemi's Borno, and from there to Makka, where he attached himself to the *khalifa* of Sheikh Ahmad al-Tijani in Hijaz, Muhammad al-Ghali. The relationship between the *murid* and his master grew very intimate: Umar remained with him for three years, during each of which they performed the hajj together. Then Umar was appointed the *khalifa* of Sheikh Ahmad al-Tijani for the whole of western Sudan. In 1831 Umar left the Hijaz armed with a mandate to 'sweep the country' of western Sudan of the vestiges of paganism and call the people to Islam.[i]

After staying for some time in Egypt, from where he is said to have visited Syria and Jerusalem, he moved to Borno. Here he had a bitter encounter with al-Kanemi. He then travelled to Sokoto where he was to stay for the next nine years or so, a period that had a tremendous influence in shaping the course of his career. It was a time of intense intellectual activity, where he wrote one of his most important works, *Suyuf al-Said*. It also offered him the opportunity to learn many aspects of *jihad* and diplomacy, which were to prove immensely valuable in the latter part of his career. Umar left Sokoto after the death of Muhammad Bello. In 1840 he established his centre at Diaguku, in Futa Jallon, a town 'strategically situated on the frontier between *dar al-Islam* and *dar al-harb*,' in the words of Willis.

Although many of his ideas had originated from contact with Shehu Usman Dan Fodio, and his *tajdid* efforts were largely influenced, if not shaped, by the experience he received during his nine-year stay in Sokoto, Hajj Umar did have a vision of his own, a vision which gave a measure of uniqueness to his revolution. Most of Hajj Umar's definitive ideas are contained in his work, *Rimah Hizb al-Rahim ala Nuhur Hizb al-Rajim*,[ii] which expounds his philosophy of revolution.

i   Omar Jah, 'The relationship between the Sokoto *Jihad* and the *Jihad* of Al-Hajj Umar: a New assessment', Studies in the History of Sokoto Caliphate, chap. 21. See generally Omar Jah's penetrating work, *Sufism and 19th century Jihad Movements in West Africa*. Ph.D. dissertation, McGill University, 1973.
ii   *Rimah* is printed on the margin of *Jawad al-Maani*, the definitive work on the Tijaniyya: it enjoys a very wide circulation especially in West Africa.

Diaguku remained Umar's centre of activities: here he raised his community, the core of which were the *talaba*, in a process called *tarbiyya wa ta'lim* – involving intensive moral and intellectual training. According to Omar Jah, this process was seen by Hajj Umar as a fundamental step in the fulfilment of one of the most important Islamic duties – the commanding of right, and prevention of wrong. Transformation of society could only be brought about, in the eyes of Hajj Umar, when fundamental changes had been brought about in the Muslim educational system and when the moral and spiritual life of the people had been improved. Accordingly, his programme of *tarbiyya* was intended to effect the necessary moral discipline, which would free the self from corruption and give the individual Muslim a conscious, inward inclination to apply the *shari'a* in his life. The programme of *ta'lim* on the other hand, was aimed at giving Umar's community the necessary intellectual nourishment.

After four years of intensive training of his *talaba*, Umar undertook an extensive tour of the Futa region, to widen his contacts and expand his community. According to Martin,[i] his route led him from Diaguku via Touba to Pakao in Casamance. At Pakao, he met two prominent Islamic figures, Modi Muhammad Bakawi and Mahmud Ba, who was later to lead an Islamic revolution in the 1860s. Then Umar moved on towards St. Louis where, in the territory of the Wolof, assassins were sent against him. These Umar dodged, and crossing Futa Toro, he arrived at his home town of Halwar, where he visited his family for the first time in twenty years. When he reached Bakal, French troops, under Hecquart, at first prevented his entry. Upset by this blatant colonial high-handedness, Umar told the French commander, 'Go back to your own country, accursed man: leave God's wide land to His servants.' Eventually Umar was admitted. From here he moved to Futa Bondu to be received by important dignitaries of the region, especially Imam Said.

His tour had been a huge success. He had been seen, Martin points out, where he had wanted to be seen, and met people who really mattered in the region, with whom he had discussed matters connected with his forthcoming *jihad*. He had greatly added to

---

i    B.G. Martin, *Muslim Brotherhood in 18th century Africa.* Cambridge University Press, chap. 3, especially pp. 78-79.

the number of his followers and had come in direct contact with the Muslim masses. During his tour he is said to have distributed manifestos urging people to join his struggle including, as Martin suggests, a posthumous message from Muhammad Bello, urging the people of Futa Toro to rise in the cause of Islam. In this message, partly reproduced by Willis, Muhammad Bello extolled the qualities of Hajj Umar, saying, 'He appeared to us on the horizon of guidance – it is most surprising that dawn comes from the West. But in him was found our lost treasure. He has completely won our hearts and minds.'

Umar was, at this stage, certainly at the threshold of revolution. His followers were now so numerous, his influence immense. His *talaba* were trained not only spiritually but equally militarily. Hajj Umar had all along been highly involved not only in extensive trade but also in the massive acquisition and manufacture of arms and ammunition. His headquarter was both a zawiyya and an impressive arsenal – fitting squarely into his own conception of life. So naturally Umar's return to Dinguku with a great number of men ready to lay down their lives in the cause of Allah, together with the weapons already at his disposal, alarmed the authorities in Futa Jallon, making his continued stay there virtually impossible. Perhaps for the first time in his career, Hajj Umar came face to face with the reality of vested interests.

In 1851, Hajj Umar made his *hijra* from Diaguku to Singuiray, which was immediately renamed Daybata – derived from one of the names of Madina, so as to commemorate the Prophet's *hijra* from Makka to Madina, Martin suggests. Here Hajj Umar intensified the military training of his *talaba* and procured more arms and ammunition. In the second year of the *hijra*, Umar completed one of his last engagements before the *jihad*, teaching the *talaba* the exegesis of the Qur'an he himself had written. Meanwhile, the pagan power of Tamba, under its ruler Yimba, alarmed by the strength of Umar's ever-growing army, attacked the Muslims. Thus began what was perhaps the most controversial and bloodiest revolution that had ever taken place in the history of West Africa.[i]

---

i    For the details of the *jihad* see especially Willis, Omar Jah, and Oluruntimehin.

## The Revolution in Yorubaland

Before going into the immediate effect of the Sokoto Revolution in Yorubaland,[i] it is pertinent to put that area of West Africa briefly into historical perspective, especially the beginning of the nineteenth century when the revolutionary fervour in Hausaland to the north was on the verge of exploding. The Yoruba people were largely pagan, sharing, as Prof. Ajayi has noted, 'a common language and basically the same culture – as reflected in religious and social values – a common pantheon, the same monarchical system, in which all paramount rulers claimed to have originated at Ile-Ife, as well as politically.' So there were several Yoruba kingdoms, each with a distinct dialect and cultural traits of its own.

Of these kingdoms, Oyo Empire was clearly the largest, strongest and the most homogenous politically and culturally. It maintained an economic and political hegemony over its neighbours, including Borgu and Nupe to the north. But towards the end of the eighteenth century revolts emerged in different provinces, ushering in a prolonged and bloody interregnum of nearly forty years when the empire did not have an effective leader. The interregnum gave birth to new situations of historic proportion: the collapse of the Oyo Empire itself and the emergence of the Emirate of Ilorin, marking the beginning of the remarkable expansion of Islam among the Yoruba people.

Four dominant factors were instrumental in effecting the change. The first was the presence of the Imale Community – a foreign Muslim merchant community, which clustered in commercial centres, not only in Oyo but all across Yorubaland and beyond. Prof. Abdullahi Smith suggests that by the end of the eighteenth century this community, 'while preserving the traditions of their Northern origin and their Islamic culture, had assimilated persons of Yoruba origin', and had become very large and influential, especially in

---

i    This part on Yorubaland is based on three sources: Prof. Ajeyi's article 'The aftermath of the fall of Old Oyo' in *History of West Africa*, ed. Ajayi and Gowder (124-166), T.G.O. Badamusi's useful work, *The Growth of Islam Among the Yoruba 1841-1908*, Longman, 1978; and Prof. Abdullahi Smith's 'A Little Light on the Collapse of the Alfinate of Yoruba', in Studies in Yoruba History and Culture, (ed) Olusanya, 1983, University Press Limited, Ibadan.

the empire's capital. This community, he elaborates, may well have been financiers of government, providing also advisors, secretaries, and much more, so that as early as 1787 the Alafin had ambassadors who 'knew how to write and calculate in Arabic', and who conducted their business in Arabic. It was this merchant community, together with their *'ulama* which provided the intellectual background for the revolution in Yorubaland.

The second factor was the existence of Hausa slave communities, the Gambari, who were almost entirely Muslim. These played a crucial role in the economic, and particularly military, sectors of Oyo, serving, as Prof. Abdullahi Smith has said, as artisans in a variety of occupations, and as stablemen tending the metropolitan cavalry. Thus, the Gambari, together with Imale communities, worked together to wield tremendous influence on the economy, maintain a crucial stake in Oyo cavalry, and above all, serve 'as a source of urban welfare and prosperity, and the support of law and order.'

The third factor was the revolt in Ilorin in 1797 by a Yoruba chieftain, Afanja, which marked the beginning of the end of Oyo Empire. It was Afanja, ironically, who introduced the fourth and most crucial factor: Sheikh Salih, known simply as Alimi, a student and standard bearer of Shehu Usman Dan Fodio. Afanja invited Alimi to Ilorin in 1817 to solicit his support in resisting Alafin's army, and to create an empire of his own. Alimi had spent some time mobilizing the Muslims, particularly the Imale and Gambari communities, preparing the ground for the revolution. In Ilorin, Alimi was concerned to spread and consolidate Islam, in direct contrast to Afanja who, in all probability, sought worldly power for himself.

Soon the inevitable happened. The alliance between Islam and *kufr* collapsed after the death of Alimi in 1823. In the ensuing battle, the *Jama'a*, now under the command of *Amir al-Muminin* Abdus Salam, Alimi's son, defeated Afanja's forces and burned their houses. 'When Afanja saw that,' said Ahmad Kokoro, 'he threw himself into the fire and died in it, burned to ashes.... This army of Afanja did not know what would befall them. Then the Emir ordered their dispersal in all the villages, and they did not know where to go.' The Hausa slave communities, the Gambari, saw an opportunity to throw off the yoke of bondage; they revolted against their masters and made their way *en masse* to Ilorin. The Imale communities and other Muslim elements also converged on Ilorin. Freedom had come at last.

Oyo panicked. 'Toleration was replaced by persecution,' says Gbadamosi, 'The Alafin massacred such of the Muslims as could be gathered into the palace... This massacre terrified the Muslims and made them bitter against the entire traditional system. They were now clearly in danger of their lives, and whether they could survive the policy of persecution and extermination must have seemed doubtful.' Ilorin provided a haven for Muslims to live in dignity under a system that was their own – the Islamic government. Henceforth many battles took place between Ilorin Emirate, which became part of the Sokoto Caliphate, and what remained of the Oyo Empire.

In 1837, the Alafin, in alliance with Borgu, gathered a formidable force in one last effort to crush Ilorin once and for all. Alarmed by the scale of this force, Ilorin appealed to Gwandu, and ultimately to Sokoto for help, and the response was a strong force in aid of the beleaguered emirate. The Muslims won the decisive battle, in which the Alafin and the most prominent men in Borgu's army were killed. 'With this defeat,' says Johnston, 'the ancient Kingdom of Oyo, which had already lost its Empire, more or less disintegrated. The old capital was never rebuilt nor did the Alafins ever recover their paramountcy. Thereafter, Oyo was hardly more than one of the city-states into which Yorubaland now broke up.' Although Ilorin did not continue its initial success by integrating the whole of Yorubaland into *dar al-Islam*, it nevertheless laid the foundation for the spread of Islam in the region. 'The same Ilorin,' Gbadamosi remarks, 'that had been so richly reinforced from both Yoruba and Hausa Muslim sources became ... a particularly nourishing source for the regeneration of Islam in Yorubaland.'

One further aspect of the far-reaching effects of the Sokoto Revolution that needs to be noted is that it created, as Prof. El-Hajj has said, the intellectual climate that gave rise to the Mahdist Revolution in the Sudan. But a consideration of the relationship between the Caliphate and that revolution is unfortunately outside the scope of this study.

## Why This Phenomenon?

What meaning can we give to this extraordinary wave of Islamization in West Africa? First, we can see the phenomenon as the triumph of piety and knowledge over moral decadence and pervasive ignorance. Wherever we look, whether in the direction of Sokoto, Masina, Futa or Yorubaland, we can see that the revolutionary process centred on discipline and knowledge and thus aimed at effecting a moral and intellectual revolution in the new communities that were raised. The larger community, hemmed in by decay and stagnation was no match for the energy and self-confidence of the emergent new order.

Secondly, we can see the phenomenon as involving a profound reaction to a universal state of corruption and oppression. There is no doubt that most of the rulers that were swept away by the revolutions were either genuinely inept – being pagans or syncretics – or blatantly oppressive. Nor can there be doubts about the fact that most of the people who rallied to the cause of Islam were the dispossessed – slaves, oppressed and weak tribes, women and those at the very bottom of the social ladder.

Thirdly, the phenomenon can be seen as the release of the moral and intellectual energy latent in the Muslim *umma*. This energy had been suppressed by the dead weight of pagan, or at best secular, rule which the Muslims had had to endure for many decades. It was a humiliating experience, one that was later transformed into social anger. This anger, on its part, fuelled the emerging revolutionary processes. The resultant force – at once intellectual, moral and social – became explosive and uncontrollable, sweeping away all in its way: governments, states, empires. It was Islam's response to tyranny and false systems, and the awakening of Muslims to their moral responsibilities. It may be said that this energy is latent in all Muslim communities, in all ages; Muslims today in all regions of the world can perform the same feat if only they raise themselves to the level of moral and intellectual heights which Islam requires.

Chapter Four

# The Theory of Government

The conception of government that evolved in the Sokoto Caliphate took many years to develop. It started, perhaps, in 1803 when the Shehu wrote his *Masail al-Muhimma*, in which he indicated that it was time Muslims established a *dar al-Islam* for themselves, and continued to the end of Muhammad Bello's rule. Some of the principles emerged from the period of *hijra*, when the Muslims were forced to abandon their homes and seek refuge elsewhere; others from the period of *jihad*, when Muslims fought for several years in defence of their faith, family, property and honour; and finally, when victory came, a new set of principles relating to government, economy and defence of state evolved,

The main sources for this chapter are Shehu Usman's *Bayan Wujub al-Hijra*, *Kitab al-Farq*, and *Siraj al-Ikhwan*; Abdullahi Dan Fodio's *Diya al-Hukkam*, *Diya al-Imam*, *Diya al-Willayat*, *Diya ahl al-Ihtisab* and *Ta'lim al-Radi*; and Muhammad Bello's *Usul al-Siyasa*, *al-Ghayth al-Wabl* and *al-Ghayth al-Shubub*.

### The Imamate

The most important office in this framework is that of the Imam, who is also variously called the caliph or *Amir al-Muminin* – the commander of the faithful. He maintains, the Shehu stated in *Bayan*,[i] 'an overall leadership embracing all religious and temporal affairs – undertaken on behalf of the Prophet 🕌'. His function is, therefore, integrative, encompassing all spheres of life, in line with the all-embracing nature of Islam itself, which seeks to regulate the totality of human life. Consequently, he is the symbol of the Muslim *umma*, the head of state, the overall commander who leads the *jihad*, the guardian of Islamic values and the realm, all in one.

i   Prof. Fathi al-Masri's translation is used throughout.

The Imam must be elected to office, which places an obligation on Muslims to choose a leader to take charge of their affairs. 'It is an obligation,' the Shehu affirmed in *Bayan*, 'to appoint a just Imam; know that this is by divine precept, not the judgement of human reasoning... This law is addressed to the whole community as from the death of the Prophet ﷺ until the Day of Resurrection.' This obligation stands in all situations, whether peaceful or turbulent. And essentially, it is the entire *umma* that is given the prerogative of electing the Imam, but it is free, the Shehu added, to delegate if it deems it necessary.

The imamate, as an elective office, necessarily precludes monarchy, let alone government by seizure. This is because, according to Abdullahi, any government which is installed without *mashwara*, or consultation of the people, is illegal and un-Islamic as it effectively negates the inherent right of people to choose their leader. The imamate, Abdullahi stated further in *Diya al-Imam*,[i] is a government by people's consent, connoting mercy, and governance in accordance with the tradition of the Prophet ﷺ Muhammad. On the other hand, monarchy, which is an institutionalized abrogation of the people's right to choose their leaders, constitutes an outrage on the people; in operation it brings only torment to them. Government by seizure is despotism which can lead only to corruption.

It is the willing choice of the people alone that makes a person an imam. The people, on their part, have two liabilities in this respect: first, to elect their leader on the basis of the Qur'an and Sunna, that is, on the understanding that he will be guided by them unfailingly; and second, to elect a person who, in Shehu's words, 'is the best among them'. He should be a person of knowledge, having a pride of place in the circle of the truly learned, of high moral stature, of diplomacy, of such moral courage as to be able to fight evil and corruption with all the determination that is necessary. The Imam remains in office for as long as he remains true to the Qur'an and Sunna; if he fails in this regard, then he should be removed, by force if necessary.

All this is implicit in the *bay'a* which the community collectively gives to the Imam when he has been elected. *Bay'a* is the oath of

i   Ms in author's possession.

allegiance, binding the community and Imam together in a mutual commitment to safeguard the basic interests of the *umma*. In essence, *bay'a* is not an allegiance to an individual as such, but is rather, as Muhammad Bello states in *Al-Ghayth al-Wabl*,[i] the community's renewal of allegiance to the Prophet 🌸 and ultimately to Allah. *'Those who pledge you their allegiance pledge allegiance to Allah. Allah's hand is over their hands.'* (48:10) *Bay'a* binds the Imam to justice, to upholding Allah's law, and to an upright life; it binds the people to loyalty.

A number of conditions are stipulated to guide the Imam in the affairs of state. The first is that he should have pure and sincere motives in respect of his office, which will impel him to perform his functions for the sake of Allah alone. An important aspect of this purity of motive lies, in Abdullahi's view, in his giving a practical example of piety and consciousness of Allah 'so that people may emulate his actions before emulating his words'.[ii]

Secondly, the Imam should treat the common people with compassion and leniency, and refrain from burdening them with harsh and cruel policies. 'He should guide them with tenderness and interdict them in a mild manner. ... He should, out of kindness, lower to them the wing of humility without being either soft, which may lead to disrespect, or harsh, which may lead to hatred,' Abdullahi wrote in *Diya al-Hukkam*. Restrictive legislation should be kept to a minimum, and at no time should the 'standard of the elite' be imposed on the masses. If that happened, Abdullahi maintained, the government would ultimately fail.

Thirdly, the Imam should not have desired that supreme office himself, much less laboured consciously to obtain it. The reason, Muhammad Bello stated in *Usul al-Siyasa*,[iii] is that 'if a ruler is not somewhat removed from the love of leadership and the desire of

i   Omar Bello's translation generally has been used.
ii  Shehu Yarmusa's translation has generally, with modifications here and there, been used. See *The Political Ideas of the Jihad Leaders*, MA. dissertation, Ahmadu Bello University, Zaria, 1975.
iii The translations of Martin and Yamusa have been used interchangeably. See Martin's 'A Muslin political tract from Northern Nigeria: Muhammad Bello's *Usul al-Siyasa'* in *Aspects of West African Islam*, D, McCall and N. Bennett (eds), Boston University, 1971.

sovereignty for itself, one may fear that he is infatuated with himself and will not deal justly with his subjects.' In short, craving for this office is most likely to result in oppression and self-aggrandizement. 'Therefore whoever we see striving hard to get it, more especially if he asks for it, we know for sure that he does not deserve it. And whoever entrusts such a person with authority has committed oppression, for he has put something where it did not deserve to be.'

Fourthly, in the appointment of public officers the Imam should observe at least five rules. One, he should appoint to public office people of competence, piety and probity. Any appointment to public office which is based on favouritism or nepotism is, according to Abdullahi in *Diya al-Hukkam*, null and void. This is perhaps because the Imam is not expected to have vested interests of his own; his only interest must be the overall well-being of the people. Two, no one who has asked for a particular office, or who covets it, should be given that office, or any public office at all. This is not a mere guideline for the Imam, but a fundamental state policy: the Shehu referred to it, in *Kitab al-Farq*,[i] as the first principle of government. Muhammad Bello reiterated the importance of this policy in *al-Ghayth al-Shubub*.[ii]

Know also that most of the evil that befalls the state comes from the appointment of officers who are anxious to have the appointment because none would be keen on such but a thief in the garb of a hermit and a fox in the guise of a pious worshipper, someone who is keen in the collection of money, sacrificing for such his religion and integrity; all his endeavours are for the fruits of this world, not portraying zeal and honesty, and that is the sign of treachery... Once the rights of the Muslims are usurped and their wealth unjustly taken their souls are corrupted. Their obedience diminishes, the affairs of the state become shaky and corruption pervades the state.

To ensure an efficient public service, Abdullahi stated in *Diya al-Hukkam*, the Imam should see that the duties, powers and limits of every public officer are clearly defined. Four, all public officers

i   Hiskett's translation.
ii  See Ismail and Aliyu: 'Bello and the tradition of manuals of Islamic government and Advice to Rulers in Nigerian Administration Research Project', (second interim report), Ahmadu Bello University, Zaria, 1975.

must declare their assets and interests before they assume public responsibilities and do the same when they leave office. 'Whoever is found to have wealth above what he earns from his work, the ruler shall confiscate and restore it to the treasury,' Abdullahi stated. And finally, public offices should be so fairly distributed among the various sections of society, the Shehu implied in *Bayan*, as to exclude no individual groups from government or favour, some above others, as such a display of discrimination or favouritism spells doom for the polity.

Fifthly, the Imam should select only men of conscience, piety and probity as advisers, and be wary of corrupt scholars, sycophants, and hangers-on. It is in his own interest to long for the company of learned men, Muhammad Bello insisted in *Usul al-Siyasa*, as venal scholars propitiate and glorify the ruler, hoping thereby to obtain 'the dross of this world and ill-gotten gains ... by double-dealing and trickery'. Even so, Muhammad Bello seems to have permitted the Imam the paraphernalia of office, provided they enabled him to discharge his functions more efficiently. The Imam, he said in *al-Ghayth al-Shubub*, requires different categories of people to aid him, including 'a group of them for consultation and advice ... a group for elegance and pride, a group for propaganda and praise, a group for writing, a group for prayer and solemnity and a group for knowledge, exegesis and the protection of (religion), the basis of the community', in addition, of course, to those who direct and conduct *jihad* and those who protect the Imam's person.

The sixth condition stipulated that it is more appropriate for the Imam to take only the 'ordinary man's share of public property' as his remuneration. Ideally, he should refrain from taking anything at all, if he has an independent means of livelihood. Bello quoted Umar ibn al-Khattab as saying: 'I granted myself from God's revenue as if it were the property of an orphan [given to a guardian for safekeeping]. If I had sufficient, I abstained [from using it] and if I was in need, I used it in all fairness.' Muhammad Bello himself, as caliph, 'insisted on being self-supporting, and the ideal remained', Prof, Murray Last stated in *The Sokoto Caliphate*. Abdullahi emphasized the fact that the Imam does not have the right in Islam to 'revert to acquiring power and wealth' from the people. Nor is he, let alone his lieutenants, permitted either to receive gifts or use his position to acquire wealth in excess of his lawful entitlements.

In the Sokoto framework his duties are conceived as being very general, mainly having to do with direction and supervision of the affairs of state and the formulation of policies. In this respect, all aspects of government relate back to him and all major state functionaries are directly answerable to him. He is the captain of state, and everyone else is his assistant, appointed by him, answerable to him. Specific functions are attributed to him only by way of emphasis, for these are performed through other organs and institutions of state.

Hence, one of the Imam's foremost tasks is to maintain the structure of the state and ensure that all its organs and apparatus function properly and efficiently. This is how Abdullahi saw the Imam's function:

> ...to serve the interest of his subjects by having civil servants to manage [the State affairs] and men of wisdom to give advice. He must have trustees to keep the treasury and to spend (the funds) for the prescribed purposes. He must have scribes and accountants to take care of the tax. He must have envoys, spies, guards, scholars to serve as guides. He must have governors to collect taxes, honest persons to serve as witnesses; *muhtasibs* to inspect and correct weights and measures; policemen to keep law and order; judges to settle disputes; mediators to reconcile between the rulers and the ruled; and viziers who fear no one but Allah. He must have an impregnable fortress fully supplied with food and water ... trustworthy physicians as well as military commanders ... (and) military experts whose advice will help overcome crisis, for it is certain that victory in war depends on subterfuge and not on the numerical strength of the army, nor on speedy action.

Closely associated with the maintenance of state apparatus is the duty to safeguard the overall well-being of the people. Muhammad Bello, in *Usul al-Siyasa*, was explicit about this fundamental function:

The Imam should provide public amenities for the people of his state for their temporal and religious benefits. For this purpose, he shall foster the artisans, and be concerned with tradesmen who are indispensable to the people, such as farmers and smiths, tailors and dyers, physicians and grocers, butchers and carpenters and all sorts of trade which contributes to [stabilize] the proper order of this world. The ruler must allocate these tradesmen to every village and every locality.... [He] should urge his subjects to seek foodstuffs and keep them for future use. He must keep villages and countryside in prosperity, construct fortresses and bridges, maintain markets and roads and realise for them all that are of public interest so that the proper order of this world may be maintained.

It is the Imam's duty to safeguard the major institutions of Islam – daily prayers, fasting, *zakat* and hajj, together with the preservation of the Islamic faith. He should ensure that all people are educated to the minimum level prescribed by Islam, where they are sufficiently instructed about Islamic faith, values and social conduct, and are given the means to earn a livelihood. Abdullahi further maintained that the state should not permit anyone to remain in ignorance; those who refuse to learn should be compelled to do so. That implies that the Imam must supply sufficient scholars and schools and establish *ribat* for students and men of piety – the expenses to be secured from the state treasury.

It is the Imam's duty to uphold the rights due to Allah by enforcing the punishments prescribed in the Qur'an and Sunna – the *hudud*. The application of *hudud* rests on three basic principles, Bello stated in *al-Ghayth al-Wabl*, that all people must be treated equally before the law; that law must follow its natural course without interference; and finally, that it is an act of betrayal on the part of the Imam to seek to alter the law prescribed by Allah.

It is the Imam's duty to preserve the territorial integrity of the state, maintain internal security and undertake *jihad* in the defence of Islam. As commander of the faithful, the Imam is required, in the words of Muhammad Bello, to 'take part in the battles in person, for the Prophet ﷺ ... took part in his noble person in twenty-seven battles.' He is the symbol of the *umma*, hence the duty to fight in the cause of Allah falls on him first and foremost, before it falls on the others.

Finally, it is the duty of the Imam to establish justice and the pursuit of excellence throughout the state. Justice entails that the due process of law is adhered to in law courts; that public officers are restrained from exploiting the masses, and if they do, are punished accordingly; that even 'righteous people' can be removed from their posts if the public are dissatisfied with their work; and finally, that the ruler makes himself available to the ordinary people in order to receive their complaints and redress their grievances. If justice is not maintained, Bello warned, neither knowledge nor livelihood can ever be pursued in society: the state, as a result, will collapse. Justice, he added, is the foundation of government.

It can be seen, therefore, that the Imam possesses enormous power, and understandably so, since he symbolizes the spirit of the *umma*, its unity and solidarity. To that extent, it is not permitted to contest his authority, or subvert his government as long as he has been legally elected and he performs his functions as required by the *shari'a*. Yet the powers of the Imam are not absolute. In the first place, these powers rest on the fundamental principle that no creature or authority is to be obeyed in disobedience to Allah. Hence, if the Imam issues an order, or brings forth a piece of legislation, or establishes a policy, which conflicts with the clear injunctions of the *shari'a*, then disobedience is not only desired but obligatory. Muhammad Bello stated that 'if he orders the killing of someone, or the seizing of property by force without justification, obedience to him in that is not lawful and there should be no compliance with his command'.

Obedience to him may also be withdrawn where the Imam abandons Islamic values, neglects the establishment of *salat*, attempts to falsify the *shari'a*, or reverts to unbelief. The same rule applies if he ceases to be the true embodiment of Islamic morality, and becomes grossly immoral in his conduct. Finally, the Imam remains in office only as long as he is able to maintain justice in society. If he becomes unjust himself, or if his government is incapable of looking after the well-being of the people, then he should resign voluntarily, failing which he should be forced out of office.

An emphasis has been placed on the need to cultivate a healthy relationship between the Imam and his people. People are asked to remain loyal to him and help him to succeed. This is what is meant by being sincere towards the Imam. The people, Bello suggested in line with al-Turtushi, should try to correct him when he errs, volunteer pertinent information to him, alert him against those who wish to subvert his authority, keep him informed about the conduct and character of his lieutenants, and help to mobilize public opinion in his support. The ideal, the *sunna*, in the opinion of Abdullahi, is that the Imam, his officials and the generality of the people should interact freely with one another, without jealousy or conflict, as it is an obligation to maintain solidarity with fellow Muslims.

**The Shura**

Let us now examine the institution of the *shura* which the Shehu referred to in *Kitab al-Farq* as one of the five foundations of government. The *shura*, we venture to say, is not an ordinary institution, but one possessing, at least in theory, enormous political and moral power. It runs parallel to the Imamate. It serves as a counter-force, albeit of a co-operative and complementary nature, to the enormous power wielded by the Imam at whose behest the police and the armed forces operate; at the same time, it serves to ensure the existence of good government, helping in a fundamental way to preserve the socio-political order of Islam.

Good government, one infers from the Qur'an, depends on two qualities: compassion and consultation. The Qur'an attributes the Prophet's success in his discharge of the affairs of the *umma* to his being compassionate and lenient to the people in general, for, it says: '...*if you had been rough or hard of heart, they would have scattered from around you*'(3:159). However, this success could only have been sustained if the Prophet ﷺ had run a government based on consultation, with consent rather than disparity or discord remaining the basic characteristic of the polity.

In *Diya al-Tawil*[i] Abdullahi explained the overriding importance of *shura* in the political life of the Muslim *Umma*. He stated that *shura* has been responsible for the efficiency, firmness and strength of successive Muslim governments after they have assumed power. It has not been customary to rush to conclusions or let everyone hold his personal opinion; on the contrary they would consult with each other until they reached a consensus; and then they would act on the basis of that consensus. A nation that runs its affairs by mutual consultation, to paraphrase Abdullahi's statement invariably achieves the best results. He maintains that rulers are under a binding obligation to run their government on the basis of *shura*; if not, then it is obligatory on Muslims to depose him forthwith. The absence of *shura*, as Abdullahi would see it, spells doom not only for the polity but also for its existence as a cohesive entity. To the extent that *shura* is a means of judging the will of the people for the purposes of formulating appropriate and acceptable policies and legislation, a government which relies on it to conduct its affairs is truly a government of the people. If this *shura* is destroyed as an institution, there can be no way in which the opinions, wishes and interests of the people can be obtained or judged: a government by and for certain entrenched vested interests – a kingdom, not a caliphate, would result.

*Shura* is, in broad terms, vested in three inter-related powers: the consultative assembly, the *'ulama* and finally, the people. In essence, *shura* runs through the entire operations of the state: every single one of its institutions is involved in consultation from appropriate quarters. The consultative body, however, is the formal, constitutional body which wields enormous political power. This body comprises *mujtahid*s, scholars, leaders of thought, military and community leaders, and, as such, symbolizes the will of the people. It is only logical, as the Sokoto framework envisages it, that it is vested with the all-important power to appoint and depose the Imam. The Imam remains in office at the pleasure of this august body. In addition, this body serves in a consultative capacity: all policies of state are referred to it, its consent or dissent being regarded as the decision of the *umma*. Unfortunately, no criterion

i   Cairo edition, 1961.

has been given in the available sources as to the modality of the appointment of this body. This is obviously due to the historical background from which the Sokoto Caliphate emerged. It was the role which the individual had played during the revolution that determined his membership of this body.

There still remains a more profound *shura* body, at least from the perspective of the historical role of Islam – the *'ulama*. Its role is to guard the conscience and vital interests of the *umma*; to urge those in authority to proper conduct and remind them of their duties, rights and limits; and to rouse the people to action if those in authority begin to move towards tyranny or oppression. The *'ulama*, in this respect, may not represent a formal, constitutional body as such, but it does represent the basic opinions and sentiments of the ordinary people since it interacts with them on a day-to-day basis.

Yet all power resides in the people. It is their voice that ultimately counts. It is their *bay'a* that confirms and legitimizes the power of the Imam. The *shura* exists only as the voice of the people. The people at all times have been invested with the power to speak and raise their voices against any tendency to misuse or abuse power they discern in their government; and the government is under an obligation to listen, and above all, to permit the free flow of the criticism or expressed opinions of the people. If the people fail to voice their opinion, then there is not much good in them; if the rulers refuse to listen to the voice of the people, then there is not much good in them either.

### Key Political Institutions

Two key political institutions received prominence in Sokoto political thought: the *wizara* and *imara*. For the Shehu, an upright *wazir* – or prime minister in modern terminology — is of the utmost necessity to an imam as one 'who wakens him if he sleeps, gives him sight if he cannot see and reminds him if he forgets'. Abdullahi considered the *wazir* as 'the associate of the Imam in the management of the affairs of state ... [his] arm in administration and his refuge in time of calamity'. He is the one principal advisor from whom the Imam 'can gain ... knowledge of what he does not know, and confirmation of what he already knows'. According to

Abdullahi, the *wazir* has jurisdiction over almost all matters of state, the main difference between him and the Imam being that all officials owe their appointment ultimately to the Imam, and remain in office at his pleasure.

In the Sokoto framework, the *wazir* was both the chief advisor and the officer in charge of people's welfare. Accordingly, he was the president of the electoral college which elected caliphs, and advised the caliph on the appointment of key officers of state and, says Prof. Murray Last, 'if the issue was clear and (the *wazir*) was on the spot, he could appoint a new Emir on his own initiative... In difficult appointments ... he had to wait for explicit instruction.' He supervised the emirates and had direct responsibility over the treasury, legal and Qur'anic education and religious institutions in general. On the other hand, as *amir al-masalih*, he took care of the poor and under-privileged. Overall, his principal function was to ensure the success of the Imam's government. Mahmud Tukur sees him 'as the leader of the bureaucracy ... who supervises the general administration, co-ordinates its agencies and orchestrates its staff functions. By this central position, especially his control of chancery and public treasury, he effectively provides the mechanism for organisational unity of command.'

No wonder then that so much was expected of him in terms of qualification and experience. Abdullahi stated in *Diya al-Hukkam* that the *wazir* must be of trustworthy conduct, perceptive in the affairs of the common people with deep kindness towards them, to enable him to remedy whatever injury that might have befallen them through the action of the ruler. Muhammad Bello makes the additional demand in *al-Ghayth Al-Wabl* that the *wazir* must be a person who is well conversant with issues relating to war and economy, and competent to deal with them. Of course he has other *wazir*s to work with him, some as advisors to the caliph, others carrying executive powers.

After the wazirate comes the *imara*, or the office of the state, or provincial governor. The governor, according to Abdullahi, 'is invested with the authority to run the general affairs of his province; he is the man to whom government and authority are delegated. He stands as governors of provinces do in relation to the

Caliphs'. He exercises political, administrative and military control over his province almost as the Imam does over the whole country. The governor is therefore an imam in his own right except that his jurisdiction covers only a limited portion of the country, and he holds office, at least in theory, at the pleasure of the Imam. It is also his prerogative to establish policies aimed at improving the general condition of the people.

The nature of this office calls for the exercise of a sense of responsibility similar to that of the Imam. Hence this note of warning from Abdullahi: 'The governor has to see to the welfare of the people which we mentioned to be one of the duties of the Imam. The governor must not think that he is the owner of the province over which he is made to rule, whereby the land becomes his personal property which he can give to whom he likes and refuse whom he wishes.' Seven specific functions have been assigned to the governor. These were specified by Abdullahi in *Diya al-Wilayat*[i] and by Muhammad Bello in *al-Ghayth al-Shubub*, with a slight difference in emphasis. The first function of the governor in Abdullahi's list is to lead the people in prayer. This is perhaps because it is his appearance and leadership in prayers that assures the community of his continued loyalty to Allah and of his commitment to the fundamental values and ethos of the *umma*. As far as the Shehu was concerned, a governor who had stopped performing this function had swerved in the direction of corruption and despotism: it suggests an inward fear about facing his own people.

It is also the duty of the governor to protect both *hara'im* and *din*. *Hara'im* embraces all objects or people sacred to the state: women, whose interests, rights and persons must be protected; sacred places like the mosques; the moral integrity of the state; and finally the realm itself. *Din*, on the other hand, connotes the Islamic practices and values which the governor should protect against corruption and innovation. This duty entails, among other things, keeping venal scholars at bay and sectarianism firmly checked. Other duties include the maintenance of justice, the appointment of judges and other state officials, the organization of troops, posting them

i    MS in author's possession.

in different parts of the state as the situation demands, founding military settlements and appointing administrators over them, the collection of taxes and levies sanctioned by Islam, and their disbursement as specified by Islamic law, the enforcement of the prescribed punishments and the forwarding of pilgrims.

## Establishment of Justice

The imamate, wazirate and emirate, as well as other vital organs of state, cannot function properly unless justice is maintained and social order effectively preserved. Hence the administration of justice, the removal of injustice from society and all departments of government, and the restraining of the people from committing aggression, injustice or injury to one another, constitutes the very essence of good government. At the head of these fundamental functions is the judiciary, followed by the *radd al-mazalim*, the institution of public complaints, and the police force operating between them.

In the Sokoto framework the judiciary was highly esteemed, Shehu Usman regarded it as the second pillar of state. It centred around the chief justice who 'is not restrained by anyone's censure from upholding God's law', he stated in *Bayan*. Muhammad Bello, perhaps writing from his experiences as caliph, placed the judiciary even higher, above the wazirate, as it were. Without a judiciary, he maintained in *al-Ghayth al-Wabl*, no government can established or survive. Abdullahi insisted that only persons of integrity, piety and knowledge should be appointed as judges, and that anyone who lobbies for the office should not be appointed to it. The best person for this exalted office is one 'who knows what is right and bases his judgement on it, and who is loyal to Allah, has no fear of any criticism, and does not look for gifts or anything of self-interest'. In that situation, to be a judge is one of the highest forms of worship.

On the specific functions of the judiciary, the definitive statement has come from the Shehu in *Bayan*:

The office of *qadi* embraces ten things. The first is to settle cases between litigants either by mutual reconciliation or by compelling them to accept a mandatory judgement.

The second is to prevent oppression, from taking things by force, or from violating the law and so on, and to support the oppressed and help everyone to get his due. The third is to uphold the statutory penalties and carry out the commands of God. The fourth is to hear cases of homicide and injury. The fifth is to safeguard the properties of orphans and the insane and to appoint legal guardians over them. The sixth is to look after estates in mortmain. The seventh is the execution of wills. The eighth is to contract marriages for women, if they have no guardian, or if the guardian has stood in the way of their marrying. The ninth is to care for public utilities, such as the roads of the Muslims and so on. The tenth is to command the good and forbid the evil by word and deed.

On other matters relating to the judiciary, Abdullahi's *Diya al-Hukkam*, remains the most detailed study. He mentioned six elements involved in the administration of justice, including the judge, his jurisdiction, the law itself, the parties involved in a dispute, the witnesses and the legal procedure. He then formulated principles to be followed in the cause of justice. He asserted that the office of the judge should go to a person possessing integrity, intelligence and perception. Secondly, he should be well-paid, so as to protect the public interest: if he were poor, 'his poverty may lead him to endear and humble himself to the rich, and give them preference over the poor in cases of dispute'. Thirdly, the judge should not keep bad company, nor attend parties, except those which Islamic law has made obligatory, nor 'accept gifts from anyone except his close relatives'; and where he has an independent source of income, he should refrain from taking 'reward for judgement'. Fourthly, he should keep away from corruption, for the judgement of a corrupt judge, even if it is correct, is considered null and void. Similarly, be should keep his lieutenants under strict supervision in order to 'restrain them from insulting the people and obtaining their money through deceit'. Fifthly, he must hold all court sessions in public, 'where the strong and the weak can reach him'. Finally, he should make it a duty to inspect prisons from time to time 'in order to release prisoners who have been unjustly jailed'.

All judgements, as is to be expected in an Islamic judicial system, must be based on the Qur'an, Sunna and *Ijma'*, i.e. the consensus of the Muslim community. If, however, the judge cannot find precedents from these sources, he is required to have recourse to his own personal 'assessment and independent reasoning, after consulting the scholars'. But if his knowledge of the *shari'a* is not profound enough to entitle him to an independent reasoning, then he should rely on the most widely accepted opinion, and failing that, 'he must compare various opinions with a view to finding the most sound one'. He is not permitted to give rein to his own whims in passing judgement, or worse still, pass judgements which contradict the clear injunctions of the Qur'an, Sunna or *Ijma'*. Nor is the judge permitted to give a judgement based on his personal knowledge of the issues involved in a case before him; he must base his judgement only on the evidence set before him. The judge, Abdullahi continued, is not permitted to 'pronounce a judgement in favour of himself', and if he has a case against someone else, 'the case has to be taken to another judge'. Similarly, he is not permitted 'to judge a case between any member of his tribe and an outside opponent; not even if the outsider consents to that'. He may not pass a judgement in favour of his close relatives, though he may pass a judgement against them; he may not judge against his enemy, he may however judge in his favour. In short, the judge must be absolutely fair, and be seen to be so.

Abdullahi stated that the judge has exclusive jurisdiction over 'all legal rights' – matters concerned with wills, trust estates, guardianships, cases of injury and bloodshed. 'All these matters must be taken to the judge alone, and must be dealt with only in his department. Should the judge lose control over these matters, he shall be at fault.' Matters which border on state policies and administration are generally considered to be outside the jurisdiction of the judge. These pertain to the office of the Imam. 'The judge may not pronounce on a general policy with regard to such matters as the distribution of spoils of war, allocating funds from the treasury for various projects of public interest, executing prescribed punishment, organising armed forces ... distribution of lands for agriculture or for [the exploitation of its] mineral resources and the like. Such policy making is not permissible for anyone except with the permission of the Imam.' Even so, the separation of powers between the judiciary and the executive is not absolute. For the judge may sometimes follow up his decisions to see that they are executed as an 'extra duty', especially where there is despotism and his orders are likely to be disregarded.

Ideally, the judge should steer clear of policy making or playing an executive role. Being aloof from society most of the time, he is detached from the intrigues and intricacies of power and not conversant with politics. If he takes over executive functions his actions could lead to instability and public dissent because they are not likely to be based on sound political judgement. All these are the concerns of the Imam.

Thus, after stating that, according to Ibn Farhun, the exclusion of the judge from supervising policies is not binding under all circumstances and that in certain situations a judge has the right to supervise many policies, depending on custom and practice, Abdullahi agreed with Ibn al-Qayyim, that 'the nature of public offices whether they have general or limited powers is derived from the words [used to describe them] as well as from [the prevailing] circumstances and customs'. The *shari'a* does not set specific limits to such offices. What in a particular situation may fall within the purview of the war office, may in another situation come under the judiciary, and so on. Similarly, the Imam is not entirely excluded from exercising judicial powers: indeed, one of his required qualifications is that he should be a *mujtahid*, a scholar capable of making decisions based on his own assessment of the issues confronting him.

In the Sokoto setting, the caliph also exercised judicial powers. Muhammad Bello, in particular, used to review the judgement of his judges, ordering a retrial if he found signs of miscarriage of justice. In short, there is nothing sacrosanct about the so-called separation of powers. The Shehu, in theory and practice, established a judiciary of pyramidal structure, with the chief justice at its apex. The Imam, he stated in *Kitab al-Farq*, 'shall appoint a *qadi* in accordance with the *shari'a*, to be with him, to review under him the judgement of every [other] *qadi*... Then the judge in his turn appoints a deputy under his command in each province of each country as he wishes, and for this reason he is customarily called 'Chief Judge' and none shall be called thus except he who answers to this description, and any other judge shall be called "judge" only.' There is also provision for judges with specific as opposed to general jurisdiction over matters relating to personal status only, or land, or criminal issues and so on. Finally, there is also a provision for one additional office directly connected with the judiciary – *wali al-radd*. Its function is to review cases in which there are doubts as to whether or not a judge has upheld the principle that he cannot be a judge in his own cause. It may well be exercised by the Chief Justice, but in Sokoto, it was exercised by the caliph himself. It may be worthwhile to note that Abdullahi cautioned against misuse of appeal procedures, because of the effect it could have on the judicial system itself. 'Legal decisions,' he said, quoting the authoritative Qadi Ismail, 'may be regarded as sound and valid so long as injustice is not established against it... . Reversing judgements causes harm to people and weakens the judges. For no judge is without enemies accusing him of injustice.'

The sister institution to the judiciary in the Sokoto system is the *wali al-mazalim*, a public complaints commission or office of ombudsman. It was an innovation, the Shehu wrote in *Bayan*, established in Islamic history when people became corrupt, and despotic rulers 'weakened the *qadis* so as to be in a position to oppress their subjects and put people in need of them – they would then sit back and the injustices would continue'. Basically, therefore, this office falls within the jurisdiction of the judiciary but the force of circumstances made it necessary to establish it as an independent institution in its own right. It is conceived as an institution with greater political, though not necessarily moral, power than the judiciary.

This office is concerned with cases beyond the *qadi*'s power, and which, therefore, a man of greater authority has to look into. Ideally, this is the Imam himself. 'The case arises when there is a dispute between two weak persons, one of whom has been favoured, or if it is between a weak and a strong man or between two strong men but one has the advantage of being supported by men in authority such as amirs and provincial governors acting unjustly; these are the cases which the caliph took it upon himself to settle.' The office is necessitated by the stipulation that the Imam should remain accessible to his people, and therefore it is his binding obligation to hear their complaints, particularly those by women, those against himself, his governors or his officials; for unless he deals with such matters promptly, he will undermine his own government.

Seven specific functions are assigned to this office, from the details available in Abdullahi's *Diya al-Hukkam* and *Diya al-Wilayat* and Bello's *al-Ghayth al-Wabl*. Muhammad Bello, whose line of thought we shall be following, suggests that the custodian of this office must be more powerful than the *qadi*, since he deals essentially with complaints against the mighty, whom he should restrain from governing by intimidation or coercion. 'It is essential that he be seen to have knowledge of the law and to the pious.' He is to be assisted by the police, judges, jurists, clerks and witnesses.

According to Muhammad Bello, *wali al-mazalim* has the fundamental responsibility to ensure that government policies are neither harsh nor cruel, and do not constitute an excessive burden on the people. He should see to it that the taxes imposed are lawful, fair and not excessive; that the method of collecting them is guided by 'equitable regulations'; that overtaxing is duly refunded; and, above all, keep a vigilant eye on the treasury. In addition, he is responsible for ensuring that public servants are paid promptly and in full, without deductions. Furthermore, he should ensure that citizens' goods seized legally by authority, or some other powerful elements in society, are restored to their legitimate owners. It is also his duty to implement those laws of Islam regarding the rights of ordinary citizens which the judges and the inspectors of public morality may have been 'too weak to put into effect'. Finally, the *wali al-mazalim* looks after endowments – such as schools, hospitals, and similar public institutions – and has a say in the upkeep of mosques and matters affecting the hajj.

Let us say a word or two about the police. The Shehu referred to this institution as the 'third pillar of sovereignty', whose function fundamentally is to ensure that 'the weak obtain justice from the powerful'. Though Bello has not given any prominence or importance to this office, Abdullahi praised it as 'the most noble of all responsibilities.' It is the police who, at the behest of either the Imam or the judge, effect arrests, take people to prison, or restrain one person from oppressing another and enforce the law generally.

### Preservation of Social Morality

We can now move on to look into another vital organ of state: the *hisba*. This institution, which is supervised by the *muhtasib*, is charged with commanding the good and prohibiting the wrong, in other words, with the preservation of Islamic social morality. The details about the functions of this institution are to be found in Abdullahi's *Diya Ahl al-Ihtisab,*[i] his *Diya al-Imam*, and Muhammad Bello's *al-Ghayth al-Wabl*.

Ideally, the responsibility for ensuring social morality should be carried out by the *'ulama*, since it is in principle a matter of public education aimed at awakening individual Muslims to their basic moral responsibilities. But as an institution *hisba* rests on the notion that every member of society should be sufficiently educated to know what his responsibilities to the *umma* are, and how they can be discharged. As long as even one individual is left without this minimal social consciousness, the Islamic government, Abdullahi implied, has yet to discharge its obligations in full. In broad terms, the *muhtasib* deals with three matters: regulation of the market; promotion of justice in society – especially as it relates to economic dealings – and finally the preservation of public morality. With regard to the market, or commerce, the *muhtasib's* main function is to control the quality of goods being sold.

The Shehu had complained that some tradesmen were in the habit of embellishing copper and passing it for silver; others refused to separate gold dust from sand; others increased the weight of meat by means of aeration; others mixed milk with water. It was the duty of the *muhtasib* to put an end to all these practices. Muhammad Bello decided that adulterated, ill-prepared, or sub-standard commodities should be destroyed, the offenders apprehended, and that all commodities should bear the stamp and name of their respective manufacturers. Secondly, the *muhtasib*, according to

i    MS in author's possession.

Abdullahi, is responsible for preventing monopolies; ensuring an unhindered flow of goods to the market; and preventing artificial and unwarranted price rises, without, however, imposing artificial prices of his own. In addition, the *muhtasib* should strive to eliminate all forms of *riba* – or unjust enrichment – in commercial transactions.

A further crucial aspect of the *muhtasib's* role in the market is the standardization of weights and measures, and the elimination of fraud in this regard. Shehu Usman agreed with al-Maghili that the country should be divided into economic zones, each zone having one standard of weights and measures, which should be checked constantly. The Shehu specified in detail the relevant procedures: 'The [correct] method of measuring is as follows: the one who is measuring should set the measuring container on the level. Then he gently pours into it what is to be measured until it is completely full, without pressing it down or buoying it up or shaking it or using any kind of trickery. He simply sets down the measuring container in a level position and pours into it until it fills up naturally.'[i] He demanded that the *muhtasib* prevent ignorant people from acting as tradesmen or agents in Muslim markets, only those acquainted with the basic Islamic rules guiding transactions should be permitted.

In the sphere of social morality, according to Abdullahi, the *muhtasib* has the following responsibilities: to safeguard the spiritual values of Islam, the most important of which is public worship; to ensure that proper standards of hygiene are maintained in homes and that health hazards are avoided; that public health is maintained; that streets are kept clean and free of waste; that the sewage is properly organized; and that animals are fairly treated and not physically abused. Similarly, the *muhtasib* must make sure that the layout of houses agrees with Islamic law, in that roads are not obstructed, and homes are not deprived of fresh air by ill-placed walls and so on. In addition, the *muhtasib* should safeguard public decency by ensuring that the interaction of the sexes in public, as well as their dress, complies generally with the *shari'a*. Food should not be wasted, especially at official banquets. The rich must be

---

i    See John Junwick's *Al-Maghili's Replies.*

prevented from making an immodest and extravagant display of wealth in public. Finally, he should ensure that the fundamental purposes of the *shari'a*, such as the preservation of the human intellect and the strengthening of family institutions, are realized. To that end he should control the flow of alcohol in society, and block any paths leading to indecency and permissiveness, such as prostitution

Since the *muhtasib* is concerned mainly with raising the moral tone of society, it is essential for him, Abdullahi realized, to observe high moral standards in discharging his duties. He must limit himself to unanimously agreed offences against fundamental moral values, and which are therefore known to be such by the majority of the people. Secondly, the *muhtasib* must observe maximum respect for individual rights. He cannot, for example, apprehend a person for an offence being committed in private; he cannot break into a house without the owner's permission; nor can he go out of his way deliberately to seek information about people, or subject them to instant searches, or eavesdrop on their conversations, or smell their mouths for wine, or otherwise spy on them. The *muhtasib* cannot apprehend a person on the basis of intent to commit a moral crime. 'We are ordered [by *shari'a*] to keep as secret what Allah has Himself kept secret, and to censure only what we see being committed in the open.'

Above all, the *muhtasib* is required to employ a blend of firmness and leniency, and offences committed out of ignorance should be dealt with 'in a kindly manner, not with roughness or causing injury'. Common offences should similarly be disposed of 'with compassion, not with harshness or anger', and, in some cases, with exhortations, appeals and education. It is only when all this fails to deter an offender that recourse can be made to strong language. Where wilful damage is being done to property, or where there has been a blatant violation of other people's rights, such as illegal occupation of another person's house, the *muhtasib* can resort to force, but without the use of arms. Incorrigible criminals may be subjected to threats and beating when all peaceful means of approach have been exhausted. Lastly, criminals who carry lethal weapons and are not amenable to appeals and moral education may, with the explicit permission of the Imam, be fought until they are overpowered. Any of the *muhtasib's* men killed in this fight, Abdullahi maintained, would have died a martyr in the cause of Allah.

From its functions as elaborated in Sokoto, one cannot but agree with the Shehu that *hisba* is the most versatile and extensive of the organs of state. Under Caliph Muhammad Bello, the *muhtasib* maintained a considerable influence in the state hierarchy. In addition to overseeing commerce, supervising buildings and streets to ensure that they complied with the law in respect of their upkeep and layout, Muhammad Julde, the *muhtasib*, administered the capital whenever the Caliph was away.

**Public Welfare**

The next issue is concerned with methods of securing the well-being of the people. What we have seen so far, whether it be in relation to the office of the Imam, the *qadi* or the *muhtasib*, suggests that the ultimate purpose of the state is to ensure that the overall welfare of the Muslim *umma* is promoted. Thus whatever other provisions there are, such as the ones we shall be examining presently, they constitute an integral aspect of a political and social process consciously engineered to fulfil the objective of safeguarding the *umma* from social degradation, deprivation and injustice, and providing its individual members with the necessary means and opportunities to live honourably and decently.

We shall now examine two matters which at all times have a profound bearing on the life of any given people: land and the *bayt-al-mal*. Our sources on land use in general are Abdullahi's *Ta'lim al-Radi*,[i] unquestionably the definitive work on land policy in the Sokoto Caliphate, which was adapted by the Shehu in *Bayan*, and Bello's *al-Ghayth al-Wabl*. *Al-Ghayth* adds a touch of experience and practice to the basic principles formulated in *Ta'lim al-Radi*.

Land policy in the Sokoto Caliphate, as in the Prophetic period and that of the rightly-guided caliphate, was generally dictated by the historical process, which gave it a central and crucial place,

---

i   Sani Zahradeen's translation. See Appendix A of his *Abd Allah Ibn Fodio's contribution to the Fulani Jihad*.

not only in matters concerning agriculture, individual pursuit of livelihood, the establishment of new cities and settlements, but also equally in matters relating to taxation, distribution of state resources and above all, *jihad* in the defence of Islam and the realm. This is in addition to man's inherent attachment to the earth, or his dependence on the soil, to which the Qur'an calls our attention time and again: *'After that He smoothed out the earth and brought forth from it its water and its pastureland and made the mountains firm, you and for your livestock to enjoy.'* (79:31-3) For the purpose of simplification, we shall examine land policy in the Sokoto framework under three headings: (i) land which falls into the category of *fay'* and therefore constitutes a common property of the Muslim *umma*; (ii) land subject to individual ownership, which can be assigned as such by the Imam; and (iii) products from the earth, such as water and mineral resources.

Land is considered *fay'*, that is, sacred, inviolable and the inalienable property of the *umma* under the following circumstances: first, if it is acquired in the process of *jihad*, or as a result of revolution, where a political and social system has been overturned and replaced by an Islamic one; second, if it is annexed as a result of a peace treaty; and finally, if it reverts to the *umma* as a result of its abandonment by its non-Muslim owners, who might have fled at the advance of Muslim forces. This category of land belongs to the generality of the Muslim *umma* and cannot be owned privately either by an individual or a group in perpetuity nor alienated in any circumstances. The revenues accruing from such land by way of tax, if it is annexed by a peace treaty, or by its beneficial use by the state or individuals who have been granted usufruct rights to it if it is acquired by war and so on, all belong to the *umma*, to be used for its welfare. This is a policy derived directly from the Qur'an and is therefore immutable: neither the Imam, nor the *umma* itself, is authorized to change this as stated in the Qur'an: *'They will ask you about booty. Say: 'Booty belongs to Allah and the Messenger.'* (8:1) Muhammad Bello elaborated on this policy in *al-Ghayth al-Wabl*:

It is not lawful to expend anything [from *fay'*] for the benefit of a particular person, nor his children, because the yield from it is for the benefit of the Muslims in general and it should not be set aside for one who is not useful to them in a general way... The assignment (of these lands) in perpetuity to a man and then to his children and his posterity or offspring for as long as they survive is not permissible. Nor is it permissible to assign it as an endowment to an individual man, then to his children or his posterity or his offspring. Nor is it permissible to assign it to an infidel or to one to whom the assigning of it is not in the interest of the Muslims.

Individual ownership of land is permissible in two instances: by an outright grant of a piece of land by the Imam acting in the interest of Muslims; and by an individual person's act of putting 'dead' land to beneficial use, with the express permission of the Imam. Abdullahi stated that whoever has been granted land by the Imam becomes its exclusive owner 'and he may sell it, give it to someone or bequeath it. The law remains the same as above whether the piece of land granted to him by the ruler is situated in desert lands or within populated areas.' However, the Imam has no right to grant arable plots of *fay'* land for individual ownership.

Abdullahi enumerated the ways in which the effort which a person puts into a piece of 'dead' or virgin land can earn him the ownership of it. These include: establishing an irrigation system; land reclamation; putting up substantial constructions; 'considerable planting'; 'cultivation by ploughing and breaking up the ground' as well as 'breaking the stones ... and levelling the ground and its steep holes' – in short, heavy investment in labour in the land. Even so, the ownership does not become absolute, as it is based solely on the piece of land being put to beneficial use. The right to ownership lapses as soon as the owner neglects the land. In that case, the man who recultivates the plot has more claim to it than the previous owner. Abdullahi's definition of 'dead' land demonstrates his concern to restrict private ownership of land to the barest minimum. In the end what emerges as a 'dead' land is land which is not useful for the cultivation of grain, and which is thus not needed by the peasantry because it requires heavy investment in money and labour.

The Imam is authorized, indeed under an obligation, to reserve land as *hima* – to be used either as pasture or grazing for the animals meant for state use, or animals of Muslims in general, or specifically for the animals of the poor who cannot otherwise obtain grazing facilities. This land remains within the jurisdiction of the state and is in excess of land required by the people to sustain their livelihood. In addition, the Imam is required to reserve spaces as *hurum*: 'where ... people get their firewood and graze their flocks'. Accordingly, individual communities and the public in general have their own *hurum*, each in accordance with their circumstances and needs. The *harim* (singular) of a house surrounded by virgin land constitutes 'areas used as entrances, exits, outdoor stone benches, drainage system ... and where earth is stored [for building purposes) by the people who live there'. The *harim* for a well used for general purposes constitutes those 'spaces [around it] which do not cause any damage to its water or to who come to drink from it'. Public roads have their own *harim* too. 'It is therefore illegal,' concluded Abdullahi, 'to sit or stand on a footpath ... anyone who puts up a building on public paths or adds part of the pathway to his property should be prohibited from doing so ... anyone who puts up a building on public paths which inconveniences the flow of traffic should be instructed to demolish it ... the building should also be demolished, even if it causes no harm to the people [so long as it was on public paths).'

Water and mineral resources belong to the *umma* and cannot be owned privately. Abdullahi classified water resources into four categories. The first is 'ownerless water', such as rivers and springs. This is meant for the general public and 'people have equal right of access to this water and no one should have exclusive rights over it'. The second is water obtained through individual effort, such as that from a well dug by a person or located on his land. Abdullahi insisted that 'it is a desired act if he allows other people free access to it but he should not be compelled to do so'. However, if people are in dire need of drinking water, it is obligatory on him to permit them access to it, and if he refuses, 'they have the right to use force against him'. Similarly if his neighbours' source of water has been damaged, they have an automatic right to his water. The third is water collected from rainfall: according to Abdullahi, it 'should be distributed among the people through whose land the water flows'. The fourth category of water is one from the wells dug in the wilderness for grazing animals. 'The person who digs the well,' Abdullahi stated, 'has priority over its water but he is not permitted to prevent other people from using the excess.'

Mineral resources fall under the jurisdiction of the Imam, who deals with them as he deems fit in the interest of the *umma*. He can, depending on the quality or quantity of the minerals, 'enter into transaction with people concerning [their exploitation] according to what is lawful'. The general principle, however, is that minerals such as gold, salt or sulphur are the property of the *umma* and cannot under any circumstance be subject to private ownership.

As for the *bayt-al-mal* or the state treasury, the conception in Sokoto is that, as defined by Bello, it is the totality of the resources 'to which the Muslims have an unqualified right and which does not belong to a particular group of them, nor to specified people,' As the support system for many of the citizens of the stare, it is essential that the *bayt-al-mal* should not be tainted with illegality: hence the insistence that it be derived from lawful incomes and by strictly lawful means. To start with, all taxes which come into it must be those sanctioned by Islam, and no more. 'The Imam,' Abdullahi stated in *Diya al-Hukkam*, 'must strive to collect taxes through lawful means and spend it where Allah has decreed that it should be spent'. He is forbidden [to] 'touch property acquired unjustly ... the use of such property is unanimously regarded as illegal', because such a method of acquisition 'corrupts the religion and opens the door wide ... to oppression of the poor'. Similarly 'punishment by confiscation' of people's property is illegal.

Legitimate sources of state income are of three categories. The first constitute all resources from *fay'*. They are to be spent on the defence of Islam and its people, to pay the salaries of soldiers, public servants and imams; and, said Abdullahi:

> [The Imam] will pay the indigents their allowances until he covers all of them, male and female, minors and adults, on the basis of the amount they need, and the nature of their

needs... If the money is more than enough, the surplus shall be kept in the treasury for what may possibly occur in form of calamity, or for building mosques, or freeing of captives, or settling debts, or assisting bachelors to get married, or helping pilgrims, or for any other purpose that may possibly arise.

It is essential that the proceeds from a given area should be spent on the needs of that area because 'the citizens of the territory where the property is located have more right [to it] than anyone else'. Another source of state income is the legitimate taxes levied on non-Muslim citizens in an Islamic state. These are: the land tax paid to the state which is the ultimate owner of land; then *jizya* paid to the state for the protection it provides and in lieu of military services; then the custom duties levied on the merchandise brought by non-Muslim foreigners to sell in the Islamic state, which protects the foreigners and their goods. A third source of income is the property of those who die without legal heirs and all properties whose owners are unknown.

There is a parallel treasury to the *bayt-al-mal*: the treasury to which belong the proceeds from *zakat* paid by Muslims. These proceeds do not belong to the state but specifically to the needy, and the underprivileged of its members. It is thus a fund intended to alleviate the condition of the dispossessed and the hard-pressed. The overall purpose of *zakat* as an institution is the elimination of poverty and keeping the *umma* as a socially cohesive entity. It is not a tax as such but a spiritual obligation which a Muslim owes to Allah by virtue of his faith. Its payment to the Islamic state by the individual Muslim represents an affirmation of loyalty to the Islamic state, just as a refusal to pay it, when a Muslim has the means to do so, represents a lack of loyalty, and a deliberate refusal to contribute his own quota to the strengthening of economic justice in society.

Taxation in general is governed by very strict regulations. The first and perhaps the most important of these rules is that all taxes and levies outside the categories we have listed are considered, in the Sokoto framework, as illegal and unjust. Muhammad Bello referred to such taxes as mucus or extortions, 'which the *shari'a* does not permit, and which [the demand of) justice does not allow'. Abdullahi made perhaps the only exception to this general rule: 'If, however, there is a calamity, the harm of which engulfs all Muslims and which cannot be removed except with money and there is no money left in the treasury, the Muslims are under obligation to help with their money,' provided, of course, that this is not turned into a permanent tax.

The second rule about taxation is that even legitimate taxes should in no way be beyond the means of the people. For example, *kharaj*, Bello stated categorically, should be levied with due regard to 'what the land bears in relation to its fertility or infertility, and in relation to the current prices of its produce, the decrease or increase thereof, and in relation to the irrigation of the land and the burden [which this imposes]'. The ultimate purpose of taxation is to establish an equitable balance between the needs of the individual and those of the state – between the purse of an individual citizen and the treasury of the state. The third condition relating to taxation is that the state must presume that the citizens are honest in respect of the declaration of their assets for the purpose of tax assessment. 'Therefore,' Abdullahi insisted in *Diya al-Hukkam*, 'the ruler and his deputies have no right to violate the privacy of people and search houses in order to collect [*zakat*], nor do they have the right to put people on oath on account of it, unless the people concerned are known to be evildoers.'

The payment of *zakat* by Muslims and of *jizya* by non-Muslims presupposes one fundamental fact: that all citizens of the Islamic state do have a right, and indeed a duty, to seek a legitimate means of livelihood without hindrance. In *Siraj al-Ikhwan*, the Shehu, following al-Barnawi, listed the various opportunities available to the citizens of an Islamic state to earn their livelihood and enrich their lives: these include trade, manual labour, hunting on land and in the sea, industry and of course agriculture. This is a right which the state cannot usurp from the people, and for which it should provide ample facilities and opportunities.

On the whole, a citizen pays, under this scheme, only one form of tax at a time; if he is in a legal position to pay two kinds of taxes, then one lapses automatically. For example, a person does not pay *zakat* and *kharaj* at the same time even if he lives on land subject to *kharaj*. He pays only *zakat*, and *kharaj*, which otherwise is binding on him, lapses. Similarly, all poor people, Muslim and non-Muslim alike, are exempt from taxes and in the case of *jizya*, women, monks, old people, etc. are exempt. Indeed all such people, the poor, the old, the infirm and in some cases, women, are recipients of state subsidies.

## The Defence of Islam

The last matter for our consideration is *jihad*, on which the ultimate defence of the *dar al-Islam* is dependent. It is the Imam's duty, Muhammad Bello emphasized in *al-Ghayth al-Wabl*, to mobilize Muslim forces in readiness at all times for *jihad*. Therefore, Islamic policy is that each citizen of the state, male and female, is in one way or other a potential defender of Islam, and must therefore be given military training. The Prophet 🕮 emphasized this fact in one of his sermons: 'Prepare to meet [the enemy] with as much strength as you can afford. Beware, strength lies in archery.' In contemporary terms, archery could well mean the effective use of guns. He also said that anyone who had had a military training and forgot it was guilty of disobedience to Allah and His Messenger.

For the purpose of convenience, we may classify *jihad* into two categories: (i) internal *jihad* – corrective wars aimed at preserving internal stability and peace; and (ii) the external *jihad*, aimed at eliminating injustice, and defending Islam and the realm against its enemies, and exalting the Word of Allah. The first kind of *jihad*, the corrective war, is fought principally, the Shehu explained in *Bayan*, against three forces: the forces of apostasy, social destabilization and rebellion. Apostates are those who undermine the ideology of the state by reneging on their belief in Islam and actively seeking to subvert it by force of arms. In general, they are treated as total enemies of the state. Thus, 'no truce can be concluded with them permitting to remain in their land; no peace treaty can be made with them which allows them to remain as apostates on the payment of sum of money ... [and] no marriage contract with them is valid'. They have forfeited their citizenship of *dar al-Islam* and cannot be permitted to live within its borders unless they first renounce their apostasy and stop their active subversion of the Islamic faith.

Rebels, or *bughat*, as defined in *Bayan* (and also in *Diya al-Hukkam*), are 'those who revolt against the Imam or refuse to come under his sway, or withhold a lawful due such as *zakat* and the like', or prevent others from obeying the Imam. The first thing is to call them 'back to the truth'; if they respond favourably, then they are re-absorbed immediately into the Islamic fold; if they refuse, they should be brought under control by military means. This is, however, governed by certain conditions as stated in *Bayan*. These include:

(i)     Rebels are fought with the intention of stopping their rebellion, not necessarily of killing them.
(ii)    Their injured and captives may not be put to death.
(iii)   Their women and children may not be held captive.
(iv)    Their property may not be taken as booty.
(v)     No truce can be concluded to enable them, in any form, 'to continue with their innovations' or to stay in the territories under their control as rebels.
(vi)    Neither their homes nor their economic base may be destroyed.

The reason for these liberal and generous stipulations, it seems, is to make reconciliation possible when rebellion is eventually crushed. Rebels are regarded in all circumstances as Muslims; their rebellion is considered as fundamentally political. According to Abdullahi, rebels are not liable to pay compensation for the damages they have caused to lives and property during the disturbances if 'the motive behind their rebellion was based on a certain interpretation of the law of Islam'. It is, however, a different matter altogether if, from the overwhelming evidence available, it appears that the standard of rebellion has been raised deliberately to weaken the *dar al-Islam* and undermine the cohesion of the *umma*.

*Muharibun* were described by Abdullahi as people who intercept travellers on highways, in cities, or in the wilderness, in order to commit robbery by violent means; or those who draw weapons against people without any just cause; or those who enter people's houses by night and fight the occupants in order to take away their property; and those who trade in premeditated murders. In short, they are those who disturb society by making life, property and honour unsafe, and subvert the social peace of the Islamic state. The Shehu stated that they should first be admonished; if that failed, a fullscale *jihad* should be waged against them.

The *jihad* against external enemies, on the other hand, may be waged in order to defend the *dar al-Islam* against aggression; to bring the enemy into the fold of Islam; or alternatively, to bring them into a peace agreement with Muslims. But in all these cases the object should be to exalt the *shari'a* and destroy unbelief. The conduct of war is governed by a strict moral code. This, as we read in *Bayan* and *Diya al-Hukkam*, includes the following conditions:

(i) In principle, unbelievers should first be invited to Islam; if they refuse, then they should be asked to enter into a peace treaty with Muslims; if they refuse, they may be fought.

(ii) While numerous kinds of weapons may be used against the enemy, poison – or in modern terminology, chemical warfare – may not be used.

(iii) Women, the disabled, priests, children, old people – in short, noncombatants – may not be killed.

(iv) If the enemy shield themselves with women and children then they should be left alone unless they pose serious strategic danger to Islam – danger that could lead to the irretrievable defeat of Muslims or the annihilation of Islam. The same situation applies if they shield themselves with Muslims.

(v) The Imam has a choice of keeping prisoners of war captive indefinitely, or else releasing them by ransom or unconditionally.

(vi) 'It is forbidden to betray a captive, who loyally gave himself up, after assuring him of a safe conduct': in Abdullahi's words, prisoners of war may not be killed.

(vii) 'It is permitted,' he also said, 'to kill a spy who transmits information about Muslims to the infidels.'

(viii) 'It is not permissible to separate a woman [captive] from her infant child."

(ix)   Mutilation of the bodies of fallen enemy soldiers is prohibited.

Non-Muslims, who become citizens of the Islamic state, either by outright conquest or through a peace treaty, are similarly governed by well-defined regulations. In the case of the latter, the Imam must abide by the terms of the treaty, which includes the inbuilt provision that they keep their land and property if they pay the *jizya* for the security they enjoy from the state. And in all cases, the obligations of the Islamic state towards them include the following:

(i)    The non-Muslim citizens shall maintain their religious and social autonomy and preserve their distinctive characteristics. They shall apply their own laws as they relate to personal status and social and moral life.

(ii)   They shall be permitted to 'settle in our land' as the Shehu has stated.

(iii)  They shall have a guarantee of protection for their lives, property and honour and shall live in peace in the Islamic state.

(iv)   We should not, said the Shehu, interfere with their places of worship, nor with their wine or pigs unless they make them public.

(v)    They shall be required by the state to adhere to their religion.

Their obligations to the Islamic state include, principally, that they shall pay the *jizya*, respect the laws and symbols of Islam and should not subject either Islam or Muslims to abuse or slander. They may not commit aggression against Muslims, but they have the right to self-defence against any Muslim aggressor. They may not rise in arms against the state, nor outrage the honour of Muslim women; nor spy against the Islamic state; nor renounce their citizenship except where they have been oppressed. The Islamic state may insist that its non-Muslim citizens practise their own religions as a precondition of citizenship.

The Sokoto Caliphate took exceptional care in following these principles to the letter. A typical example of its treatment of its non-Muslim citizens can be found in the case of the Jukun. Dr. Tesemchi Makar has made the observation that after the Jukun had accepted their *dhimmi* status by their payment of *jizya*, 'they maintained their traditional religious systems of beliefs ... whether the Jukun people really embraced Islam or not they [Muslim authorities] did not care to know'. But the Muslims went further than that. The Caliphate carried out *jihad* against the Tiv people to protect its *dhimmi* population, the Jukun, from being colonized by the Tiv. Dr. Makar remarks that in general, 'conquered people were not compelled to practice the Islamic faith. This fact alone seems to explain the presence of large non-Muslim communities found today in the Emirates of Lafia, Keffi and Nassarawa'.

The Imam, or indeed any member of the Muslim *umma*, is permitted to grant an *aman*, or safe-conduct, within the length and breadth of the Islamic state to non-Muslims belonging to a country at war with the Islamic state. *Aman* operates to accord sanctity and invioliability to the life, property and honour of such people who come for one purpose or other into *dar al-Islam*. The granting of *aman* is ultimately the prerogative of the Imam, especially when those to be granted are many; but in general, any *bona fide* member of the Islamic state – male or female – can grant it to others, and the state is bound to honour it.

Three matters may be noted in respect of *aman*. First of all, there are categories of people who, by virtue of their occupation or political status, are entitled to *aman* as of right. These are the business community and diplomats. 'A man engaged in trading,' said the Shehu, 'or on an embassy does not need an *aman* because that mission automatically gives him protection.' Diplomatic and commercial channels must remain open between all states even in times of war.

Secondly, the Islamic state is encouraged to grant *aman* on very liberal terms and to give those who seek it the benefit of the doubt, or return them to a place of safety if the state cannot grant them *aman*. The following is how Abdullahi illustrated this magnanimous Islamic gesture in *Diya al-Hukkam*:

> If a Muslim said to the enemy, 'Do not be afraid' and the enemy thought that to be *aman*, while the Muslim had no intention of granting one, but the enemy came along [into

the Islamic State] in the belief that be was given *aman*; or if the Imam had forbidden the Muslims to give *aman* but they disobeyed and gave it without permission; or if the people were not aware of the Imam's prohibition to give *aman* or had forgotten about it, or were ignorant about the obligation of obedience to the Imam in that respect; or if the enemy thought that the person who had given him the *aman* was a Muslim but later he discovered that he was a *dhimmi* – the *aman* in these five cases should be honoured subject to the approval of the Imam. If the Imam does not approve, the enemy must be returned to the place of safety in which he was before. He may neither be killed nor put into slavery.

Thirdly, emphasis is laid on the inviolability of the property of those granted *aman*. If a person who is granted *aman* dies within the Islamic state, his property, according to Abdullahi, 'should be sent to whom his property is normally sent'. Abdullahi stated further: 'Know that a deposit left with us by a person who has been granted an *aman* should be sent to him wherever he may be, even if he had fought against the Muslims.'

One of the possible reasons for maintaining this liberal policy of *aman* could be to keep the door of peace and reconciliation between the Islamic state and its non-Muslim adversary wide open, so that peace treaties can be concluded between Muslims and non-Muslims. The Islamic state is under strict obligation to honour all the terms in the treaties it concludes with others. It is reported in the hadith that 'Whoever kills a man who is under the protection of a pact shall not smell the air of Paradise.' It is also reported that 'If a people betray a treaty, Allah shall cause their enemy to prevail over them.' It is on this basis that the scholars are unanimous on the prohibition of breaking a pact. Nevertheless the Islamic state is not authorized to enter into a treaty which, in the final analysis, is bound to be detrimental to the cause of Islam.

To conclude, two points need to be re-emphasized. Firstly, that the whole conception of state which we have just seen is built on the premise that an Islamic dispensation begins with the *hijra*, which, as a moral, intellectual and physical flight from the domain of evil, cancels all excuses to return to pre-Islamic habits and methods of government. *Hijra* imposes on the Islamic community the obligations to do justice, uphold the *shari'a* and keep a safe distance from all practices and policies that are known to be repugnant to Islam. *Hijra* also imposes on Muslims the obligation to befriend all other Muslims and enter into solidarity with them, and to abhor friendship with unbelieving powers in opposition to Islam. It is no accident, therefore, that the two principal manuals of government, *Diya al-Hukkam* of Abdullahi and *Bayan* of Shehu, start with chapters dealing with *hijra* and the attendant obligation to identify with Muslims wherever they are. The other point has been stated by Mahmud Tukur: 'It can be said on the basis of the available evidence, that, under the Shehu and Bello at least, public business was conducted within the framework of the accepted value system and in tune with the ideals which inspired the revolution and created a novel political order.'

## Chapter Five

# The Conception of Law

### A New Legal Process Advocated

Our next task is to explore the conception of law that finally emerged from this climate in which theory and experience blended together to create revolutionary approaches. To have a better picture of the process, it is necessary to look back to the days of Shehu Usman when the foundation for this legal procedure was established. He set in motion certain trends that were to have beneficial results many years later when the Caliphate became an established reality.

The first of these trends was the attempt to resolve the two issues which, owing to their emotive nature, were the most likely to be the greatest source of friction in society: faith and sufism. The Shehu's position expressed particularly in *Tabsirat al-Mubtadi fi Usul al-Din*[i] can be summed up as follows. The essential faith which is binding on a Muslim is that which is contained in the Qur'an and Sunna: any other demands on Muslims, which are of philosophical nature, are at best the *ijtihad* of scholars, and therefore, not binding. In short, philosophical arguments about God and other aspects of faith do not strictly fall within the sphere of Islamic faith. No one can be censured for not understanding those arguments, nor should society waste its efforts in delving into such issues. All that a person requires to be a full member of the Muslim *umma* is to affirm that there is no God but Allah and Muhammad is his Messenger. Once this is done, the person has all the rights and obligations of a Muslim and no one has a right to remove him from Islam, or investigate his faith to determine whether it is genuine or not. In addition, every believer is considered a full member of the *umma*, regardless of the sins he commits. As long as people 'beckon to Allah' then Islam

i    MS in author's possession.

embraces them. The genuineness of one's faith is known only to Allah, who has reserved judgement till the ultimate day.

The Shehu noted that the sufis are mainly concerned to attune the human mind to the most excellent conduct and to turn it away from evil deeds. They impart qualities such as consciousness of Allah, repentance, patience, reliance on Allah, as well as self-discipline, remembrance of Allah and contemplation. They train people to overcome moral weaknesses such as envy, greed, arrogance, inordinate ambition, miserliness and so on. From this perspective, sufism is the quintessence (*zubda*) of human endeavour to apply *shari'a* in life. The development of sufism in Islam is akin to the development of *fiqh*: they are both the outcome of *ijtihad* or human reasoning, except that one emphasizes the spiritual, the other the legalistic, aspects of Islam. And to the extent that *ijtihad* is not absolutely binding on the *umma*, neither is *fiqh* nor sufism; therefore neither of them should be a source of friction in society.

The Shehu also set in motion a trend to relieve his society from excessive and uncritical reliance on the intellectual heritage of the past. He stated that Muslims have an obligation to be perceptive in the practice of Islam and that Allah had perfected Islam during the lifetime of the Prophet ﷺ. Two things flow from this standpoint. First, reasoned and clear-sighted approach to Islam is imperative – it is one of the sources of Islam itself – so whoever follows Islam with blindness is disobeying the clear injunctions of the *shari'a*. Secondly, since Islam is essentially complete, it follows that all its binding elements were established in the lifetime of the Prophet ﷺ. It is from this core that branches have developed, through the effort of *'ulama*, such as *ilm al-kalam* or theology, *fiqh* or jurisprudence and sufism. As long as all these constitute human understanding of the Book and Sunnah, they are not binding on the *umma*. The only exception to this rule is where all the *'ulama* reach a consensus on a particular issue, which then becomes an obligation. However, in *Kashf ma alaihil Amal minal Aqwal*,[i] the Shehu urged the *'ulama* of his time to expand the frontiers of knowledge, take a fresh look at the Qur'an and Sunna, and bring forth *tafsir*s or exegesis of their own, pursue *ijtihad* vigorously

i   MS in author's possession.

with the aim of solving the issues of the day, and above all, reduce their reliance on the works of earlier scholars and depend more on their own initiative and intellectual output. Since contemporary scholars see at first hand the condition of their time, their works are necessarily of greater benefit than the works of yesteryear.

The third trend is of a legal nature. The principles gleaned from the Shehu's *Hidayat al-Tullab* and *Tawqif al-Muslimin ala Madhabib al-Mujtahidin*,[i] can be condensed as follows. The *shari'a*, the absolutely binding body of laws, is contained in the Qur'an and Sunna, and no more. All else is the result of human effort and therefore not binding on the *umma*. The schools of law emerged from those human efforts: so it is not obligatory on Muslims to follow any specific school, nor do the founders of those schools themselves insist on being followed. But even so, the schools have been accepted by the Muslim *umma* as being within the *shari'a*, and constituting roads leading to Allah and to Paradise. One can therefore adhere to a school of one's choice, or move from one to the other, or take certain principles from one, and certain others from another, as long as the intention is to improve the practice of Islam. The key elements in this trend are the universalization of the schools, making it possible for people to set aside aspects of their own school, which are no longer applicable in their circumstances, and adopt aspects of other schools which prove to be more relevant and appropriate. The other element is the clear-cut distinction between the *shari'a* and *fiqh*: the *shari'a* is what Allah and his Prophet have made binding on all and for all times. *Fiqh* is what men understand from the *shari'a*, and which is therefore time-bound and ephemeral. We have here hints from the Shehu which suggest a call for a new process of jurisprudence, to cope with a new age and a social condition not contemplated by the founders of the schools.

But it was left to Muhammad Bello to translate these trends into practical social and political policies. In the event, he found himself, rather predictably, in the midst of opposition and criticisms from a section of the *'ulama*. His immediate reaction, in *Shifa al-Asqam fi Marifat Madarik al-Ahkam*, was to show that he possessed the requisite credentials to make far-reaching policies in the interests

---

i    *Hidayat al-Tulab* was published in the 1960s by the then Northern Nigerian Government with a Hausa translation; *Tawqif al-Muslimin* remains a MS.

of the people, referring to the hadith and pointing to the power which the Imam possesses to formulate new policies to safeguard the interests of the *umma*. As to his personal credentials, the Caliph related how he was educated, the numerous books he had studied, who his teachers were, and what he had attained in terms of knowledge and spiritual standing. He had acquired first of all the mastery of the Qur'an. 'As for the transcendental abilities, Allah has opened my mind's eye to comprehend the secrets of religion and the true direction of its purpose... According to al-Qastallani, this kind of knowledge cannot be obtained except by complete veneration and worship of Allah and emulating the Prophet ﷺ. In this way true comprehension of the Qur'an and Sunna is achieved.'[i]

Moreover, his position as a caliph required him to establish such new policies as were needed to put the Caliphate on a sound political footing. Referring to the hadith which enjoins the *umma* to adhere to the sunna of the Prophet ﷺ and rightly-guided caliphs, Muhammad Bello, who obviously considered himself as one of the rightly-guided caliphs, said that the Prophet ﷺ had meant to say: 'Take to my traditions so long as the conditions are the same as those which prevailed in my time. When times and conditions change, and innovations increase, take to the traditions of the caliphs after me. They know that my traditions for those times and conditions were from the Qur'an and the Sunna. Were I to be around at your time, I would have shown you the same.'

Bello proposed that the role of an Imam or Islamic government is to introduce policies, interpret laws and organize society in such a way as to relieve hardships and make life easier and better for the people. If, in so doing, the letter of the *shari'a* needs to be sacrificed to safeguard its spirit, so be it. Referring to his role as the Imam, he said: 'This learned man [meaning himself] has been established by Allah as the expounder of his time and the legislator for his generation. He teaches them what is allowed and what is forbidden. He introduces new policies for them. In this respect his decisions whether something is forbidden or permissible will be based on prevailing conditions. He [the Caliph] will allow a thing

---

i   All quotations from *Shifa al-Asqam* have been taken from Tukur's *Values and Public Affairs*.

which was previously forbidden if he has strong reasons for so doing. Where [some] people decide on matters on the basis of their obvious meanings, he bases his decisions on the results [which are likely to follow].' Muhammad Bello proposed and followed an empirical approach in the application of Islamic Law, an approach he considered absolutely necessary if the purposes of the *shari'a* itself were to be realized.

## The *Shari'a* in a Changing World

It is in *Kitab al-Tahrir*, above all, that the Caliph put his ideas about how the *shari'a* should be applied in the most definitive terms. But for a more comprehensive understanding of his views one needs to refer to three works that we shall presently examine.[i] Being a product of a revolutionary climate, Muhammad Bello did not appear to have the cautionary attitude which was evident in his two mentors, Shehu Usman and Abdullahi. He almost threw caution to the winds in suggesting that, in formulating policies, leaders do not have to look at the *fiqh* books, they only have to make an objective assessment of the existing realities and deal with them accordingly.

According to Muhammad Bello the *shari'a* has two components: the absolute and the relative. The absolute comprises 'the essential matters', such as belief and unbelief; these are matters which do not admit of more than one meaning, nor varying interpretations. Each of them has 'a single fixed meaning' and in application, it is 'either entirely praiseworthy or entirely blameworthy'. Such matters of absolute, unvarying and fixed nature are very few indeed. The relative component of the *shari'a*, which is the Caliph's concern in *Kitab al-Tahrir*, has many aspects in line perhaps with the requirements of human nature. 'Most things are relative and subjective and vary according to different individuals, goals, times, places and states.' All relative matters, being in themselves subject to varying interpretations and containing many possibilities, necessarily 'incur differing judgements' depending on the reasons or intentions behind them, and the circumstances which give rise to them. 'Thus,' said Muhammad Bello, 'a thing can be correct

i   Abdalhaqq and Aisha Bewley's translation of *Kitab al-Tahrir* is used throughout this chapter.

because of what is intended by it in one instance and incorrect because of what is intended by it in another. This thing is permitted in this first instance and forbidden in the second – permitted at one time and not at another – permitted in one place and not in another – permitted in one state and not in another.' But even so, most relative matters have 'a predominant element,' making judgement about them easy. The predominant elements can be set aside at the intervention of temporary factors.

A temporary intervening circumstance can turn what is otherwise blameworthy into a permissible act when the aim is to bring benefit to oneself, or better still, to Islam. Similarly, another temporary circumstances can turn what is otherwise praiseworthy into an objectionable act where the practice of Islam is bound to suffer, or harm to oneself is feared. In the words of Muhammad Bello:

'They [scholars] have said that something forbidden can be permissible if that will prevent something worse happening – as is the case when a man tells lies in a gathering in order to break up the unity of the unbelievers ... or to protect the property, honour, lineage or person of a Muslim or on his own behalf when he is questioned about an act of rebellion he has committed or some property which someone is trying to seize from him by force or from someone else. This is because truthfulness would have a detrimental effect in this instance and would lead to worse results. This is also the case when he fears that his wife and child would be alienated by the truth. In other words it is permissible to do this to avert corruption, or in order to bring about a beneficial result.'

Yet, not all relative matters are intrinsically either blameworthy or praiseworthy. Many are essentially neutral, with blame or praise dictated by circumstances, like possessing rank or leadership. It is the intentions which lie behind them, or their use, that determine their outcome.

On the basis of the axiom that circumstances alter judgement, the Caliph formulated further principles of state policy or *siyasa*. The first is that intention plays a predominant role in determining the quality of an act, even to the extent that an act which is barely permissible in the *shari'a* can, depending on the intention behind it, 'bring you closest to Allah'. Perhaps not unintentionally, the Caliph gave dress as his example: it was his policy of permitting his governors, ministers and other public officers to dress in splendour that had evoked the heaviest criticism from some *'ulama*. He started with the proposition that if pride or showing superiority is the intention behind wearing a particular dress, then it is forbidden; but where the intention is 'luxury and delight', there is no blame in it although it is hardly commendable. This is a matter of individual preference, and one in which the *shari'a* is rather liberal.

'If [a person's] aim [in dress] is to receive delegations and those he loves, wearing good clothes is recommended for leaders of the people who can afford them. The Prophet, may Allah bless him and grant him peace, commanded the great Companions to wear good garments when receiving delegations and he encouraged them to do that. If the aim is adornment for the Id prayer, wearing good clothes for the Id is recommended for everyone who can afford it... . [The Messenger of Allah) said: It is prescribed that you should exalt the deen and strike terror into the enemy.'

Since imams and governors change according to different levels in civilization as well as times and circumstances, 'it is necessary to institute new adornments and political systems which did not exist in the past'.

This logically leads to the principle that each age produces new situations and creates specific requirements, a factor which requires the Islamic policymakers and the *'ulama* to examine and evaluate matters continually so that they do not go outside the dictates of the *shari'a*. The Caliph emphasized that it is a continuing *sunna* of Allah to relax his laws whenever the moral stamina of the people has weakened. When one considers the high moral standards which prevailed in the time of the Prophet 🌿, one can only conclude that 'the best of our time is the worst of that time'. Since this was the case, the policymakers in Sokoto had to take into account that, 'What was ugly then is now considered good and what was narrow is now wide; judgements vary according to different times.' The policy implication of this fact was that people of such a low moral quality, as compared with the Prophet's men, were having to run an Islamic government, even though the strict position of the *shari'a* is that 'government by the worst is corruption'. Once again the Caliph insisted that matters of this nature were not to be taken from *fiqh* books, but dealt with on the basis of objective assessment and appraisal of the totality of the situation. Establishing policies on the basis of *fiqh* texts would lead to corruption.

The Caliph developed the principle that custom or *'urf* must necessarily play a leading role in the formulation of policies and legislation and in the running of government in general. Custom, defined by the Caliph as a usage which extends over a whole country or part of it, can be assumed to mean the totality of the historical and cultural experience of a given people, which gives them traits, instincts, tastes and other characteristics that distinguish them from others. And since history is an on-going process, it follows that societies are inherently dynamic, as they must undergo changes on a continuous basis. This fact of life, as far as the Caliph was concerned, implies that laws and policies must suffer change as well as reflect the experiences of the people. He then laid down the following rules for *'ulama*, judges and policymakers:

(i)    All laws which derive from a given custom must be set aside as soon as that custom loses its relevance or ceases to exist. 'If a new custom develops,' it is taken into consideration, and if a custom is abandoned, judgements based on it disappear and you never need to refer to the texts in the books.*

(ii)   Fatwas must deal with the issues at hand, taking into account the existing social realities. Again the Caliph cautioned the *'ulama* against relying on legal theories developed in an entirely different social milieu. 'Rigidity regarding texts' is always misguidance in the religion and ignorance of the goals of the *'ulama* of the Muslims and the *salaf.* Similarly, government must respond appropriately even if their policies conflict with the position of the schools of law. For when a statute produces the opposite result to what was originally intended, it then loses its status as an *ijma'*, and has to be set aside. Moreover since the schools themselves developed from a particular historical background, it follows that their *fatwas* emerged from that period too.

(iii) Lastly, it is necessary for each country or region to develop a legal system appropriate to its situation. No legal system of one country should be superimposed on another. This is how Bello saw it, in agreement with al-Qarafi: 'If we leave one land for another land where the custom is different from the custom of the land where we were at first, we must give *fatwa* according to the custom of that land... It is the same when anyone comes to us from a land whose custom is different from our land. We can only give him a *fatwa* according to the custom of his land.'

Muslims are not required to close their eyes to the historical experiences of other people or civilizations which can be of benefit to them. 'If people do something', Bello said, 'which is in harmony with what is recommended, obligatory, or permitted in our *shari'a*, we do not reject that simply because they use it, because the *shari'a* is not prejudiced by the act of resemblance. The Prophet ﷺ, may Allah bless him and grant him peace, dug the ditch around Madina imitating the Persians.' The Caliph included coinage, furniture, weddings and business transactions among matters which fall within the concept of custom.

Finally, the Caliph put forward the principle that where there is a constraint then there must be an accompanying dispensation. This is especially desired in cases where a rigid adherence to the letter of the law will jeopardize occupations and livelihoods, compromising people's welfare. 'Grapes can be cultivated, in this world,' the Caliph explained this principle, 'even though that might lead to wine-making and wine-drinking. In the same way, you have to go out to get necessities of life and go into the market place even though that might lead to you seeing a woman unrelated to you or falling into arguments or indulging in forbidden behaviour.'

### Siyasat al-Shar'iyya

What then is the relationship between the *shari'a* and *siyasat al-shar'iyya*, or *siyasa* for short? Perhaps there is no harm in proposing from the onset that *siyasa* is simply the human effort, through the agency of government, to ensure that the fundamental purposes of the *shari'a* are realized in society. *Siyasa* is, therefore, the application of reason, intellect and realism to safeguard the *shari'a* against corruption or extinction. It is easy to see therefore why, in the conception of Sokoto leaders, *siyasa* came to be seen as an integral part of the *shari'a* itself - the divine and human are fused together to keep the word of Allah supreme. Abdullahi expressed this fact in *Diya al-Hukkam* as follows: 'Know that there are two types of policies [*siyasat*]: the unjust policy, which is forbidden by the *shari'a* and the just policy which extracts a right from the oppressor, redresses the wrongs and suppresses the corrupt people. *Shari'a* prescribes that just policy should always be relied upon.' The golden mean must be adhered to in this delicate task of establishing the right balance between the *shari'a* and *siyasa*. If *siyasa* is neglected and not applied, people will eventually lose their rights, the *hudud* may be suspended and corrupt people will gain the upper hand. On the other hand, if *siyasa* is given a free reign, and goes beyond the boundaries of the *shari'a*, the inevitable outcome will be the prevalence of injustice, bloodshed, and confiscation of property. So the Islamic government must follow the middle course.

According to Abdullahi, the basis of *siyasa* is to be found in the hadith: 'no harm may be inflicted or reciprocated'. This implies, in broad terms, 'looking after the welfare of the people and repelling corruption by means of exposing the wrongs through methods which show the truth.' In this endeavour, the Imam, whose function is 'to prevent corruption on earth and suppress evildoers and aggression', should be in the forefront to apply *siyasa*, followed closely by the *qadi*. As long as *siyasa* involves principally the employment of human initiatives in promoting the goals of Islam, any office or organ of government is required to avail itself of its use, provided, as Abdullahi cautions, that piety and support of Islam are the sole motivation; not personal whims or the desire to settle personal scores.

The scope of *siyasa*, from the perspective given in *Diya al-Hukkam*, is almost unlimited, covering every aspect encompassed by *shari'a*, as well as innumerable others. But its purpose must always be kept in sight: to keep the Islamic government viable, to uphold the law, to suppress evil and corruption. Abdullahi has given many examples of how corruption can be suppressed. He suggested a temporary sequestration of the estate of a person who has usurped the property of another; imprisonment for recidivists; compulsory sale of houses which serve as centres of crime and corruption; or the compulsory ejection of the perpetrators of crime from them. But he also stressed that government, law enforcement agencies and the public must behave responsibly. Government has no right to spy on people. The police have no authority to violate people's privacy: homes may be searched only when several reports have been received about it, or where it is notorious. People are advised not to expose the private affairs of others, especially their neighbours.

*Siyasa* is concerned with protecting the weak against the strong, and ensuring that the strong are brought to book. Public officers must not carry out unjust or unlawful governmental instructions, or they will be held personally liable for the injustices they commit. If a public officer, for example, tortures, flogs, or kills a person unlawfully, or confiscates his property on the instruction of the government 'he shall be liable to retaliatory punishment'. To protect the property of ordinary people, Abdullahi proposed that any commercial transaction which involves compulsion be neither permissible nor binding, that those who have donated part of their wealth out of fear of a tyrant, can reclaim their money when there is a turn of events. But Abdullahi shows no sympathy for an oppressor who is himself being oppressed: 'The sale of property owned and sold by an unjust person, when someone more powerful than him wants to confiscate it, is valid and binding. Such will be the case when a ruler imposes heavy fines on his unjust officials as a result of which they become compelled to sell their property in order to pay the fine. For imposing a fine on them in that respect is justified.'

It is the function of *siyasa*, to establish an equitable criminal procedure law to deter criminals and protect the innocent. And even more important, it is a function of government to institute laws to deal with offences known as *ta'zirat*: offences which do not fall strictly within the ambit of *hudud*; or which do not warrant *hadd* punishments; or for which punishments are not specified in the *shari'a. Ta'zir* covers all kinds of offences, ranging from bestiality, the protection of corrupt people, perjury, market frauds, usury, and giving false evidence to refusal to pay *zakat*, settle debts, restore trusts, deposits or orphan's property. Punishments range from mere rebuke to severe penalties. Nevertheless there is an important caveat: since the aim of *ta'zir* is deterrence, punishments should be reasonable with safe consequences. The state is permitted here to accept intercessions made on behalf of offenders by responsible citizens, and is at liberty to exercise pardon, which is not the case in *hadd* offences.

*Siyasa* also encompasses almost the entire province of torts, when the purpose is mainly to settle the conflicting claims of citizens, prevent discord and safeguard professions which help sustain society. We may note here three of the many examples of the operation of *siyasa* in this sphere given by Abdullahi in *Diya al-Hukkam*. First, professions and occupations are governed by the principle which imposes on manufacturers, artisans and vendors the liability to guarantee their commodities, and absolves those whose work necessarily involves high risks, such as physicians, surgeons and dentists, of liabilities for any damage that they may have caused, where neither negligence, incompetence, deception, nor pretence has been established against them. In addition, the principle confers the right of compensation on employees who sustain injuries in the course of their work, especially where high risks are involved.

Secondly, *siyasa* regulations are also intended to create the right balance between the individual and society, where the public is protected without, however, severely compromising individual initiatives, interests or liberty. For example, a person who digs a well on a public road, or fastens his animal in the road, shall be held responsible for whatever damage that is caused. But he shall not be held liable for damages which result from a lawful action such as 'digging up a passage for rain, or a latrine on the side of his wall ... [or] digging a well inside his house, if it is not intended to harm anyone, or halting his animal in the middle of the road for a need, or by the door of a mosque, or by the door of the emir's palace or in a market place'. But a person who deliberately refuses to straighten a 'bent wall' shall be liable for any damage that may result from its collapse. 'Warning coming from any person other than the ruler,' wrote Abdullahi, 'is not valid except in a town where there is no ruler, in which case the warning of the neighbour and the people shall be sufficient.'

Thirdly, *siyasa* seeks to protect persons who act in good faith. A guest, for example, is presumed to have permission to use facilities available in his host's house for his basic needs. There is also the assumption of the right to use private facilities open to the public, such as private water reservoirs situated on the roadside, without having to obtain permission of the owners, and so on. Finally, *siyasa* is applied generally to ensure primacy of public over private interest, protect society from powerful vested interests, or people causing harm to others. The examples given by Abdullahi in this regard cover the prevention of neighbours from infringing on the rights and conveniences of one another, prevention of injuries to the public and minimizing occasions when the privacy of people might be violated.

Since 'all harm must be removed' in Islamic society, the state must deny a person 'the right to build an animal stable on the side of his neighbour's house,' or a grinding mill, a blacksmith forge and so on. Thus all sources of discomfort, which cause pollution, noise or constitute health hazards, must be prevented. And where materials which endanger the health of the public accumulate in a neighbourhood, for which no one person can be held responsible, the residents should be held collectively responsible for removing them.

The state must also ensure that the privacy of individual citizens is protected. Hence, according to Abdullahi: 'If a person causes injury by opening a door or a window to peep at his neighbour, he shall be restrained ... If the offender is ordered to close the door or window, he should close it thoroughly well and remove the lintel. If, on the other hand, the window or the door is of old standing, the [aggrieved] person has no right to demand its closure. In the opinion of some jurists, however, the closure is mandatory as a right of Allah since it is Allah's law that no one shall be allowed to infringe on others' privacy.' Similarly, the state must ensure that the basic needs of one neighbour, like ventilation or water, are not blocked by another. In all cases the rights of the general public take precedence over individual rights or conveniences. Hence, said Abdullahi, 'Ibn al-Qasim states, in the case of a public road going through a land owned by a particular person, that the owner has no right to alter the course of the road, even if that may be better for him and the road users. No one has the right to divert a public road even if its existence [in the place] does harm to him.'

### Shari'a in the Political Process

Let us return finally to the Caliph to see how he sought to integrate the principles of *siyasa* in the political process. It is worth suggesting from the outset that he must have had at the back of his mind Abdullahi's enthusiastic endorsement of *istihsan* in state policies. The state is permitted, he said in *Diya al-Hukkam*, to resort to *istihsan*, by choosing the more remote, and even 'less appropriate' options in cases where two principles of *shari'a* come into conflict, in order to protect the interest of the people, fend off harm and maintain the continuity of a 'common practice' or convention which can only be broken at public expense. To the extent that the state exists precisely to enhance public well-being, remove harm and ensure harmony or 'continuity' in society, the Caliph may well have agreed with his uncle that ninety per cent of the science of *shari'a* is based on custom and practice. Our examination of the Caliph's method in this area is based on two works of his: *al-Qawl al-Mawhub fi Ajwibat Asila al-Amir Yaqub*[i] and *Tanbih al-Raqid ala ma Yatawir al-Hajj min al-Mafasid.*[ii]

In *Al-Qawl*, the Caliph was confronted with questions as to how Islamic law should operate in the Bauchi Emirate, perhaps the most complex of the emirates in the Caliphate. The peculiar difficulties encountered in Bauchi are summed up by Ismail and Yahya:

The difficulties derive their significance mainly from the nature of political, social and geographical conditions of

i   Edited and translated by OE A. Ismail and A.Y. Aliyu and published in Nigerian Administration Research Project (Second Interim Report) Institute of Administration, Ahamadu Bello University, Zaria, (1975), pp. 34-53.
ii   Translated by Abdalhaqq and Aisha Bewley.

Bauchi region itself. Unlike other emirates in Hausaland which, having been established on old political and cultural centres and anchored among largely Muslim populations, retained substantive features of their earlier past, including a considerable proportion of their earlier boundaries as well as internal administrative divisions, Bauchi was an entirely new phenomenon. It was created by the conditions of the *jihad* and institutionalised among predominantly non-Muslim populations. It was also one of the largest, most heterogeneous and mountainous regions in the Caliphate, posing enormous difficulties in the maintenance of political control, communication and administration.[i]

So when the Emir Yakubu sought guidance from the Caliph on a number of issues, the latter's reply stressed extreme caution in the application of the *shari'a*. He allowed the Emir considerable discretion and extensive application of *siyasa*.

Emir Yakubu asked what his government should do about Muslim communities who lived as minorities among pagan populations, but were reluctant to be incorporated into the Muslim *umma* because they had entrenched interests in the pagan economy. The Caliph answered as follows:

> Their amir will deal with them in the light of their *maslaha* (welfare). Either he will add to them some people so that they can protect themselves against the infidels or he will order them to move to a place where they can be secure. He should not neglect their affairs or leave them to their own opinions because he is their shepherd and the shepherd is always responsible for his flock. This is the more so since you mentioned in their regard that they love the place because of their love of their property there; surely the love of a thing blinds and deafens. If their amir neglects them and does not give them sound advice on their affairs, he indeed betrays them.

i   'Bello and the tradition of manuals of Islamic Government and advice to rulers', Nigerian Administration Research Project, Ahmadu Bello University, 1975.

Ismail and Yahya have suggested that, in compliance with this directive, Emir Yakub embarked on extensive resettlement schemes aimed at boosting Muslim populations, providing defences for them as well as improving agriculture. The overall result was the emergence of new towns with absolute Muslim majorities, serving at the same time as new urban centres in Bauchi Emirate.

In *Tanbih al-Raqid*, the Caliph was faced with a situation where the desire of his people to perform the hajj conflicted with the need to defend the Islamic state and secure its economic and social well-being. His frequent reference to lack of security and dangers on the roads suggest that the book was written in the turbulent years of his rule, when rebellions and insurrections were rampant. The Caliph stated that he himself had a desire to perform the hajj, like others in the Caliphate, and that 'I have taken note of the fact that it is incumbent for anyone who has not gone on hajj to the Sacred House to be disturbed and to yearn to undertake it and also to have yearning to visit and be aggrieved if he has not visited the Noble *Rawda*.' Yet people must weigh the obligation of hajj against the obligation of *jihad* and the establishment of social justice in society. He then advanced the following principles.

When the Imam is faced with the choice of going on hajj or remaining to protect the realm against its enemies, then he must choose the latter, for in this case he is considered as having lacked the ability to perform hajj, which is then no longer obligatory on him. In other words, the Caliph was most probably giving the reason why neither Shehu Usman, Abdullahi nor he himself had undertaken the hajj.

Secondly, where hajj conflicts with the need for social justice, then the latter should have preference. 'Bringing happiness to the heart of a Muslim and relieving someone's grief and removing hardship from someone in need and helping someone whose belief is uncertain is better than a hundred hajj's after the obligatory hajj of Islam.' The resources meant for such hajj should rather be given to 'a debtor to discharge his debt, a poor man to set him back on his feet, the father of a large family to provide nourishment for it, and to someone bringing up an orphan to help him out'. The Caliph referred to those who amassed wealth 'from the dirt of trade and doubtful things' and used part of it to go on hajj as having gone only on an excursion, not the sacred hajj.

Thirdly, where a person has to perform the hajj at the expense of personal honour, or the welfare of his family, then hajj is not obligatory. Some people contracted debts, cheated or begged for the sake of going on hajj 'even to the point where some of them will petition tyrants who oppress Muslims when it is in fact incumbent to dissociate oneself from them'. Such an attitude, said the Caliph, gave encouragement to tyrants who were boosted by seeing people 'seeking good at their doors, kowtowing to them in this way and asking them for the leftovers from the filth of their *haram* [illegal] worldly wealth'. Similarly, others put their families in difficult circumstances thereby flying in the face of the Prophet's condemnation of putting one's dependents at risk; some others use the hajj 'as a market place to get hold of people's wealth'. If hajj can be performed only with unlawful income, then it is better not performed.

Finally the all-important question of *jihad*: the Caliph affirmed that *jihad* is certainly of greater benefit than hajj. The Prophet ﷺ made only one hajj, 'then he continued to fight in *jihad* until he met Allah'; the *mujahid* strives to defend the faith and defend the Islamic state, for which he shall reap the reward of all those who have gone on hajj from the state he defends in addition to the reward of *jihad*.

In conclusion, we give the final word to the Caliph. 'Rulers have dared to oppose the *shari'a* under the false apprehension that the policy of the *shari'a* is not capable of dealing with people and the best interest of the community. They overstep the limits of Allah and abandon the *shari'a* by rebelling in various ways and making innovations in government in a way that is not permitted. The reason for this is ignorance of the *shari'a*. There is a sound hadith from the Prophet ﷺ, "Whoever holds the Book and the Sunna will not be misguided".'

## Chapter Six

# The Encounter with the West

'I saw with infinite pleasure the great object of my mission – the long sought for majestic Niger, glittering to the morning sun, as broad as the Thames at Westminster, and flowing slowly to the eastward. I hastened to the brink, and, having drank of the water, lifted up my fervent thanks in prayer to the Great Ruler of all things, for having thus far crowned my endeavours with success.'

Those were the jubilant words of Mungo Park, spoken on July 21, 1796. This achievement was yet another stage in the historic process which was to culminate in the colonization of Africa, and, what is of interest to us presently, in the overthrow of the Sokoto Caliphate. Yet such is the wonder of history that on this fateful day, when the 'majestic Niger' revealed itself to the searching and greedy eyes of Europe, the process of Shehu Usman's transformation was just gathering momentum, not ready to burst forth into a revolution until some seven years later. Thus two forces were at work at about the same time: firstly, the force of Islam, striving to lift a people from the abyss of decadence to a state of uprightness, strength and felicity, and secondly, the force of *Yajuj wa Majuj* – Gog and Magog – getting ready to burst upon Africa, to destroy, to plunder, to enslave. In this chapter we shall be dealing with three people, Mungo Park, Major Denham and Captain Clapperton, whose exploration of Africa – whether intentionally for the purpose of spying or for genuinely scientific reasons – was effectively used by the powers of greed and destruction to further their own ends.

## Mungo Park's Mission to the Niger

Mungo Park, at the behest of those whom he termed in his *Travels* as 'my noble and honourable employers, the Members of the African Association', set sail for Africa from Portsmouth, Britain, on 22 May 1975. His mission was to explore the Niger, for as John Keay states in his introduction to *Travels*: 'Like the Nile in Egypt the [River Niger] was still, however, considered to be the key to the geography of Nigiritia and the focus of its society. Cities on or near its banks ... were believed to be fabulously rich and populous; and somewhere in its vicinity lay Wangara whence came most of North Africa's gold.' Mungo Park was therefore, if we may say so, not only on a journey of exploration, but also on a journey in search of gold and natural resources. We shall follow his tracks, and the unfolding of his ideas, as he related them in his *Travels*, which he described as 'a plain unvarnished tale, without pretensions of any kind'. All along the journey, Mungo Park represented himself as a botanist, interested only in plants, rivers and mountains.

He and his team arrived in the Gambia region in June 1795 to begin his African activities in earnest. He found the region especially rich in fish, 'some species of which are excellent food', and covered generally with woods – a feature which appeared 'gloomy and tiresome' to him. 'But although nature has denied to the inhabitants the beauties of romantic landscapes,' he wrote, 'she has bestowed on them, with a liberal hand, the more important blessings of fertility and abundance. A little attention to cultivation procures a sufficiency of corn; the fields afford a rich pasturage for cattle; and the natives are plentifully supplied with excellent fish, both from the Gambia river and the Walli creek.'

Even though the object of European interest in Africa was not to know its people but to discover its resources, the people around the Gambia region came under Mungo Park's close scrutiny. He noticed that 'among all these nations, the religion of Mahomet has made, and continues to make, considerable progress.' His eurocentric perspective meant that he saw the people merely in racial terms; the Feloops 'are of a gloomy disposition and are supposed not to forgive an injury', yet 'they display the utmost gratitude and affection towards their benefactors; and the fidelity with which they preserve whatever is entrusted to them is remarkable'. His ideological limitations are evident in his wish for this remarkable people: 'How greatly is it to be wished that the minds of a people, so determined and faithful, could be softened and civilized by the mild and benevolent spirit of Christianity!'

The Jaloffs were described as an 'active, powerful and warlike race', and the Mandigoes – 'who have made ... the laws of the Prophet 鬱 their peculiar study' – were mild, sociable and having an obliging disposition. 'The men are commonly above the middle size,' said Mungo Park, 'well shaped, strong, and capable of enduring great labour; the women are good-natured, sprightly and agreeable.' The Foulah (or Fulani) were

'of a mild and gentle disposition but the uncharitable maxims of the Koran have made them less hospitable to strangers. Their government differs from that of the Mandigoes chiefly in this, that they are more immediately under the influence of the Mahomedan laws ... and the authority and laws of the Prophet 鬱 are everywhere looked upon as sacred and decisive.'

Park observed further that the Fulani were except-ionally tolerant and religious persecution was unknown among them, having been rendered unnecessary by their policy of advancing Islam through universal education.

'By establishing small schools in different towns, where many of the pagan as well as Mahomedan children are taught to read the Koran, and instructed in the tenets of the Prophet 鬱, the Mahomedan priests fix a bias on the minds, and form the character of their young disciples, which no accidents of life can ever afterwards remove or alter.'

Park claimed that after visiting some of these schools he 'observed with pleasure the great docility and submissive deportment of the children, and heartily wished that they had better instructors and a purer religion' – meaning, of course, Christianity. He also credited the Fulani with having a remarkable industry and great skills.

Mungo Park moved on from town to town and kingdom to kingdom in West Africa, encountering on his path different beliefs and attitudes: but almost everywhere the fact of his being a spy lingered on in the minds of his rather benevolent hosts. At one time, he encountered some Arabs who seemed to have intentions similar to his: plunder and pilferage. He claimed he was taken prisoner and subjected to insults and indignities for days on end.

'With the returning day commenced the same round of insult and irritation: the boys assembled to beat the hog, and the men and women to plague the Christian. It is impossible for me to describe the behaviour of a people who study mischief as a science, and exult in the miseries and misfortunes of their fellow creatures. It is sufficient to observe that the rudeness, ferocity, and fanaticism, which distinguish the Moors from the rest of mankind, found here a proper subject whereupon to exercise their propensities. I was a *stranger*, I was *unprotected*, and I was a *Christian*; each of these circumstances is sufficient to drive every spark of humanity from the heart of a Moor... From sunrise to sunset was I obliged to suffer, with an unruffled countenance, the insults of the rudest savages on earth.'

The sense of indignation felt by Mungo Park is understandable; yet, as he thought those harsh words, his own people – who thought of themselves as the most civilized of all mankind – were perpetrating the most inhuman, the most savage of all human actions: the transportation of human beings across the Atlantic as slaves. For over 300 years Africa suffered this colossal human tragedy, costing her, Walter Rodney has suggested, well over one hundred and twenty million people! 'It is impossible,' to borrow the very words of Mungo Park, 'to describe the behaviour of a people who study mischief as a science, and exult in the miseries and misfortunes of their fellow creatures', and, if we may add, who make a profit out of the miseries of others and build their nations on the wealth and ruin of others. This subjection of a continent to three centuries of human plunder is perhaps the greatest savagery of all: or, does history provide a parallel?

Mungo Park was able to make his escape from his Arab captors and continue his journey towards the Niger. We are now in the month of July 1796, and the traveller was on his way to a town called Segu, in the Muslim Kingdom of Bambara, where, on the 21st of the same month, he at last saw the Niger. The town was entirely Muslim. 'The view of this extensive city, the numerous canoes upon the river, the crowded population and the cultivated state of the surrounding country, formed altogether a prospect of civilization and magnificence, which I little expected to find in the bosom of Africa,' he said.

On his return journey to the Gambia, Mungo Park went through a rather bitter experience. He claimed that he was robbed by a group of Fulani and, what is more, stripped naked. Perhaps more than anything else, his reaction to this experience provides an insight into the personality and conscience of this servant of the British Empire.

'After they were gone, I sat for some time looking around me with amazement and terror. Whichever way I turned, nothing appeared but danger and difficulty. I saw myself in the midst of a vast wilderness in the depth of the rainy season, naked and alone; surrounded by savage animals, and men still more savage. I was five hundred miles from the nearest European settlement. All these circumstances crowded at once on my recollection; and I confess that my spirits began to fail me. I considered my fate as certain; and that I had no alternative, but to lie down and perish. The influence of religion, however, aided and supported me. I reflected that no human prudence or foresight could possibly have averted my present sufferings. I was indeed a stranger in a strange land, yet I was still under the protecting eye of that Providence who has condescended to call himself the stranger's friend.

'At this moment, painful as my reflections were, the extraordinary beauty of a small moss, in fructification, irresistibly caught my eye. I mention this to show from what trifling circumstances the mind will sometimes derive consolation; for though the whole plant was not larger than the top of one of my fingers, I could not contemplate the delicate conformation of its roots, leaves, capsula, without admiration. Can that Being (thought I) who planted, watered and brought to perfection, in this obscure part of the world, a thing which appears of so small importance, look with unconcern upon the situation and sufferings of creatures formed after his own image? — surely not!'

This was Mungo Park at his best: a man of faith, a firm believer in justice, possessed of a heart overflowing with compassion. Man, being of the very highest order of creation, cannot, he believed, be condemned to suffering and degradation by his fellow man, without God, his creator, showing concern. Yet this outpouring of emotion, of inward compassion and sense of justice, was evident only because it was Mungo Park - a white man - that had been affected. Unfortunately, it is this partial, parochial and racial sense of justice - which assigns to one race alone the right to fairness, compassion and dignity and condemns all others as fit only for exploitation, murder, slavery and all forms of indignity - that formed the basis of European enterprise in Africa. And not surprisingly, this believer in Providence embarked for his homeward journey on an American vessel carrying, of all things, 130 African slaves - apparently without any qualms whatsoever.

The belief that Africa can justifiably be plundered by the European race and that Islam must be wiped out from the face of Africa, remained the dominant theme of Mungo Park's account, and his mission was primarily to explore the means through which that ambition could be realized. Of the abundant resources of Africa, Mungo Park wrote in detail, describing the extent of the commercial connections with Europe; with slaves, gold and ivory constituting the main 'exportable commodities'. Other crops were noted incidentally: 'such as grain of different kinds, tobacco, indigo, common wool, and perhaps a few others; but all of these ... the natives raise sufficient only for their own immediate expenditure; nor under the present system of their laws, manners, grade and government, can anything further be expected'. Park added:

'It cannot, however, admit of a doubt, that all the rich and valuable productions, both of the East and West Indies, might easily be naturalised and brought to the utmost perfection in the tropical part of this immense continent. Nothing is wanting to this end but example, to enlighten the minds of the natives, and instruction, to enable them to direct their industry to proper objects. It was not possible for me to behold the wonderful fertility of the soil, the vast herds of cattle, proper both for labour and food, and a variety of other circumstances favourable to colonization and agriculture – and reflect, withal, on the means which presented themselves of a vast inland navigation – without lamenting that a country so abundantly gifted and favoured by nature, should remain in its present savage and neglected state. Much more did I lament that a people of manners and dispositions so gentle and benevolent should either be left as they now are, immersed in the gross and uncomfortable blindness of pagan superstition, or permitted to become converts to a system of bigotry and fanaticism [ie. Islam], which, without enlightening the mind, often debases the heart.'

In his second mission to Africa, which began in January 1805, Mungo Park finally revealed his true colours: he came not as a mere explorer but as a commandant in charge of a gunboat, the HMS Joliba. His mission was no longer exploration but, as Johnston and Muffen put it in *Denham in Borno*, for 'grabbing the trade, the gold, and the glory before France or any other power should pre-empt them'. All along their route Park and his gang launched a campaign of terror, banditry and murder. In the words of John Keay: 'On the earlier leg of the journey Park had been driven to order his men to shoot all robbers on sight. Now they seem to have let fly at anyone who so much as approached the Joliba ... All attentions were treated as hostile and each shower of native spears was ruthlessly repaid with gunshot.' This dog of war with the rest of his men, at last, drowned in the River Niger.

**The Mission to Borno**

The next mission which concerns us in this chapter is that of Major Dixon Denham, Commander Hugh Clapperton and its leader, Dr. Walter Oudiney. Its immediate purpose was, as Johnston and

103

Muffett have said in their introduction to *Denham in Borno*[i] – our main reference here – to 'clear up the mysteries of Lake Chad, Bornu, Hausaland and of the course of the lower Niger'. This fits in squarely with the larger purpose of British imperialism: to explore the means of wresting control of the resources of this part of Africa from their legitimate possessors, and expanding the frontiers of the British Empire.

The expedition was arranged to take off for the Sultanate of Borno – part of it now in the present northern Nigeria – from Tripoli, where they were to take a letter of introduction from the Pasha to the Sheikh of Borno. Tripolitania had all but become a vassal of Britain, from whose officials the Pasha took what appear to be direct instructions. For, as we read in Denham in Borno: 'The English name, in fact, is of such importance in Tripoli that there is scarcely a point to carry or a dispute to settle in which the Pasha does not request the interference of the British Consul.' This explains, in part, how the Arabs came to enter into an alliance of conspiracy, even if somewhat unwillingly, to subvert Islam in West Africa and expose the honour and possessions of the Muslims to colonial powers. In March 1822, the mission set off across the great Sahara desert, armed with Pasha's letter of introduction. As planned, it joined an Arab trade caravan, under a wealthy and influential Fezzan merchant, Abubakar Bu-Khalum, heading for Borno and Hausaland from Murzuk.

On their way through the Sahara, Dr. Qudney and his men constantly came upon heart-rending and awful scenes: the human detritus, to use the words in *Denham in Borno*, that the slave trade had deposited:

'During the last two days we had passed on an average from sixty to eighty skeletons each day, but the numbers that lay about the wells at El-Harmmar were countless. Those of two women, whose perfect and regular teeth bespoke them young, were particularly shocking; their arms still remained clasped round each other as

---

i    See generally *Denham in Borno*, Johnston and Muffett, Duquesne University Press, 1973, and *Narrative of Travels and Discoveries in Northern and Central Africa in years 1822, 1823 and 1824*, Dixon Denham, Hugh Clapperton and Dr. Oudney, London, 1826.

they had expired, although the flesh had long since perished by being exposed to the burning rays of the sun and the blackened bones only left. The nails of the fingers and some of the sinews of the hand also remained and part of the tongue of one of them still appeared through the teeth.'

Although the bulk of the slaves who managed to survive the harsh and unbearable conditions of the passage across the desert were eventually sold to European slave merchants, it is impossible to absolve the Arabs of blame in this historic tragedy. And when their role in this abhorrent trade is considered along with several other campaigns of plunder and devastation they waged in Africa – especially the Moroccan invasion which effectively sealed the fate of the Muslim state of Songhay – it is difficult to escape the conclusion that, on the whole, the Arab role in the history of Islam in West Africa is not only negative but lamentable. It is perhaps fair to say that Islam has spread and taken hold in this region, not because of the Arabs but in spite of them.

On February 4, 1823, the English spies achieved one of the objects of their mission: they sighted Lake Chad. 'The great lake, Chad, glowing with the golden rays of the sun in its strength,' as Denham exultantly recorded this moment, 'appeared to be within a mile of the spot on which we stood. My heart bounded with me at the prospect, for I believed the lake to be the key to the great object of our search, and I could not refrain from silently imploring Heaven's continued protection.' And almost two weeks later, another object of the mission, the meeting with the formidable Shehu of Borno, Muhammad al-Amin al-Kanemi, was realized. The following, in the words of Major Denham, described the great occasion:

'This was to us a momentous day, and it seemed to be equally so to our conductors. Notwithstanding all the difficulties that had presented themselves at the various stages of our journey, we were at last within a few short miles of our destination; were about to become acquainted with a people who had never seen, or scarcely heard of, a European; and, to tread on ground, the knowledge and true situation of which had hitherto been wholly unknown. These ideas of

105

course excited no common sensations; and could scarcely be unaccompanied by strong hope of our labours being beneficial to the race amongst whom we were shortly to mix; of our laying the first stone of a work which might lead to their civilisation, if not their emancipation from all their prejudices and ignorance, and probably, at the same time, open a field of commerce to our country, which might increase its wealth and prosperity.

'We found him [the Shehu] in a small dark room, sitting on a carpet, plainly dressed in a blue Hausa gown and a shawl turban … His personal appearance was prepossessing, apparently not more than forty-five or forty-six, with an expressive countenance and a benevolent smile. We delivered our letter from the Pasha and, after he had read it, he enquired "what was our object in coming?" We answered, "to see the country merely, and to give an account of its inhabitants, produce and appearance, as our Sultan was desirous of knowing every part of the globe." His reply was that "we were welcome and whatever he could show us would give him pleasure".'

This historic moment was but the beginning of a historical process full of ironies and paradoxes. From the very start, it seemed clear that this was an encounter between two opposite forces and world views: Islam and colonialism. Al-Kanemi, taking the Pasha's letter on its face value – for he seemed apparently unaware of Tripoli's subservience to Britain – accepted these Englishmen as their country's envoys; and accepted their word when they claimed their purpose for visiting his domain was without evil intentions. And such was the irony that al-Kanemi was full of kindness to them, concerned for their safety and well-being. As Major Denham conceded: 'It is impossible to describe the value of his kindness to us on all occasions. … Knowing us through the medium of the Pasha of Tripoli only, his disinterested conduct could have been alone the dictation of a generous confidence, and his own penetration and sagacity had long since convinced him of the perfect innocence of our intentions in visiting his country.' One can only wonder at how far the forces of materialism can go in deception and treachery in the pursuit of their goals.

Before we consider some of Major Denham's observations on Borno, it is pertinent to highlight two of the issues that persistently recur in the course of these Europeans' stay in Borno. The first, of course, was their inevitable encounter with Islam. They found that when they crossed the boundary of the Arab world into *Bilad al-Sudan* they had entered a region where Islam constituted the most fundamental issue: indeed, the sole issue in the relationship between the region and the outside world. They were questioned everywhere they went as to whether they were Muslims or not, in a marked contrast to their experience in Tripoli where the issue was that they belonged to a very powerful nation.

In one instance, Major Denham encountered one of the Borno *'ulama* who had accompanied the army to Mandara on a *jihad* expedition, which Denham was permitted to join. This scholar, Mallam Chadili, straight away discerned the treachery involved in the European visit. Major Denham arrogantly referred to the scholar as a charm-writer, who he said, always eyed him with suspicion and dismay. At one time, during the dawn prayer, the dialogue that took place between Mallam Chadili and Denham went as follows:

> "'Do you wash and pray?"
> "Yes."
> "Where?"
> "In my tent."

'This Mallam who continued throughout my mortal enemy and annoyance, now asked Bu-Kahlum [the Arab merchant] what these English were? Were they Hanafi or Maliki? Still believing that, as we appear a little better than the pagans, we must be Moslem in some way or the other. Bu-Khalum answered, with some hesitation, No: that we were unfortunate; that we believed not in "the Book", the title always given to the Koran; that we were not circumcised; that we had a Book of our own, which did not mention the Prophet Muhammad ﷺ, and that, blind as we were, we believed in it. "But inshallah," added he, "they will see their error and die

Moslems, for they are beautiful people, very beautiful." This account was followed by a general groan and the Mallam clasped his hands, looked thoughtful, and then said, "Why does not the great Pasha of Tripoli make them all Moslems?"'

A second issue, which continued to recur, concerned the credentials of these Europeans: were they ordinary people driven by innocent curiosity to see the wonders of Borno, or were they on a mission of spying and subversion? At Mandara, Denham was caught gathering geological specimens. This aroused sufficient suspicion to warrant his being brought to General Barka Gana for questioning. Major Denham claimed that he was driven merely by curiosity to collect those specimens and that 'to take anything from any of the inhabitants of these countries is not the wish of the English king'. Perhaps history has lied!

The whole issue was brought to a head when the Shehu himself received the information that Britain had occupied India. The following conversation took place between Denham and his team, and Shehu of Borno: Al-Kanemi asked about the distance between England and India, and the reply was that it took four months by sea. 'What could induce you to go so far from home – to find it out and fight with the people?' he asked. The Englishmen replied that it was the love of discovery and their determination to outbid the French and the Dutch. 'And now it is all yours and governed by your laws!' al-Kanemi said. They replied that England took possession only of the Indian coast, that the Indian people were allowed to keep their laws 'but that even Moslems often preferred the English laws to their own'. Said al-Kanemi, 'Wonderful! And you went at first with a few ships, as friends?' They replied: 'We are friends now, and by trade have not only made ourselves rich but the natives also.' What about Algeria, and other Muslim countries in North Africa, what right had Europe to dictate to them? al-Kanemi demanded. The Algerians, replied the Englishmen, were unfaithful to their words and little better than pirates.

Major Denham's observations of Borno, its people and government betray his racist attitudes. He described the Shuwa Arabs as 'a deceitful, arrogant, and cunning race' possessing 'pilfering propensities'. The Kanuris, who constitute the bulk of the populace of Borno were described as 'peaceable, quiet and civil'. Even so, we are told, the best of them would commit petty larceny at every opportunity. The builders of one of Africa's greatest civilizations were described as 'being no warriors, but revengeful' and 'extremely timid'. Even their strict adherence to Islam was a fault. 'They are Moslems and very particular in performing their prayers five times a day,' Major Denham wrote. 'They are less tolerant than the Arabs and I have known a Bornoese refuse to eat with an Arab because he had not washed and prayed at the preceding appointed hour.' Borno's legal system, based almost entirely on the *shari'a*, was considered by Denham as 'arbitrary'.

Major Denham also provided descriptions of the commodities, and animal and natural resources to be found in Borno. 'Gold is neither found in the country nor is it brought in,' he wrote. 'Iron is procured in the Mandara mountains, but is not brought in large quantities, and it is coarse.' In the appendices to his *Narratives* an exhaustive and painstaking list is made of the animals, plants and rock specimens found in this region of Africa. Major Denham spoke of the Shehu of Borno, al-Amin al-Kanemi, as having all the qualifications of a great commander: 'an enterprising genius, sound judgement, features engaging with a demeanour gentle and conciliating: and so little of vanity was there mixed with his ambition that he refused the offer of being made Sultan and, placing Muhammad, the brother of Sultan Ahmad, on the throne, he first doing homage himself, insisted on the whole army following his example.'

Only one power in central Africa could be compared to the Sheikh of Borno in importance in Denham's opinion – that of Bello:

'He has turned all his victories to the advantage of those whom he conquered, by attending to their improvement in moral and religious duties. His subjects are the most strict Moslems in all the black country, and their respect for us gradually increased on ascertaining that we really had a religion of our own, and obeyed its ordinances by praying, if not by fasting – which they at first doubted. ... Whenever El-Kanemi has power, Europeans, and particularly Englishmen, will be hospitably and kindly received. ... I consider the establishment of a friendly intercourse with this potentate beyond the Great Desert, by whose means the unknown parts of Africa may at no distant period be visited, of the greatest importance, in every point of view'

## Clapperton in Sokoto Caliphate

Our next task is to follow Captain Clapperton's mission to the Sokoto Caliphate, where he was to have several audiences with the *Amir al-Muminin*, Muhammad Bello. The first mission, comprising Dr. Qudney, the leader of the Borno mission, and Captain Clapperton and several assistants, including a Jew, set off from Borno on 14 December 1823. The third member of the Borno mission, Major Denham, had returned to Tripoli. The Shehu of Borno, 'with some degree of reluctance', gave the team permission to cross into the Sokoto Caliphate from his territory and, what is more, gave them two introductory letters, one to the Emir of Kano, and the other to Caliph Muhammad Bello. The letters were to prove very decisive in the success of the mission.

The Shehu wrote of them as 'English travellers; whose nation, out of all the other Christians, has maintained with the Muslims uninterrupted treaties of religious amity and friendship, established since ancient periods.' He reminded Muhammad Bello of what is written in the Qur'an on the subject of honour, recalling that true Muslims have always avoided shedding the blood of Christians, but have assisted and protected them with their own honour. 'Be then attentive to these travellers, and cast them not into the corners of neglect; let no one hurt them, either by words or deeds, nor interrupt them with any injurious behaviour: but let them return to us, safe, content and satisfied, as they went from us to you.' In his letter to the Emir of Kano, the Shehu of Borno stated that: 'There never was between them and the Muslims any dispute; and whenever war is declared by the other Christians against the Muslims, they are always ready to help us, as it has happened in the great assistance they gave to our nation when they delivered Egypt from the hands of the French.'

Clapperton was received in audience by the Emir of Kano, who was then on a *jihad* expedition, at a *ribat* outside Kano. After he had read Sheikh al-Kanemi's letter, Clapperton wrote, he 'told me he expected to return to Kano in fifteen days, and would then send me to his master Bello, who, he knew, would be very glad to see me. We shook hands again at parting. The governor is a Felatah [Fulani], of a dark copper colour and stout make, and has the character of being very devout and learned.' Meanwhile a message had reached the Caliph in Sokoto of Captain Clapperton's arrival in Kano and he gave instructions that he should be conducted to Sokoto and be supplied, in Clapperton's words, 'with everything necessary for the journey'. On March 16, 1824, Captain Clapperton arrived in Sokoto. Of his first audience with the *Amir al-Muminin*, he said:

'He asked me a great many questions about Europe, and our religious distinctions. He was acquainted with the names of some of the more ancient sects, and asked whether we were Nestorians or Socinians. To extricate myself from the embarrassment occasioned by this question, I bluntly replied we were called Protestants. ... He continued to ask several other theological questions, until I was obliged to confess myself not sufficiently versed in religious subtleties to resolve these knotty points, having always left that task to others more learned than myself. ... The sultan is a noble-looking man, forty four years of age, although much younger in appearance, five feet ten inches high, portly in person, with a short curling black beard, a small mouth, a fine forehead, a Graecian nose, and large black eyes. He was dressed in a light blue cotton robe, with a white muslin turban, the shawl of which he wore over the nose and mouth in the Tuarick fashion.'

Clapperton was again received in audience by the Caliph later in the afternoon where the discussion centred on the need to put an end to the Atlantic Slave Trade. He told the Caliph that there were no slaves in England and that 'whenever a slave sets his foot in England, he is from that moment free'. Several other audiences were held. In one, Clapperton sought permission to proceed to Nupeland, in the western part of the Caliphate; in another, the possibility of opening a commercial channel with England was discussed, and so on. On the whole, the following points came out of those discussions: the need for a steady commercial and economic co-operation with England; the 'establishment of an English consul and physician at Sokoto' and the sale of arms by England to the Caliphate. The Caliph inquired why the Christians were at war with Algeria and about the subjugation of India. Clapperton replied that the Algerians were 'a ferocious race' who had been 'making slaves of Europeans' and that India was not in actual fact subjugated; 'we merely afforded it our protection'. In another audience, the Caliph delved into the history of Europe and of Muslim Spain. 'He asked me,' said Clapperton, 'to send him, from England, some Arabic books and a map of the world and, in recompense, promised his protection to as many of our learned men as chose to visit his dominions.' The Caliph also hinted at the possibility of prospecting for gold and silver and Clapperton, again falsely, asserted that England was not at all 'anxious about gold mines', its interest being more in commerce and science.

On May 3, 1824, Clapperton made his farewell visit to Muhammad Bello. 'At seven o'clock in the evening,' he wrote, 'I went to take leave of the Sultan. He was at the mosque and I had to wait for about two hours till he came out. I followed him, at a little distance, to the door of his residence, where an old female slave took my hand and led me through a number of dark passages. ... I could not imagine where the old woman was conducting me, who, on her part, was highly diverted at my importunate inquiries. After much turning and winding, I was at last brought into the presence of Bello, who was sitting alone, and immediately delivered into my hands a letter for the King of England with assurances of his friendly sentiments towards the English nation.'

In his second mission to the Sokoto Caliphate, Clapperton took a route from the coastal town of Badagry, ensuring that he passed through Yorubaland and substantial parts of the Caliphate. In October 1826, he was received in audience by Muhammad Bello. The mission this time was somewhat dramatic. Clapperton was even permitted to join the army on a *jihad*, staying very close to the *wazir*, Gidado Dan Laima. The Caliph in the meantime had received a letter from the Shehu of Borno who, incidentally, was then at war with Sokoto, to the effect that Clapperton was indeed a British spy and that 'if the English should meet with great encouragement, they would come into Sudan, one after another, until they got strong enough to seize on the country, and dispossess him, as they had done with regard to India, which they had wrested from the hands of Muslims'. Al-Kanemi suggested that Clapperton be put to death, as that is the punishment for spies, but Bello felt that in Clapperton's words, 'it would be a most disgraceful thing in him to cause an unprotected man to be put to death'. On the strength of this letter, Clapperton was summoned to the Caliph, whom he found engrossed in reading. The Caliph told him of al-Kanemi's letter, and referred to the colonization of India as proof of English motives towards Muslims. The Caliph ordered a search of his luggage, and prevented him from proceeding to Borno. On 13 April 1827, after a long illness, Clapperton died in Sokoto.

Of Clapperton's observations on the Caliphate not much is worth mentioning because they contain so much impropriety and foulness except, 'The laws of the Koran were so strictly put in force ... and the whole country, when not in a state of war, was so regulated, that it was a common saying that a woman might travel with a casket of gold upon her head from one end of the Fellata dominions to the other.'[i]

## The Wall had been Breached

Clapperton was closely followed into *Bilad al-Sudan* by Henry Barth and several others, until trade missions on a large scale began to pour in. It can be said, therefore, that when Clapperton died in Sokoto in 1827, the seeds of colonization had been effectively sown. The wall that protected the Caliphate and the Muslims of *Bilad al-Sudan* had been breached by *Yajuj wa Majuj*, even though they were not to scale it and surge into this blessed land until seven decades later. So many things regarding this land had these travellers gathered: they had noted in great detail the vegetation and soil; they had amassed knowledge of the natural

i   *Journal of a Second Expedition in the Interior of Africa*, Clapperton, London, 1429.

resources; they had seen Muslims and studied their way of life; and, above all, they had acquired first-hand knowledge of the military capability and war strategies of these two most powerful nations in West Africa.

For their part, the rulers of Borno and Sokoto, together with their people, can be said to have lived up to expectations of Islam. They proved themselves to be absolutely free from the slavish and timid mentality which the Arabs, perhaps overawed by European power, had developed at that time. No one in *Bilad al-Sudan* seemed to be impressed by the admittedly awesome European power, not even when it was clear to them that Algeria and India had fallen. For indeed, as it was firmly believed in this region, 'There is no power nor strength save in Allah'. Perhaps this explains why the visit of these Europeans has not featured in either Borno or Sokoto literature. It was perhaps not considered sufficiently important to merit a mention.

Secondly, the Muslim rulers had treated these harbingers of death and destruction almost exactly as Islam had instructed. They were, on the strength of the letter of Pasha of Tripoli, received as diplomats and treated as such. Clapperton was himself surprised that, in spite of his being told in clear terms by Muhammad Bello that Sokoto took him for spy, he was nevertheless treated with respect and supplied with all that he needed to live comfortably. And thirdly, the Muslim rulers had shown where their interest lay: in Islam, and nothing else. At no time was Islam compromised.

In all of its encounters with Britain, *Bilad al-Sudan* had been consistent in upholding Islam, in defending it with all the power at its disposal, and in refusing, even against overwhelming odds, to compromise Islam's vital interests to European powers. Whereas Muslims treated Europeans with kindness and honour, this gesture was repaid, as history has shown, with acts of treachery, massacres and extermination. The reason perhaps is that both the *Bilad al-Sudan* and Britain have operated from opposing world views: the former believing that it was dealing with a people worthy of trust and confidence; while Britain believed that might was right, and that as 'barbarians' it was perfectly fitting that Muslims should be robbed, plundered and betrayed.

Two treaties were conceded by Borno and Sokoto to the British Government, but not by either Muhammad al-Kanemi or Muhammad Bello. They were negotiated in 1851 and 1853 respectively by later rulers, but nevertheless express clearly how these states had maintained their sovereignty and upheld the *shari'a*. This attitude, as Adeleye has observed, marked these Muslim states distinctly from their non-Muslim counterparts.[i] Instead of merely signing a model draft treaty brought to them by the British envoy, the two rulers wrote a fresh treaty of their own, containing such concessions as they were ready to grant.

In Borno's treaty, British citizens were granted the right to trade throughout the length and breadth of the Sultanate but with certain provisos. 'They shall not be hindered,' says the document, 'from buying and selling whatever is legal for them according to the *shari'a* of Muhammad. But with regard to illegal things such as slaves, copies of the Qur'an and the like, no.' It should be noted that Britain had asked to be given preferential treatment over other European countries, but this was rejected, since 'the religion of all Christians is one and the same religion to us and as such [they are entitled to] the same protection (*dhimmi* status)'. Britain also asked for the right to appoint a consul in Borno, who 'shall be honoured and protected and his words shall be heeded', a subtle reference to a desire to have Borno under its influence. The Borno treaty stipulated that Britain could appoint a consul and his personal safety and property would be guaranteed, 'But other than this he shall be treated according to what is enjoined on us by the *shari'a*, since it will not be proper for us to exceed its limits.'

The Caliph in Sokoto granted British merchants the right to trade under *aman*, or safe conduct, in the Caliphate 'with their children, their property and their mounts and they shall lose nothing. ... Neither in speech shall they hear that which may be loathsome to them nor shall any oppressor harm them'. However, 'they shall traffic in everything except slaves, for the *Amir al-Muminin* will not allow them to purchase slaves'. Sokoto, like Borno, was cautious of possible designs by Europeans against the sovereignty of the

---

i    *Power and Diplomacy in Northern Nigeria: The Sokoto Caliphate and its Enemies*, R.A. Adeleye, Longman, 1977.

state. Adeleye observed that 'it was an explicit aspect of the policy of the Caliphate that, legally, political concessions prejudicial to the Caliph's sovereignty could not be granted to Europeans, whom they classified as Christians. Further, the Christians must accept the position of protected peoples under the Caliphate.' He believes that this policy, which remained remarkably consistent throughout the century, proved later to be a major obstacle to the ambitions of European imperialism.

Now we come to the charge of barbarism, which was consistently levelled against the people in *Bilad al-Sudan* and almost every other non-European race in the world. While it is perhaps natural for everyone to see in their own culture only what is best, for which we may excuse the Europeans, when we look at history we are apt to be disappointed by the lack of European sense of fairness and objectivity. When we ask in Africa who is it that has caused the greatest damage to our continent, robbing it of one hundred twenty million souls in an unbroken period of three full centuries, the answer obviously is the Europeans. When we ask where have our gold, diamonds, silver, tin and other assets gone, the answer inexorably points to Europe. And there we can clearly see the impact of our plundered resources in the prosperity and beauty of the European cities and the 'grandeur' of its civilization.

# Chapter Seven

# Abdullahi Bade His Farewell

We move now from the hustle and bustle of politics and statecraft to pay a final visit to Shehu Abdullahi Dan Fodio as he approached the final year of his life in this world. The purpose of this visit is to explore, albeit briefly, some of the fundamental ideals of life as expounded in the Caliphate – ideals which Shehu Abdullahi came to embody and symbolize. It needs to be stressed at this point that Shehu Abdullahi had been concerned, perhaps more than any other scholar in Sokoto Caliphate, with emphasizing the ideals of Islam – the Sunna – so zealously and persistently with the hope that they might ultimately be realized, in the future, if not in his lifetime. He had devoted his entire life in the search for those ideals, refusing even for one moment to bow to the currents which sought to wash away his hopes.

### Abdullahi on Foundation of Life

Let us begin with what Shehu Abdullahi had to say on two most important pillars of Islam, faith and prayer, which together with *zakat*, fasting and hajj constitute the very foundation of Islam. Our examination is based on Shehu Abdullahi's *Diya al-Umma* and *Al-Targhib wat-Tarhib fis-Salat*. In the former work, Shehu Abdullahi emphasized the importance of *niyya* – intention – to an Islamic way of life: all actions are, in the final analysis, judged by the intentions that lie behind them, and people can obtain by way of recompense only what they have intended; faith depends largely on the purity of motive; and the success of the *umma* lies in four things: protection of the weak and dispossessed, supplication to Allah, *salat* and purity and strength of conviction. Any action which is done for a purpose other than the pleasure of Allah is void and irrelevant.

Faith consists in belief in Allah, his angels, his books, his messengers, the day of judgement and in *qadr* or Allah's ultimate decision – good or bad. But since faith is basically a matter deep in the heart and in the conscience, a person is presumed to be a believer, and therefore a member of the Muslim *umma*, if he manifests the outward attributes of faith – prayer, and identification with the Islamic culture. Yet, faith does have a social manifestation as well: in the expression of human relations by removing harm from society, showing genuine love to believers, and refraining from causing harm to mankind in general. 'A believer is he,' says the Prophet 🌸, 'in whose hands people feel utterly secure, in respect of their persons and possessions.'

Faith leads naturally to Islam, which is living in accordance with Allah's laws. To the extent that the life, property and honour of a Muslim are absolutely inviolable, to be a Muslim implies being in a contract of mutual obligations with Allah: for worshipping Allah one receives a guarantee of security in this world and the next. This contract has political and social implications as well. The Prophet 🌸 used to insist on definite undertakings from his Companions as the basis for their membership of the Islamic community. These pledges include the following: to worship Allah alone, and no one else; to 'hear and obey' the Prophet 🌸 in all matters; to live a life of self-reliance, neither begging nor depending on others; to refrain from stealing, fornication, murder or perjury; to speak the truth at all times and in all places, regardless of the consequences; and to undertake the *jihad* in the cause of Allah.

The Qur'an and Sunna are the ultimate source of guidance. Absolute values which establish right and wrong for society are determined by Allah and His Messenger alone, and are to be found only in the Qur'an and Sunna. And since these two sources are sufficient a guidance for the *umma*, innovations alien to the spirit of Islam must be rejected outright.

Islam is based on *tabsira* – insight – said Abdullahi. Islam therefore requires that society should be continually informed and educated about Islam and no one should be left in ignorance of its precepts and requirements. This implies two things. In the first place there must be learned men – the *'ulama* – whose primary responsibility is to teach and spread the message of Islam. It is in this context that scholars are called heirs of the prophets, for they bequeathed neither dirham nor dinar but only knowledge. Secondly, every Muslim – male or female – must endeavour to acquire the knowledge of Islam, since a person's religion, as a hadith implies, remains sound only in proportion to the depth of his knowledge. Knowledge, however, must relate fundamentally to one's character, if not, then it becomes a liability rather than an asset. So vital is knowledge to the practice of Islam that, as Ibn Masud is quoted as saying, when ignorance pervades society, and learned men diminish in number and stature and only a handful of people remain trustworthy, then *fitna,* or turmoil and corruption, will engulf the entire fabric of society. Imparting knowledge to enable individual Muslims to practise Islam on the basis of clear insight rather than blind imitation, is Shehu Abdullahi's recipe for a healthy society.

*Salat* is the greatest manifestation of Islam, as Abdullahi pointed out. It embodies a number of principles vital to Muslim life – cleanliness, modesty, a sense of dignity, and seriousness of purpose, to name but a few. A Muslim is expected to cleanse himself of all impurities, whether they are the outcome of answering the call of nature, sexual intercourse, menstruation or childbirth. Water is the symbol of purity, and is thus appropriately the object for purification. *Salat* is preceded by *wudu* – ablution – and where sexual intercourse has taken place, by *ghusl* – complete ritual bath. Shehu Abdullahi describes in detail how the Prophet 🕌 used to perform both *wudu* and *ghusl,* emphasizing the necessity of perfecting these aspects of cleanliness and maintaining complete composure in the process. The Friday and Id prayers should also be preceded by *ghusl*; and the body of a dead Muslim should be laid to rest in the grave only after it has been given *ghusl,* for the last time.

The Prophet 🕌 used to honour all matters relating to *salat* and made the life, property and honour of a person who prays inviolable. Children should be made to pray at the age of seven. After describing the times of prayer and similar matters, Shehu Abdullahi reiterated the ethics of *salat.* The Prophet 🕌 used sometimes to weep during prayer; he urged Muslims to remain conscious of Allah and deeply fearful of Him in the course of prayer; but dangers can be removed. 'The Prophet 🕌 once killed a scorpion whilst at prayer,' Shehu

Abdullahi wrote, 'and he would sometimes smile.' In congregational prayer rows should be straight, Muslims standing shoulder to shoulder, in complete silence and serenity, behind the Imam. The Imam, on his part, should maintain a moderate standard in his prayer by not prolonging the prayer to the point of discomfiture or leading the prayer against the wish of the people. The reading of *Sura al-Fatiha*, we are told, is compulsory in prayer, and without it no *salat* can be said to be complete. The Prophet 🕮, however, used to offer concessions to the bedouins – and, by implication, to all those with less education – in respect of the reading of other portions of the Qur'an apart from *al-Fatiha*.

Shehu Abdullahi recommended the performance of some supererogatory deeds of devotion which are most likely to bring one closer to Allah. These were practised by the Prophet 🕮 himself. These include: two or four *rak'ats* before and after *zuhr*; four before *asr*; two or more after *maghrib*, four after *isha* and two before *subh*. They also include: the night prayer – *tahajjud* and the *witr* – which together comprise between eleven and thirteen *rak'ats* – the Prophet 🕮 describes the night prayer as leading a Muslim to eminence in the sight of Allah – and in Ramadan, the *tarawih* prayers. Then the forenoon prayer called *salat al-duha*, which ranges between four and twelve *rak'ats*, 'at home or on a journey'. Others include: 'enlivening' the time between *zuhr* and *asr* with prayer, offering some *rak'ats* on entering the mosque, and following every *wudu* with some *rak'ats*. However, the more important ones are: *salat al-Haja*,[i] which is done to seek Allah's assistance for a need or favour; *salat al-Tawba*,[ii] which is an act of atonement for a specific sin one has committed; *salat al-Istikhara*, for seeking decisions and the assistance of Allah for a major undertaking; and *salat al-Tasbih*,[iii]

i   All works of Shehu Abdullahi referred to in this chapter are, except otherwise stated, in manuscripts. Most, if not all, are available in Graduate Research Unit, Bayero University, Kano, Nigeria, and in Northern History Research Project, Ahmadu Bello University, Zaria, Nigeria.
ii  'Ali said: Abu Bakr told me, and Abu Bakr spoke the truth, that he heard God's messenger say, "No man will commit a sin, then get up and purify himself, then pray, then ask God's forgiveness without God forgiving him."' (*Mishkhat*)
iii Ibn Abbas told that the Prophet 🕮 said to al-Abbas b. Abd al-Muttalib: 'Abbas my uncle, shall I not give you, shall I not present you, shall I not tell you, shall

intended solely to glorify Allah. In addition, one should make *salat* to relieve distress or pain when in difficult circumstances, as the Prophet ﷺ himself used to do.

Obligatory prayers are best performed in congregation, especially *subh* and *isha*. Women are given the concession of praying at home, for their *salat* at home is better and greater in reward than in the mosque. And one should pray in the mosque nearest to one. The Prophet ﷺ used to accept illness, rain, fear of danger and being engaged in meals as valid excuses for not attending the congregation. A man may lead a congregation comprising both men and women; and a woman may lead other women in prayer. And where the unity of Muslims is at risk, a person of lesser piety could be appointed as imam as a compromise.

The Friday prayer is an obligation on Muslims. Even if there are 'only four people' in a locality, *salat al-Jumu'a* becomes obligatory on them, for the *shari'a* does not place a specific limit on the number of people who can perform it. Friday itself is undoubtedly the most important day for a Muslim, who is asked to honour it. He must wash and adorn himself in a presentable and dignified fashion, appropriate to the day. It is necessary to glorify Allah, and supplicate as much as possible, 'for there is an hour in this day, in which Allah grants whatever request that is made to Him', we are told. Cheating and rancour among Muslims are especially prohibited on this day. It is recommended that *khutbas* should be short and precise.

*Salat* seems to determine the flow of an Islamic way of life as well as being a Muslim response to the vicissitudes of life. *Salat*

---

I not produce in you ten things, by your doing which God will forgive you your sins, first and last, old and new, involuntary and voluntary, small and great, secret and open? You should pray four *rak'ats* reciting in each one *Fatihat al-Kitab* and a *sura*; and when you finish the recitation in the first *rak'a*, you should say fifteen times while standing *Subhanallah wal hamdulillah wa la ilaha illa'llah wa'llahu akbar* (Glory be to God. Praise be to God. There is no god but God. God is most great.) Then you should bow and say it ten times. Then you should get down in prostration and say it ten times while prostrating yourself. Then you should raise your head after prostrating yourself and say it ten times. Then you should prostrate yourself and say it ten times. Then raise your head and say it ten times. That is, seventy-five in every *rak'a*. You should do that in four *rak'ats*. If you can observe it once daily do so; if not, then once weekly; if not, then once a month; if not then once a year; if not then once in your lifetime.' (*Mishkat*) *al-Khawf* provides the spiritual support needed by a Muslim army in the battlefield; *salat al-Kusuf* is the Muslim response to Allah's manifestation of his power in the universe; it is observed whenever 'something extraordinary occurs in the heaven'. *Salat al-Istisqa* is man's acknowledgement of his limitations to provide sustenance without the benevolent support of Allah. Water is the source of life and mainspring of human existence: in *salat al-Istisqa* Muslims seek the indispensable help of Allah when rains fail. In *salat al-Janaza* Muslims offer their last respects to a departing brother or sister; it is, as it were, the final gesture which helps to unite them in the *umma*. The Prophet ﷺ, Shehu Abdullahi told us, would urge Muslims to go in large numbers to *salat al-Janaza*, saying that a large attendance elicits Allah's forgiveness for the dead. And he himself used to supplicate to Allah after *salat al-Janaza* on behalf of the dead, saying: 'Allah, this is your servant coming as Your guest, and You are the best of hosts, so forgive him and offer him a comfortable home.'

In *at-Tartib*, Shehu Abdullahi linked the fortunes of the *umma* to the way in which it observes the *salat*. Two examples may be noted here. First, in the days of the Prophet ﷺ, Muslims felt extremely sad whenever they missed a congregational prayer. In the days of Shehu Usman the same situation occurred, so is there any wonder then that the phenomenal successes achieved by the Muslims in Sokoto were similar in many respects to those of the early days of Islam? Secondly, Shehu Abdullahi established a correlation between the diminishing fortunes of the earliest *umma* to the diminishing quality of their *salat*. In the Prophet's time, people's concentration in *salat* was almost perfect. In the time of Abu Bakr, it was near-perfect; and a little less so in the time of Umar. During Uthman's era, however, 'there occurred the *fitna* – political and social upheaval – and people looked right and left [in the course of *salat*).

### Abdullahi on Ethical Values

We can now move a stage further to examine briefly Shehu Abdullahi's ethical and cultural values. Our main reference here is his *Kitab Adab al-Adat ala Sunnat ar-Rasul*, supplemented by *Diya al-Umma*. To start with, Shehu Abdullahi conceived of a man of ethics as one with an occupation or independent means of livelihood. 'Let it be known,' he said in *Kitab al-Adat*, 'that earning pursued in order to strengthen one's practice of the religion, is one of the commandments of the religion.' For that reason it is an obligation on every Muslim to have a means of livelihood which will earn him self-reliance. The only exceptions are those who, by virtue of their work – such as pietists, teachers, judges and public officers – have to be supported by the state. Earning, however, has its own set of ethics. Some of the legal rules governing occupation in general, and especially trade, were reaffirmed by Shehu Abdullahi in *Kifayat al-Awam fil Buyu*. He warned people against illegal trafficking, saying, as rendered by Prof. Zahradeen:

> 'The selling of free men and making servants of them by force, and withholding their wages is illegal, and in the *shari'a*, fraud and cheating have been prohibited. The use of deceitful charms has also been forbidden. O you sellers (of wares) in the markets, beware of these actions of the godless, as well as the hoarding of cotton or food because they are all illegal acts.'[i]

All economic activities must be conducted with justice, made free from *riba*, exploitation, or cheating. A Muslim, to return to *Kitab al-Adat*, does not hoard essential commodities, especially in a time of scarcity. The Prophet 📖 warned that whoever defrauds Muslims is not a member of the *umma* and that cheating and treachery lead to hell. Weights and measures must be perfected and faithfully observed, for failure in this regard has led in the past to the collapse of many a nation, as the Prophet 📖 warned. Similarly, a Muslim observes faithfully the following ethics in his economic dealings with others: he does not sell things which are indispensable to life, such as water, salt or sources of energy, for these are items of common ownership; he does not deal in commodities expressly forbidden in *shari'a*, such as wine or pork; he does not enter into any major agreement without having witnesses attesting to it. He endeavours to offer loans to Allah, that is to be charitable not hoping

---

i    MS Zahradeen, *Abd Allah Ibn Fodio's Contributions to the Fulani Jihad in 19th century Hausaland*. Ph.D. dissertation McGill University, 1976.

for a favour in return, to give respite to those who are unable to pay their loans, and to be helpful in general to neighbours and those in less favoured circumstances. The sincere Muslim refrains from leading an extravagant lifestyle, especially with regard to buildings, for the Prophet ﷺ has warned that massive and opulent buildings are a means of self-destruction.

The Muslim, in his dealings with others, refrains also from *ghasb*, economic exploitation. He takes nothing from a fellow Muslim without the latter's consent; he does not appropriate any part of public land for his personal benefit, nor usurp the land of other people; as a public treasurer he is faithful and trustworthy; as an artisan he guarantees his work; as a physician he masters his work well; as an employer he pays his employee 'even before his perspiration dries out', that is, promptly. Child labour is improper and best avoided, so also is using less privileged women as unskilled labourers: the former could corrupt children, and the latter is likely to lead to prostitution. Partnership should not involve betrayal of trust of taking undue advantage by one party over the other.

A Muslim is careful to avoid living off illegal income, distancing himself from all sources of illegality. He avoids the outcome of *zulm* – injustice – or *riba* – unjust enrichment. He is careful to avoid dealing with those associated with oppression. If he is a public servant he ensures that his salary comes only from the state treasury. Gifts from rulers should be avoided since 'the wealth of rulers is predominantly illegal'. All forms of bribery are unlawful, particularly those given for the purpose of 'perverting the course of justice'. Public officers, especially judges and governors, should avoid bribery since whatever they are given outside their legal entitlement by virtue of their office is illegal. Shehu Abdullahi's best known work on the issues of legality and illegality is *Diya al-Anam fil Halal wal Haram*. In it he stressed the necessity for a Muslim, especially the scholar, to avoid dealing with oppressors and urged whoever had taken anything from the public treasury to restore it, and he cautioned Muslims not to pollute lawful wealth with fraud, usurpation or oppression.[i]

i   For more details, see A.A. Gwandu's 'Abdullahi b. Fodio as a Muslim Jurist,' PhD. dissertation, Durham University, 1977, especially pp. 140-147. Says Gwandu,

Food is essential for life, but as Shehu Abdullahi reasoned in *Kitab al-Adat*, its very importance necessitates the observation of certain ethical values. Some of these are as follows: food should be taken purposely to gain the strength to serve Allah and promote his cause; food must be lawful as well as wholesome, untainted by illegality or impurity; it should be taken in accordance with the *Sunna*, with sublime etiquette. Moreover, it is preferable that a family should eat together rather than separately. Meals should start with *bismillah* and end with *alhamdulillah*, and the cultured Muslim should eat with his right hand and eat what is nearest to him. A Muslim may not offer his guests food that he would loathe. When Muslims meet together to study the Qur'an, or for any other noble purpose, they should not disperse until they have taken a meal together. Similarly, Muslims should make a habit of inviting upright and poor people and close relatives to meals. Eating in company is a virtue. Food may not be wasted. A person may not attend a meal to which he has not been invited, but one who is invited should honour the invitation. A guest should stay for only such length of time as would not constitute a burden on his host – preferably just three days. There should always be a guest room in the house; this is in keeping with the injunction of the Prophet 舞, which says there should always be at least three rooms in a house: one for the householder, one for his wife and one for guests.

A cultured man, in the eyes of Shehu Abdullahi, is a family man. He suggested that three factors are essential for a good marriage. First of all, the choice of a spouse should be based on righteousness. Secondly, there should be the ability or willingness on the part of the husband to look after his wife properly and uphold her rights. Thirdly, only a person with a legitimate income which is sufficient to maintain a family decently, should marry. A Muslim guardian may not, Shehu Abdullahi stated, give a woman in his

inter alia: 'Abdullahi's conclusion was that most of the possessions of these [Hausa] rulers were unlawful. However, the welfare of the people who needed the services of public servants and professionals had to be taken into consideration. Necessity and common sense, therefore, required that salaries and wages paid to these public servants should be declared lawful. To do otherwise would have been to defeat one of the main purposes of the *shari'a*, namely the promotion of public good.'

care in marriage to a person known to be of evil repute, or not strongly committed to Islam, or who from all indications would be incapable of safeguarding her rights. Nor should he surrender her to an oppressor or a corrupt person. A husband has a moral obligation to 'ward off all harm' from his wife, to be gentle and just to her and to endeavour to please her heart in a legitimate manner. He should ensure that she is educated. It is best to conduct marriage in the month of Shawwal, and hold the ceremony in the mosque. A cultured man, in Abdullahi's view, treats his wife well and is respectful to her. The Prophet 餐, we are told, said: 'The best of you are those who are best to their wives.' A woman may neither be beaten nor insulted. Although a woman has a distinctive nature of her own, and a disposition which is clearly distinct in many respects from that of a man, she should enjoy the same lifestyle as her husband in respect of lodging, food and clothing, as the Qur'an has commanded.

Parents are not permitted to show favour to their sons at the expense of their daughters or in any way to discriminate against the latter, for the Prophet 餐 has enjoined that both sons and daughters must be treated equally. Wives in a polygamous family must be treated fairly. As for divorce, Shehu Abdullahi stated that the Prophet 餐 discouraged it, but when it is unavoidable Islamic rules should be observed. These include, in addition to the well-known regulations, that the husband should offer the divorced wife gifts to 'please her heart', and keep all her secrets to himself, as a trust, as we read in *Kitab al-Adat*. A woman who seeks a divorce from her husband, where the latter has committed no fault nor caused her injury will have to compensate him; but her request for divorce should be granted, as the Prophet 餐 invariably did.

Shehu Abdullahi also touched on the treatment of servants. 'An ill-mannered master,' the Prophet 餐 warned, 'will not enter Paradise.' He enjoined Muslims to feed their servants with the same food that they eat and to clothe them with the same clothing that they themselves wear and not to overburden them with tasks beyond their power. Servants should be forgiven 'more than seventy times a day'. The Prophet 餐 prohibited their working at night: 'You have taken all their day, the night is theirs.'

Pets and domestic animals are to be treated fairly, Abdullahi maintained in *Diya al-Umma*. They are entitled to maintenance and *ihsan*, or kindness. A certain woman suffered divine punishment for starving her pet cat to death. Domestic animals may not be overburdened with loads; nor even insulted. They may not be branded on the face.

The man of ethics relates with people in order principally to foster harmony, love, brotherhood, comradeship and social intercourse. Harmony, said Abdullahi, emanates from good character; it entails associating with those who seek to cut off a relationship with you; forgiving those who have wronged you; and giving to those who have denied you. Genuine love is that which is inspired by the love of Allah and aimed solely at reaping the good of the Hereafter. For example, a husband is duty-bound to love his wife, and the wife her husband, but this love is valuable only when it is aimed at self-fortification against sin. 'But love whose purpose is to obtain worldly glory, rank and wealth,' said Shehu Abdullahi, 'cannot be counted as love for the sake of Allah.' And of course genuine love is to be extended only to upright people, and never to unbelievers who should be resisted at all times, and fought if need be.

Brotherhood, Shehu Abdullahi explained, is based on the following obligations: to extend greetings of peace to a fellow Muslim; to honour his invitations; to invoke Allah's mercy on him when he sneezes; to visit him when he is sick; to accept his apologies in good faith and honour his plighted words; to offer him sincere advice when he seeks it; to defend his integrity in his absence; to love for him what one loves for oneself and hate for him what one hates for oneself; and to attend his funeral in the event of his death. If the Muslim is also a neighbour, there are additional obligations towards him: to extend moral and material help to him when he is in need; to share in his happiness as well as sorrow; to share food with him and to honour his privacy and refrain from exposing his weaknesses.[i]

Social intercourse is permissible only with those who are of good character. Evil people are bound to be harmful to others, for even

---

i    For more details on Islamic brotherhood see Shehu Abdullahi's *Al Tibyan li Huquq al-Ikhwan*.

when they are intelligent, they easily succumb to 'passion, anger, miserliness, or cowardice'. No one can be safe from the treachery of the profligate and 'associating with the greedy is a deadly poison'. Social intercourse may be avoided only for the sake of retiring for worship or escaping from disputes, or to save oneself from causing harm to others, or from coveting their possessions. For withdrawal from society, especially by learned people who are best capable of changing it, may have calamitous consequences. Scholars may be compelled to withdraw for social and political reasons; but it should be undertaken only as a last resort, with the object of coming back, if possible, to effect change.

Travelling is an integral part of Muslim culture, whether in search of knowledge, hajj or *jihad*, for trade or in search of a livelihood. The ethics of travelling as Shehu Abdullahi enumerated them include: purging oneself of all acts of oppression one might have committed; settling debts; organizing the maintenance of dependents; returning all deposits to their owners; and wishing goodbye to the family. In addition, *salat al-Istikhara* should be observed before setting out on a journey. Concessions which are offered by Allah for travellers, such as the shortening of prayer, should be fully utilized. On returning from journey, thanks should be offered to Allah.

Finally, Shehu Abdullahi, in *Kitab al-Adat*, reiterated the obligation of a responsible Muslim to command the good and forbid the evil, in his home, locality and society as a whole through education, exhortations, counselling, warning, and, failing these, the use of arms. The man of ethics is thus an active and robust member of society, a soldier ever on the alert to defend its social and moral integrity.

### Abdullahi on Morality

Of the three who made up the Sokoto intellectual and political leadership – Shehu Usman, Abdullahi and Muhammad Bello – Shehu Abdullahi appears to have shown the greatest interest in the moral development of the individual. On several occasions he showed his disgust openly at the moral commitment of some of the people with whom he was struggling to establish a better society.

His experience at the Battle of Alwasa, where the indiscipline nearly brought the whole cause to a disastrous end, must have confirmed his suspicions about the new society. Most of the men who had embodied the spirit of Islam – the spirit of the revolution – had died as martyrs. Now, Shehu Abdullahi lamented, 'I have been left among a remnant who neglect their prayers, and obey, in procuring pleasures, their own lower selves, and the majority of them have traded their faith for the world.' Shehu Abdullahi thought at first that the best course of action was for him to take refuge in Madina. Eventually, however, he realized that there was no shortcut to the moral regeneration of society and he had to face the reality of the situation with the courage it required.

He then devoted himself to writing books on practically every aspect of morality and to producing scholars to serve as teachers, judges, administrators and guides to society. He wrote probably no less than twenty works on this subject alone. At least three of his *Sabil* series, *Sabil al-Najat*, *Sabil al-Sunna* and *Sabil Ahl al-Falah* are devoted exclusively to issues of morality. To this may be added *Tahdhib al-Insan, Masalih al-Insan, Kitab al-Nasaih, Tariq al-Salihin, Diya al-Fawa'id*, to name but a few. In all these works, Abdullahi's basic concern was to espouse the moral ideals which individual members of society should pursue. Since *Sabil Ahl al-Falah* seems to be the quintessence of what Abdullahi wrote on morality, it will form the basis of our discussion.

A person who seeks to achieve success in life is morally bound to spare no effort in making adequate provisions and in preparing himself for his ultimate destiny: the Hereafter. These provisions and preparations entail making sincere repentance on a continual basis for his sins, not causing injury or injustice to others, avoiding the prohibitions of Islam, resisting the temptations of the lower self and lamenting over those parts of life not spent in obedience to Allah. He should also make the necessary effort to learn about his Islamic obligations, and consult the *'ulama* before taking any course of action to ensure compliance with Islam. A person is advised to cultivate the quality of social restraint. He should control his vital organs, always keeping in mind that death inevitably awaits him, limit his association with people to what is absolutely necessary, content himself with what he possesses by lawful means and live strictly in accordance with the Sunna. He counselled:

'Do not hurt those who seek to hurt you, nor intrude into what does not concern you. Withhold your tongue from backbiting and listen not to backbiting, rather, be true of tongue. Keep away from dubious things, give generously – especially to your relatives. Be long of silence, patient in adversities and blows of fate. Stand for long periods in prayer during the night and be in the habit of fasting constantly. Let your body be with people while your heart keeps company with the dead, by constantly bringing death to mind... And know that Allah keeps watch over you. Beware, therefore, lest He should find you where He has forbidden you to be, or miss you where He has commanded you to be; and apportion some of your time to the remembrance of Allah.'

A Muslim is further advised to enhance his standing before Allah by fulfilling his obligations to him, and avoiding sinful practices. He should in fact do more than that through the observance of supererogatory acts. 'Do not be a fool, who rejoices at the increase in his wealth; rather let your rejoicing be at the increase of your knowledge and good works,' Shehu Abdullahi advised, for they alone constitute the imperishable assets of a person. 'And be content with the minimum requirements of this world in respect of food, clothing, marriage, lodging, transport and furniture.' A Muslim must not try to make wealth by any means: 'for whoever does not mind whence his wealth comes, Allah will not mind as to which of the gates he is thrown into hell'. He should rather try to emulate the Messenger of Allah who took only the minimum of what he required in this world, and refrained from luxury and comfort, and heed the advice which the Messenger of Allah gave to his wife, Aisha, namely to take from the world only the equivalent of what a traveller needs for a journey, avoid rubbing shoulders with the wealthy, waste and self-indulgence. For as long as things in life come in pairs, decline follows power, death follows life and the Hereafter follows this world.

The Muslim in search of *falah* – felicity – should strive to gain greater intimacy with Allah every day. This can be achieved by observing three practices: *du'a*, or supplication; *dhikr*, or remembrance of Allah; and *nawafil*, or supererogatory devotional acts. *Dua* is the most precious thing in the eyes of Allah, and one of the most important *du'a* is an acknowledgement of one's moral failures, a prayer for Allah's forgiveness and mercy. Shehu Abdullahi assured Muslims that prayers are bound to be answered by Allah either in the form of direct granting of what is asked for, or by the warding off of evils which would otherwise have afflicted them. Allah does not, however, accept a *du'a* which involves sin or breaking the ties of relationship. Nor does he accept a *du'a* which is made without full concentration of the mind, or the *du'a* of one who lives off unjust earnings. But even so, there is the firm assurance that Allah will never destroy a person who supplicates to him.

*Dhikr* consists of bringing Allah to mind at every possible moment and situation in one's life, and in seeking Allah's forgiveness at all times. Shehu Abdullahi related the hadith which states that when a person retires to bed the angel says to him, 'End your day with some good,' whereas the devil says to him, 'End your day with evil.' If the person remembers Allah and celebrates His name, he then enjoys the protection of angels throughout the night. The same process is repeated when he wakes up in the morning, and if he praises Allah, he is then protected, and is assured of grace should he die on that day.

*Nawafil* or supererogatory deeds of devotion should be performed by one who 'seeks deliverance from punishment' on the Day of Judgement. Most of these have already been mentioned in this chapter. Shehu Abdullahi, however, stressed the particular importance of the night prayer, *qiyam al-layl* or *tahajjud*, which he described as a means of obliterating sins and illuminating the heart and countenance. A person who wishes to find this devotional deed easy to perform should, among other things, develop the spirit of penitence, free himself from despising fellow Muslims and from being materialistic. The highest stage of *qiyam al-layl* is to stand the whole night, which is 'the practice of the strong and the robust' followed by standing half the night; then a third; then a fifth; then a sixth; then standing from the early part of the night until one is overcome by sleep; and then, for the weak, observing four or even two *rak'ats* in the night. There is still another stage, for those who cannot manage four or two *rak'ats*: they can engage their hearts in *dhikr* and *du'a* as they lie on their beds; this is counted for them as *qiyam al-layl*. Night prayer, as Shehu Abdullahi emphasized, is a sign of a person's love for Allah.

The issues of death and the Hereafter take up the larger part of the treatise. Remembrance of death, he said, curbs inordinate ambition and gives contentment to the heart. He warned against making light of this fact, because those who do so usually give rein to their appetites. They live in perpetual self-delusion, and their greed and ambition increase as their days in this world.' Shehu Abdullahi then discussed the Day of Judgement, the Resurrection, the Final Judgement and the Life Hereafter, stressing the importance for the Muslim to prepare himself for this everlasting life. Judgement, he said, quoting authorities, will centre on four things: how a person has spent his life; how he has used his senses and organs; how he has utilized his knowledge; and how he has acquired and spent his wealth. The judgement will be so thorough that everyone who has been oppressed in this world will have adequate compensation. The morally poor will eventually perish. Finally, Shehu Abdullahi described both Hell and Paradise, stressing the intensity of the punishment in Hell, and the grace and mercy that characterize life in Paradise. 'I have prepared for my righteous servants,' as Allah stated in a hadith quoted by Shehu Abdullahi, 'what no eye has seen and no ear has heard, nor has it occurred to human heart.'

### Abdullahi on *Uswatun Hasana*

Shehu Abdullahi's life was one of relentless search for the ideal. His lecture tours early in his life with his mentor, Shehu Usman, across the lands of Gobir, Kebbi and others, his *hijra* from the domain of injustice to Gudu in search of a home for Islam; his *jihad* against the forces opposed to Islam; and, above all, his numerous writings – about one hundred and seventy works – all indicate his devotion to the ideal, which is none other than the Sunna of the Prophet 🌸, or what the Qur'an terms *uswatun hasana*, the perfect model of life, the epitome of human excellence, the standard for distinguishing the good from the bad. Shehu Abdullahi took every opportunity to remind Muslims of the character of the Prophet ﷺ. Many of his works are exclusively devoted to explaining the character of the Prophet ﷺ but our attention here will be focused solely on *Sabil al-Sunna*, a concise and meaningful work, which if followed will lead a person to Paradise.

In the first chapter, Shehu Abdullahi stressed the point that all Muslims owe certain obligations to the Prophet ﷺ, which they should do their best to discharge:

> 'Let it be known that it is obligatory on us to have faith in the Messenger of Allah, to obey him and to adhere to his Sunna... Allah, Most High says: *'But no, by thy Lord, they can have no [real] faith until they make thee [Muhammad] judge in all disputes between them, and find in their souls no resistance against thy decisions, but accept them with the fullest conviction.'* (4:65) And He says: *'Ye have indeed in the Apostle of God a beautiful pattern [of conduct].'* (33:21)

The Islamic way of life is rooted in three attitudes: following the example of the Prophet ﷺ in both conduct and deed; living only on what is lawful; and being a person of sincerity and good faith.

The obligations of Muslims towards the Prophet ﷺ include having a genuine love for him – love which supersedes the love for parents, children and above all the self – loving what he loved, and hating what he hated, doing what he has ordered to be done, and refraining from what he has prohibited, and placing obedience to his commandments above all personal interests. It entails remembering him, yearning for his company, loving those who love him, and hating those who hate him. The love of the Qur'an, being compassionate to the Prophet's *umma*, being abstemious regarding the good things of life, preferring the Hereafter to this world – all fall within the obligations of Muslims to the Prophet ﷺ. It is necessary to show profound reverence for the person of the Prophet ﷺ whenever he is mentioned. Reverence for his household and his Companions is part of these obligations. Above all, is the obligation to invoke constantly Allah's blessing.

From here, Shehu Abdullahi, in the second chapter of *Sabil al-Sunna*, moved on to highlight some aspects of the character of the Prophet ﷺ. The Prophet ﷺ had a natural disposition for goodness which emanated from his being in possession of a perfect intellect. Thus he was able to display the necessary political wisdom, forbearance and patience in nurturing and taming the Arabs, who, in the words of Shehu Abdullahi, had been like 'wild beasts', until they turned to him, 'obeying the commandments of Allah on account of him, fighting at his behest even against their fathers, sons and kinsmen, preferring him above their own selves, making the *hijra* to seek his acceptance from their homeland and loved ones'. This perfect intellect of the Prophet ﷺ also enabled him to endure patiently the rejection, insults and persecution of his people, and to refuse to have them punished for their injustices to him. In fact, he used to ask Allah to forgive their excesses and overlook their faults, in spite of the harm they continually inflicted upon him and his followers.

The Prophet ﷺ was also humble, to the extent that when Allah gave him the choice of being either a prophet and a king or a prophet and a slave, he chose the latter. He cheerfully shared in the household chores with his family, oblivious of his exalted status, and lived contentedly with them, judging between them whenever there was a dispute. He would stitch his clothes, mend his sandals, draw water from the well, milk his goats. He would serve himself, even when a servant was on hand, and serve his guests personally. He disdained to be marked out from his Companions, and used to say, 'I hate to be distinguished from you, for Allah detests to see a servant of His being distinguishable from his companions.' He also had a love for the poor, whose invitations he always honoured and he would visit the sick and attend funerals.

It was the Prophet's habit to engage in jokes with his Companions, but 'saying nothing but the truth'. He gave equal attention to those around him, so that everyone felt honoured. He appreciated food, and never found fault with it. He was not in the habit of using gatemen, except on rare occasions 'when he needed absolute privacy'. The Prophet ﷺ, Shehu Abdullahi stated further, was extremely modest: he was shy, never fixing his gaze on a person, nor exposing his nakedness, even to his wife; nor confronting anyone with what the latter disliked. He showed a tremendous awe of Allah in prayer – sounds of weeping could be heard coming from his chest like 'the boiling of the cauldron'. But he was also a man of extraordinary courage and generosity. 'He gave preference to others over himself and his children. All his generosity was for the sake of Allah, in pursuit of His pleasure; at times, he gave to the poor, at other times in the cause of Allah, and at yet other times, to draw people into the fold of Islam.'

In the third and last chapter of *Sabil al-Sunna*, Shehu Abdullahi highlighted some of the Prophet's 'sublime characteristics' especially those relating to personal discipline. The Prophet never ate his fill; he did not reserve choice food for himself; he would eat with three fingers, and where the nature of the food did not permit that, with five. He was also modest in his dress and was particularly so in his bedding. His bed was a skin stuffed with palm fibres. 'At times', said Shehu Abdullahi, 'he slept on a bed; and at other times on a leather mat, or on ordinary mat and even, at times, on bare floor.' The Prophet had an excellent relationship with his family. His sexual life had four objectives: preservation of health; attainment of sexual joy; fulfilment of the fundamental aim of marriage, which is the preservation of the human race; and safeguarding chastity. Shehu Abdullahi maintained that prolonged suppression of sexual desire does give rise to some emotional and spiritual ailments, if not physical ones.

The Prophet would hold his tongue and restrain his eyes when he went out. He would retire to bed in the beginning of the night, wake up in the middle to perform ablution and pray. 'He did not partake of sleep beyond what was necessary nor deny himself that minimum of it he required.' He used to honour any delegation that came to him: he would welcome, accommodate and feed them well, and then imbue them with knowledge of Islam.

As if to underline the pre-eminent position of *jihad* in the cause of Allah, Shehu Abdullahi ended with describing the various *jihad*s fought in the course of the Prophet's life. Then we are told of his illness, when he sought the permission of his wives to stay his final days with Aisha; that he ordered that the money in his possession – seven dinars in all – be given as charity. On a Monday, the Prophet

🕌, unable to go himself to the mosque to lead the prayer, watched from his room, and was impressed by their intense devotion to it. A smile of supreme satisfaction and sense of fulfilment suffused his face. And on that same Monday the Messenger of Allah died.

## Abdullahi on Sufism

As the year 1244/1828 moved towards its end, Shehu Abdullahi began, perhaps, to sense that his life in this world was coming to an end. This sense of parting with the world occasioned a final reflection on the meaning and purpose of life and a gesture of gratitude to Allah, expressed in *Shukr al-Ihsan ala Minan al-Mannan*. It is his meditation, after a passage of forty-three years, on his first published work *Minan al-Mannan*, as if to show his indebtedness and commitment to sufism.

*Shukr al-Ihsan* represents an articulation of the fundamental principles and objectives of sufism, as well as being a testimony of Shehu Abdullahi's commitment to it. Indeed, it was his belief that an Islamic way of life, which is not illuminated by the light of sufism, is deficient and that the best Muslim is the sufi. Sufism, to him, is not a spirituality extraneous to Islam, it is rather the striving on the part of a Muslim to attain to excellence and perfection in the practice of Islam. It is man's effort to turn his entire being towards Allah, a feeling engendered by the realization of the omnipresence of Allah. In the final analysis, then, every sincere Muslim is a sufi, as long as he seeks to attain not only to faith and Islam, but also to *ihsan*, which is the essence of sufism.[i]

Central to *Shukr al-Ihsan* is the idea that sufism is essentially the pursuit of excellence, representing for a Muslim a desire to live in strict accordance with the Sunna of the Prophet 🕌. The sufi, or rather the pursuer of excellence, should be guided in his life by two attitudes – gratitude and patience. He should be grateful to Allah when he is in a state of *ni'ma*, when circumstances are easy for him, and patient in *shidda*, when circumstances are difficult. It is imperative for the pursuer of excellence to purge himself of all *kibr*

i    See Shehu Umar Abdulllahi's, *The Life and Ideals of Shehu Abdullahi ibn Fodio*, being an edition and translation of his work, *Diya al-Siyasat*, M.A. dissertation, Bayero University, 1983, or arrogance, for no one can be sure of what the end will be like, as we find in the famous hadith:

'By Him beside whom there is none worthy of worship, one of you behaves like the dwellers of Paradise till there is left between him and it but the space of a hand and then that which is recorded overtakes him and he begins to behave like the denizens of the Fire and eventually enters it. On the other hand, one of you behaves like the denizens of the Fire until there is left between him and it only the space of a hand then what is recorded overtakes him and he begins to behave like the dwellers of Paradise and eventually enters it.'

Abdullahi's recounting this hadith points to the fact that life is open to all kinds of vicissitudes. For example, the pious can degenerate in the last part of life and die corrupt and the corrupt can be morally transformed and die in a righteous state. The realization of this ceaseless drama in life is enough to eliminate any sense of superiority which may lurk in the heart.

It is also imperative on the sufi to acknowledge Allah's absolute sway over his life and accept with grateful and open heart what Allah has decreed for him. 'If you obey His orders and accept His decrees on you then you have confirmed that you are His servant and He is your Lord.' This attitude helps to ensure that a Muslim relates to people in accordance with Allah's laws and not in order to please them, since he knows that all good and all evil flow from the will of Allah alone. At the same time, it helps the Muslim to develop a tolerant character. His realization of the essential limitations of human power may inspire him to forgive those who have wronged him. A Muslim lives in the belief that his own life is entirely in the hands of Allah and can never, therefore, be a plaything in the hands of others, no matter how powerful they may appear to be. This is the recipe for self-confidence in life. The whole of mankind, we are reminded in a hadith, can neither profit nor harm a single person except as Allah has willed.

This absolute trust in the rightness of Allah's decrees is rooted in the understanding that the vicissitudes of life are the outcome of Allah's mercy for, as Shehu Abdullahi emphasized, 'Allah is indeed more merciful to you than you can ever be to yourself.' He is 'more merciful to the believer than a woman is to her child', and is 'the best of judges'. Therefore what one really does in accepting changes in fortunes in good faith, is to submit to a superior judgement. Allah obliterates a person's sins for every affliction that befalls him. This is why patience is a decisive factor in the success of life.

Now what are the values which the Sufi strives to realize in life? The first and indeed the most important is faith, which serves as a bond uniting all believers into a single loving brotherhood. The sufi from this perspective is a man of community – free from hypocrisy and doing things in absolute sincerity and good faith, he is loyal to a legitimate authority and abides with the Muslim community. Discipline, in its most comprehensive sense, is another value which a sufi must endeavour to attain. It begins with *al-haya*, the sense of modesty, which in itself is an integral part of faith; then discharging all obligations; then humility which implies the honouring of elders and being merciful to the young. 'Only a hypocrite belittles these three: a person who grows old in Islam; a learned man; and a just imam,' says the hadith. Humility, however, does not imply that one should kowtow to an oppressor. Restraining anger, and being of good character are also aspects of discipline. No one truly believes in Allah unless he perfects his character. Discipline also entails displaying the quality of mercy. Avoidance of lying, obscene speech, backbiting, exaggeration also pertain to discipline.

A true sufi does not keep away unnecessarily from people or remain aloof from problems in society. He is rather the one who struggles actively to establish a proper political and social order in society. He undertakes the *hijra*; he is a *mujahid* who struggles to make Islam supreme; he stands firmly for justice; he sees to the implementation of Allah's laws, and the equalization of people before the law. The sufi joins with other Muslims in co-operation to promote piety and suppress evil, and to call to the way of Allah. When in authority, he discharges his obligations to his people faithfully, avoiding treachery. In other words, he is a man of faith and a sincere scholar. The sufi is especially particular about his integrity and social standing in society. He avoids all pastimes except those which conform with the *shari'a*, such as military exercises, swimming and sporting with one's spouse. 'Military training,' the Prophet 🕌 said, 'is the best of your sports in this world.'

*Ta'affuf*, or the safeguarding of chastity, which is one of the reasons for taking a spouse, is a vital part of enhancing one's standing in society. We are reminded by Shehu Abdullahi of this hadith: 'Four things pertain to the Sunna of the Messengers of Allah: modesty, perfuming oneself, toothbrushing and marriage.' Finally, earning one's livelihood is one of the most decisive ways of safeguarding one's integrity. To remain idle on the pretext of trusting in Allah is, to Shehu Abdullahi, nonsensical. 'One who puts his seed in the soil and then puts his trust in Allah, is the true truster in Allah', he said, quoting Umar.

This, in sum, was Shehu Abdullahi's farewell message to the world and his final act of gratitude to Providence. The year 1244/1828 saw Shehu Abdullahi totally occupied in writing. He wrote, in addition to *Shukr al-Ihsan*, at least four other works: *Tazim Allah li Nabiyyina, Akhlaq al-Mustafa* and *Tahdhib al-Insan*. The first work deals with the character, virtues and way of life of the Prophet 🕌 and the second portrays the Prophet 🕌 as a model of excellent conduct. Ahmad Kani has observed that he 'is remembered in an ecstatic manner – that he was the most learned, the most pious, the most ascetic, the most virtuous and the most generous, whose characteristic was not to keep a dinar or a dirham for the following day. Abdullahi's main object was to educate his students on the Prophet's humility, abstinence, clemency, generosity, modesty, self-denial, justice and other commendable qualities'. The third deals with the means of nurturing a person to moral perfection. After that, he wrote a treatise containing the prayers to be recited at different times during the day and night. And in the month of Muharram 1245/July 1829, Shehu Abdullahi, the sword of God, the sheikh of sheikhs, the mine of sincerity and knowledge and the treasure of saints, the standard bearer of sufism – as he was variously called in the Caliphate – died at about the age of sixty-six.

### The Man, Abdullahi

How do we assess this remarkable person – Shehu Abdullahi? Let us first listen to what some contemporary scholars have said of him.

Sani Zahradeen has made the following remarks: 'He was strict and law-abiding, and insisted that others be the same almost to the point of fanaticism. His writings, military prowess and piety helped to spread the ideas of the revival beyond the confines of Hausaland. His students came from all over West Africa and beyond. In the Tartib al-Ashab, seven hundred and fifty of his companions were listed... It is in this role as a teacher and populariser of Islamic concepts and ideas that Abd Allah excelled.' Johnston remarks as follows:

In age, Abdullahi stood half-way between Shehu and Bello. In character and outlook, no less than in years, he also occupied a position between them. He shared with Shehu a distrust of worldly affairs and a bent towards mysticism. Equally, however, when the occasion demanded it, he could show talents as a soldier and administrator which did not fall far short of Bello's. If Shehu and Bello were the complements of one another, then Abdullahi was supplementary to both of them. Moreover, being a poet and a jurist as well as a mystic and a man of action, he was the most versatile of the three and incidentally the most complex in character. If Shehu inspired the *jihad*, and Bello became the architect of the Empire, Abdullahi's great though less spectacular contribution was to build up the body of theoretical knowledge necessary for the conduct of government based on principle and precept. Possessing, as he did, a marked strain of humility and self-abnegation, this is the tribute which he himself would probably have appreciated more than any other as his epitaph.

Abubakar Gwandu writes of his faith and religious conviction. 'His deep-rooted belief motivated him in all his actions. Throughout his life he was consciously trying to follow the example of the Prophet 🌼, at a time when many of his contemporaries were craving after pleasure. The strength which he derived from his faith made it possible for him to strive for his ideals – ideals in ethics and morality which he saw as part of his faith... Abdullahi was extremely kind and considerate, especially to the common people.'

In assessing the place of Shehu Abdullahi in the history of the Sokoto Caliphate in particular and of Islam in West Africa in general, three basic considerations must command our attention. Firstly, and by far the most important – for it is precisely what marks Shehu Abdullahi out distinctly from the others – is his absolute and uncompromising commitment to justice. In his unrelenting struggle he left no stone unturned. He constantly nudged his fellow rulers – not sparing even the Shehu – to stand up firmly for justice. He opposed without hesitation any tendency which he felt represented a compromise of justice or a step towards tyranny. Hence his vehement condemnation of monarchy, or of a sumptuous lifestyle by those in authority, usurpation and misuse of power or state resources. He was the most vocal advocate of the *shari'a*, which he saw as the sole and ultimate guarantor of justice and good government, and he displayed his commitment to it by making a most painstaking contribution to its understanding and its application. He never failed to warn against luxury, misrule and the creation of a gap between the poor and rich; for if the hole in the cloth might prove 'too wide for the stitcher' the social fabric of society might eventually disintegrate.

Shehu Abdullahi was never one to show respect for oppressors for whom he reserved the most vehement condemnation. What is the difference except in appearance, he asked in *Tariq al-Salihin*, between wild dogs, which terrify innocent people and tear off their clothes, and law enforcement agencies, which terrorize Muslims and cause injury to their religion, bodies and property? Abdullahi also ruled that Muslims should not give their daughters in marriage to those who perpetrate oppression and that business transaction with rich people who refuse to give *zakat* is unlawful.[i]

Secondly, we must bear in mind his immense and unmatched contribution to knowledge and the dissemination of Islam in the Caliphate and beyond. His books, as has been already observed, form the theoretical basis for the running of the Caliphate. These books include *Diya al-Hukam* (on law and constitution), *Diya al-Siyasar* (on judicial decisions and related matters), *Diya al-Wilayat* (on constitutional matters), *Diya Ahl al-Ihtisab* (on maintenance of law and social morality) and *Ta'lim al-Radi* (on land policy). Shehu Abdullahi wrote many text books for his students – or rather his

i    See Shehu Umar Abdullahi: *The Life and Ideals of Shehu Abdullahi.*

companions – who, as we have been told, were drawn from all over West Africa. These include: his magnum opus, *Diya al-Tawil*, an exegesis of the Qur'an, the only *tafsir* as far as we know to have been published so far in the Caliphate, which was abridged by the author under the title *Kifayat Duafai al-Sudani*; in jurisprudence, *Alfiyyat al-Usul*; in Islamic family law, *Kifayat al-Tullab fil Nikah* – probably the most detailed work of its kind to be written in the Caliphate; on Arabic language the monumental *al-Bahr al-Muhit*; and on commercial law, *Kifayat al-Awwam fil Buyu*. These constitute only a fraction of what Shehu Abdullahi wrote for the guidance of his students in numerous fields.

Perhaps Shehu Abdullahi's greatest achievement in the field of scholarship lies in his immense contribution to the study of the Qur'an and the *shari'a*. Dr. Abubakar Gwandu has suggested that his works on *shari'a* may well warrant his being counted as a *mujtahid*. Nevertheless, he did not hesitate to draw freely from other Sunni schools whenever he thought that necessary... For Abdullahi the preservation of the *shari'a* both in letter and in spirit whenever possible, and in spirit rather than in letter when occasion demands, is the most essential duty of a Muslim scholar.'

Thirdly, we must not lose sight of Shehu Abdullahi's unbounded love for the Prophet 🕋, whose footsteps he sought to follow even against overwhelming odds; whose qualities he had put forward as a guidance for 'those possessing insight'; and whose Sunna he had endeavoured to project as *uswatun hasana* for mankind. Ultimately, Shehu Abdullahi's sole desire was to be joined with the supreme object of his love — the Messenger of Allah, Muhammad:

I have turned towards you, a captive of my sins, shambling in shackles,
In order to overtake a heart which is with you, never to depart.
Untie my shackles; then bring me to you.
O you of noble characteristics, you are the sea of gifts.
Here am I, Abdullahi by name... [i]

---

i   These and the rest of the verses are taken from *Tazyin al-Waraqat*, Hiskett's translation.

# Chapter Eight

# The Policies

## On Principles of Statecraft

We now return to the realm of statecraft to examine some of the important policies of Muhammad Bello and the ideas which inspired and shaped them. Perhaps it is more appropriate to start this examination with a consideration of the Caliph's ideas of statecraft, as contained in what appears to be his earliest work on politics, the well-known *Usul al-Siyasa*[i] written long before his assumption of office, probably, as Shehu Yamusa suggests, in 1807-8. *Usul al-Siyasa* was meant as advice to the Emir of Katsina, Umaru Dallaji, a man described as a sincere and zealous fighter in the cause of Allah, on 'the principles of *siyasa* and the mode of conduct for a sincere man in matters connected with leadership'.

In the introduction, Muhammad Bello described power and the grave responsibility it entails as a 'most serious affliction', since the holder is obliged to account to Allah not only for his own personal deeds, which is in itself a heavy burden, but also for his management of human society. Yet, at the same time, power is 'an unending happiness, the like of which never exists' for one who knows how to discharge its obligations: 'there can be no blessing more precious to one of Allah's servants than the rank of a ruler'. It is only when rulers lose sight of the importance of this office that they 'busy themselves with oppression', thereby risking a war with Allah.

'Know that the principles of politics are seven, and their essence is derived from the meaning of justice: and politics means justice, and nothing more,' declared Muhammad Bello and then explained the essence of these seven principles of statecraft one by one. First

i   See generally Shehu Yamusa and Martin's translations, both have been used interchangeably in this chapter.

of all, government's foremost obligation is to God, whose religion it must preserve, whose law it must uphold, whose set limits it must not transgress. Rulers must be 'free from worldly desires', and not be infatuated with the desire to be in power. Upright government maintains security, acquires funds to promote human welfare and to prosecute the *jihad*. In other words, Islamic government is established 'so that the interest of religion may be guaranteed, and the entire harmony of the world likewise'. In this scheme, however, people must not be allowed to jostle and hustle for public office as if it were a booty, thereby increasing the risk of placing government into the wrong hands.

Government must necessarily be flexible, 'given to kindness, more inclined to forgiveness than to anger'. It must give liberally to those in need and treat the people with tolerance. Similarly, government must possess courage and deal with problems resolutely. Above all, it must have the 'steady support of its employees and the people'. If it lacks generosity and fails to spend money on 'fulfilling the legitimate needs of the people', people might be inclined to do without the government. Government must be conducted with intelligence and initiative, thus requiring the minds of scholars who will have the courage to give sound advice and criticize when necessary. The relationship between government and scholars is organic, one feeding the other. Scholars ensure a clean, efficient and responsive government, which becomes unassailable. Government has a responsibility to select the best hands as ministers, judges and above all as civil servants, who should be kept under vigilant scrutiny. It is in the very nature of bureaucracy to feed itself fat – 'its fatness becomes the cause for its destruction' – and to use the ruler as 'a fisherman uses his net' for their own benefit, not his. Wherever there is money, there you find the bureaucrats, Bello maintained.

It is the function of the government to orient the general public towards justice, to raise the moral tone of society as a whole. If people treat one another unjustly, then inevitably, they will have to endure an unjust government, since it is the practice of Allah to impose oppressors on oppressors, as a punishment for their conduct. And more important, government must provide public amenities, develop the economy, keep the rural population 'in prosperity', undertake urbanization projects, maintain markets and roads. Finally, it is part of good government to be lenient in respect of restrictive laws. Although criminals need to be punished, yet in principle, when dealing with ordinary people, government should 'not hurry to disavow them, or hurt their beliefs or thwart their activities or their worship'. In political matters it is necessary for the government to be liberal, tolerating, as the Prophet ﷺ did, 'the roughness of the nomads or rural people and the insults of the hypocrites', and treating leaders of the people and their noble ones with respect.

All this is, however, just one aspect of the policies advocated, and pursued, by the Caliph. The other concerns the defence of the state, which together with the enhancement of human well-being, dominated the Caliph's thoughts in his advice to Emir Yakubu of Bauchi in *Al-Ghayth al-Shubub. Jihad*, as conceived here, serves at least two important purposes: the defence of *dar al-Islam*, and the provision of an environment conducive to the flourishing and spreading of Islamic civilization. Umar's policy of establishing *ribats* on the frontiers of Byzantium, Persia and India as bastions against those powers which were preparing to overrun them, served as the model. Murray Last was right to say of Bello: Now he followed the example of the Caliph Umar when the armies of Islam had been turned to the conquest of Iraq, Syria and Egypt. Both Umar and Bello faced the problem of maintaining, in an occupied country, an army composed of largely nomadic tribes. Taking the camp towns of Kufa and Basra in Iraq and Fustat in Egypt as his models, Bello founded his *ribats* in the newly conquered areas. In these *ribats* Bello hoped to have a warrior/scholar aristocracy, dedicated to learning as well as to defence.[i] He, like Umar and the other rightly-guided caliphs, wanted to make Islam supreme in the land, and to reduce to the minimum all threats to its existence.

### Socio-Economic Development

Coming now to the actual practice, we shall first deal with the policy of economic development, the main aim of which was to safeguard

i    Murray Last, 'An aspect of the Caliph Muhammad Bello's social policy', *Kano Studies*, Vol. One, 1965-7, pp. 56-59.

human welfare. Certain historical developments, suggests Prof. Mahdi Adamu, contributed to the Caliphate's efforts. The most important was the existence of well-developed trade routes, linking much of the area covered by the Caliphate with the outside world. The extensive trading activities, involving export of foods and import of luxury items, were dominated generally by the Hausa merchant community, who had built for themselves, over the centuries, formidable experience and skills in commercial enterprises. The *jihad* had disrupted most of the trade routes, but at the same time it almost simultaneously created new centres, giving rise to new trade routes in line with the extensive political, demographic and social changes brought about by the establishment of the Caliphate. The Hausa merchant community threw the weight of their powerful economic empire in support of the new Islamic dispensation, providing the *mujahidun* with funds, essential commodities and intelligence services, as well as helping generally to create wealth and prosperity for the Caliphate and ensuring the flow of essential goods to the communities.

The sheer scale of the revolution itself made it possible for the Caliphate to appropriate a greater share of the volume of trade in the region. This new development was typified by Kano which, according to Mahdi Adamu, in the course of the nineteenth century became 'the emporium of the Central Sudan', increasing its share of Hausa commerce with the Benue Valley, taking over from Katsina the 'Hausa exploitation of trans-Saharan commerce', as well as appropriating what was formally Birni Gazangamu's sphere of commercial influence. And to some extent, Sokoto, the Caliphate's capital, grew rapidly from its inception into a great commercial and industrial centre, and new trade routes developed to link this new 'imperial capital' with the outside world.

The Islamic government established a policy of encouraging trade, by supporting craftsmen, manufacturers and merchants. Dr. Garba Na-Dama has made the point that 'the elimination of petty kingdoms and the establishment of the Caliphate administration provided a better atmosphere for the expansion and development of both internal and external trade'. He further points out that roads in the metropolis were patrolled to ensure safety and that the state undertook the responsibility of providing armed escorts for merchants all along their trade routes. Prof. Mahdi sums up the results of these developments:

The geographical area of operation of the Muslim traders, most of whom were Hausa, had expanded greatly, because the traders followed the warriors into new areas opened up. This created demand for consumer goods in places where tastes for them did not exist before and it facilitated the export of the natural produce of the new areas on a scale much larger than before. It was indeed in this regard – that is the boosting up of the Hausa import and export trade – that the Sokoto *jihad* had become a major factor in the economic expansion [indeed, a boom] which the Hausaland had enjoyed in the course of the nineteenth century.[i]

Agriculture was of course inexorably linked with commerce and industry. Saleh Abubakar[ii] has rightly observed 'that government programmes [such as the establishment of agricultural settlements, the encouragement given to nomads to settle, etc.], immigration and the response to the prospects of the local grain trade were important factors in the expansion of the frontier of agricultural production.' In addition, the establishment of agricultural colonies for the war captives, whose number was considerable owing to extensive *jihad* activities, boosted agricultural output and diversification of crops. Cotton cultivation, a beneficiary of this diversification, provided a means of occupation for a substantial number of women.

The Caliphate soon came to dominate the region of West Africa in commerce, agriculture, and of course, in military might. Its political and economic influence was, as a result, necessarily immense, if not all-pervasive. According to Stewart,[iii] the Caliphate,

i   Mahdi Adama, 'Distribution of Trading Centres in the Central Sudan in the 18th and 19th centuries', *Studies in the History of the Sokoto Caliphate*, ed. Y.B. Usman. For NaDama's view, see 'Urbanisation in the Sokoto Caliphate: a case study of Gusau and Kaura-Namoda', in *Studies*.
ii   Saleh Abubakar, 'Aspects of an urban phenomenon: Sokoto and its hinterland to c. 1850', Usman, *Studies*.
iii   C. Stewart, "Diplomatic relations in early 19th century West Africa: Sokoto-Masina – Zaouad correspondence', Usman, *Studies*.

even in the times of Muhammad Bello, was described as extending up to the areas of Nigerbend, then to the borders of Borno, as well as to Agadez. It has even been asserted that Timbuktu was under Muhammad Bello. Stewart suggests that this rather extensive definition 'may be a more accurate delimitation of what may be called "Sokoto Common Market" than the territories under the direct political administration of the Caliphate'. Whatever the case, Sokoto remained the dominant state, having a substantial portion of the West African region under its sway, politically and economically, if not ideologically.

Is it conceivable that Caliph Muhammad Bello could have established an economic policy on such a scale without providing the ideological foundation for it? His *Tanbih as-Sahib ala Ahkam al-Makasib*[i] would suggest not. He starts with the obvious proposition that Islam unreservedly encourages economic pursuits and extols 'the excellence of lawful earning'. The Qur'anic verse: '*When the prayer is over, disperse in the land and seek Allah's bounty*' (62:10) and the hadith, 'Allah likes His slaves to be gainfully employed', are cited. Then he quoted the Companions of the Prophet ﷺ and eminent sufis in support of the following principles:

Firstly, Islam requires people to strike a balance between this world and the Next and to do justice to them both. Thus, 'the best of you are those who do not neglect this world for the sake of the Next World nor the Next World for the sake of this world'. The demands of the body and the spirit are not mutually exclusive, but complementary. To neglect one's material needs, therefore, is not part of Islam. It is self-delusion when piety is invoked as an excuse for idleness. Hence: 'In our opinion worship is not putting your feet up while someone else feeds you. Rather first get your two loaves and cut them up and then worship.' And: 'I prefer to see you earning your living than to see you sitting in the corner of the mosque.'

Secondly, to be gainfully employed is an act of worship in its own right, and all occupations are accorded equal respect: they all give assurance of a place in the Garden. The Prophet ﷺ has made it known that: 'Whoever seeks this world in a *halal* [lawful] way, restraining himself from begging from others, striving on behalf

i   Aisha and Abdalhaqq Bewley's unpublished translation is used throughout.

148

of his family, keeping himself independent of other people and treating his neighbours well, will meet Allah on the Day of Rising with his face like the moon when it is full.'

Thirdly, poverty is not a virtue, but rather an affliction with calamitous consequences. Poverty weakens a person's practice of Islam, diminishes his intellect, and what is more, obliterates his self-dignity, making him contemptible. On the other hand, clean wealth will earn him a good standing in society.

Fourthly, begging is an even greater affliction than poverty because the face of begging is one of utter humiliation: 'it is the last resort of men seeking a livelihood', and its gains are worthless. The Caliph summed up his discourse: 'The upshot of all this is that to abandon earning your livelihood through inactivity or idleness is blameworthy in the *shari'a* as can be seen from the words of the Prophet ﷺ, "Allah hates a healthy person who remains idle."' The Caliph favours an economic arrangement where the individual can develop an independent means of livelihood. Dependence on other persons or on the state is to be avoided as far as possible, because it renders people defenceless against the might of vested interests.

The Caliph stipulates that the individual has the primary responsibility to 'gain wealth and keep it pure', and to make himself independent. 'The earning whose object is the acquisition of the minimum needed for one's self, one's family and to pay one's debts is obligatory.' If he is able to do that and no more, a Muslim would have fulfilled the basic requirement of the *shari'a* and absolved himself of the blame which attaches to idleness. There is perhaps a corresponding obligation on the State to help individuals secure the work from which they can adequately meet their basic needs.

The Caliph even encouraged Muslims to earn more than enough for their basic needs so that they could 'support a poor person and maintain the ties of kinship'. Indeed this kind of pursuit competes favourably with other forms of worship, such as supererogatory prayer, and can even excel them. To earn more wealth than a person needs to support himself and his family, the poor and relatives is 'permissible' in the *shari'a*, though it is hardly commendable – it is in fact to be frowned upon. It can be used, said the Caliph, for luxuries, even for erecting buildings, decorating walls and employing servants. After all, Allah has made lawful to people the good things of life and the Prophet ﷺ described rightly-acquired wealth in the hands of a rightly-guided man as 'excellent'. This, however, is the tolerable limit as far as the *shari'a* is concerned, the borderline between lawful and unlawful earning. In fact, the Caliph himself frowned at this category of earning, fearing that it might lead to arrogance, disobedience of Allah and accumulation. Accumulation of wealth on its own is forbidden, irrespective of whether the means of obtaining it is lawful or not. Hoarding of wealth harms the individual person and society.

The Caliph defined his own priorities as follows:

> The best form of earning is *jihad*. This is because its benefit is universal since it includes taking lawful booty, repelling the evil of the unbelievers and putting out their fire on behalf of the Muslims. After this comes trading. This is because traders receive benefit through time space and earn enough by their trading to suffice their needs. Because its benefit is more general, trading is better than farming whose benefit is found only at certain times. Farming comes next. This is because its object is the sustenance of man's body. The body is sustained by food and clothing and these are obtained by farming. It is also one of the means of gaining a livelihood. Then comes nomadic herding since it is also a means of earning a livelihood.

### Human Mobilization

The Caliph, as can be clearly understood from *Tanbih as-Sahib ala Ahhkam al-Makasib*, regarded *jihad* as fundamental not only to the defence of Islam but also to the economic and social development of the Caliphate. It may perhaps be safe to assume that he viewed *jihad* as an indispensable instrument in the creation and consolidation of Islamic civilization. Indeed, *jihad* is an effective means of state-creation and general human development, as Islamic history has shown. What great civilization has not employed the mechanism of war to spread and consolidate? Civilizations decline as soon as they lose their power to maintain their ascendency or to defend themselves.

It is from this consideration that the Caliph was particularly concerned about the welfare of soldiers, in whom lies ultimately the strength of the Caliphate. Those who carry arms in defence of Islam, he wrote in *al-Ghayth al-Wabl*,[i] should be provided for by the state, either in cash or in kind. Where the state is short of money, the Imam can grant the 'soldiers of Islam' usufruct rights to state lands in lieu of salaries, provided they do not reserve those rights in perpetuity. Moreover, where a soldier 'is afflicted with palsy or disease', he shall retain the usufruct rights to the land as an incentive to the soldiers as a whole, since economic security is vital to loyal service. Similarly, when a soldier dies, said the Caliph, 'his salary should continue to be paid to his daughter and to his wives until they marry, and to his young sons until they reach puberty and become independent in earning a living... and to his children who are invalid and permanently blind. All of this is to excite interest in *jihad* and devotion to it.' It may be said in passing that this pension scheme covered other public servants as well. The Caliph does not seem to have committed the state to a particular salary scheme, noting that the rightly-guided caliphs did not follow one single policy. Abu Bakr and Ali used to treat all defenders of Islam equally in the matter of salary, he said, adding:

> But the purpose of treating them equally was not with regards to the amount of the salary but rather that every person should be given according to his need and the need of his family and what suffices them in all fairness... And the salary should not exceed what is sufficient even if there is more money. And no one should be favoured above another because of nobility or genealogy or precedent in being a free man but the noble and the hero and others should be treated equally as regards salary according to what suffices for they are only given salary because of what they themselves prepared for *jihad* and its motives and all of them are equal in that.

In assessing what is adequate and fair remuneration for defenders of Islam and public servants in general, the cost of living, basic

i   Omar Bello's translation.

human needs as well as the responsibilities of each person, such as the number of his dependents, must all be taken into account.

The Caliph, in spite of his concern for the soldiers, did not maintain a standing army. It was, therefore, in his *ribat* policy that one can see how *jihad* came to be a vehicle for the transformation of society. This was a policy of establishing military settlements or *ribats* to serve both as bastions against enemy powers as well as administrative and commercial centres. Sokoto, the caliphal capital, as well as some of the emirate capitals – some of them state capitals in modern Nigeria – like Kaura-Namoda, Gusau, Yola and Wurno to name but a few, are examples. The *ribat* scheme is perhaps the most ambitious urbanization programme *Bilad al-Sudan* has ever known.

The various instructions given by the Caliph to the administrators of these settlements, suggest that he very much wanted them to serve as model communities for the Islamic dispensation. According to Murray Last in *The Sokoto Caliphate*, the Caliph instructed one of them as follows: 'to close the frontiers and protect the roads; to send out raids and night sorties and maintain spies; to establish justice and execute the law; to avoid insulting, striking, imprisoning or, above all, killing anyone without due process of law; to guard against bribes, illegal taxes and lavish spending; instead, he was to welcome righteous men and listen to their advice, to receive travellers and help the poor'. To yet another administrator, the Caliph gave the instructions that the *ribat* should be kept in strict vigilance and readiness for war; that the agreements with protected people [*dhimmis*] must be kept; that the *ribat* must be kept in prosperity; and, above all, that the ruler must beware of the trickery and strife that would surround him. In the *ribats* the policy of establishing schools, mosques, trades and workshops was maintained, and agriculture boosted, as Last has pointed out.

Dr. Mahmud Tukur sees, in his *Values and Public Affairs*, another dimension to the *ribat* system: namely, it effectively surrounded the heartland of the Caliphate with secure administrative units.

These not only supervised and protected the surrounding countryside, but also served as models for the type of selfless and committed leadership which the administrative and political system needed. Moreover, in the *ribats*, the younger children of the rulers and the *'ulama* obtained training as leaders in the administrative sphere as well as in the military. Any positive management experience in these situations added immeasurably to the institutionalization of leadership norms and to the perpetuity of the Caliphate. The opportunity for the next generation of leaders to test themselves in preparation for wider and more demanding administrative roles in the capital and elsewhere was also inherent in the system. It was a perfect device for spreading talent and employing it positively as it was being developed. Moreover it provided a technique for dispersing a potentially destabilizing cadre of individuals whose idleness and frustration could be a cause of grave disquiet.

Some of the reasons behind the *ribat* policy can be gleaned from the Caliph's *Kitab al-Ribat wal Hirasa*.[i] Of paramount importance was the fact that the Prophet ﷺ extolled the virtues of eternal vigilance and permanent readiness for war, which constitute the essence of *ribat*: an eye which keeps vigil in the cause of Allah will never be touched by hellfire. In addition it confers moral and spiritual benefits on Muslims, for Allah has promised them that whatever paths they tread *'to raise the ire of the unbelievers'* and whatever injury they receive from the enemy in the cause of Allah will be reckoned to their credit. Indeed, the Prophet ﷺ counted participating in *ribat* as 'better than the world and all that it contains', the reward of which continues to multiply till the day of judgement. Above all, death in *ribat* is martyrdom, which is the ultimate ambition of a true Muslim. There is also the equally valuable social and economic benefit *ribat* provides. *Ribat*, the Caliph reasoned, is essentially defensive: and to preserve Muslim blood is much better than to shed the blood of idol worshippers. Moreover virtuous deeds cannot be performed except in an atmosphere of peace and security which the *ribat* strategy provides.

The Caliph's final and most penetrating reason for his policy rests on the Prophet's statement: 'a time will come upon people

i    MS in author's possession.

when the best of their struggle will be the *ribat*.' It is the time when Muslims have ceased to be the models of perfect morality they are expected to be, and have become mere straws which bend with fate; when *jihad* has become merely a means of territorial or personal aggrandizement and what is held as sacred in *shari'a* – such as human life, property or women's honour – is outraged; when Muslims no longer honour their agreements with non-Muslims and do not uphold the Qur'an and Sunna. *Jihad* in those circumstances becomes no longer a wise or valid policy, *ribat* then becomes the most appropriate strategy.

The Caliph's instruction to the effect that all *ribats* must be supplied with enough teachers, imams, *muhtasibs* to ensure that Islamic standards of social justice and morality be upheld, points to his desire to see that the people were sufficiently infused with the supreme values of Islam before they were called upon to fight in its cause. And when Muslims had been recharged with moral energy, made to understand the goals of *jihad* and imbued with the right Islamic spirit and orientation, then they could again venture outside their territories, to liberate people and give them justice. The Caliph's thinking, however, was that Muslims have at all times to make a choice between *jihad* or *ribat*; those who claim that there could be a time when neither *jihad* nor *ribat* is valid are the 'fuel for the Fire'. The state of morality in the *umma* should decide which of the two options be adopted.

The net result of the *ribat* policy was that, firstly, it gave peace and security to a substantial part of the Caliphate, allowing trade, agriculture and learning to flourish. And secondly, it gave a quite remarkable and unprecedented impetus to urbanization and general human development. Indeed, as pointed out by Saleh Abubakar, the policy sparked off a process of urban development, at once revolutionary and far-reaching in scope, whose pace continued throughout the century.

Muhammad Bello's definitive views on urbanization are contained in his *Jawabun Shafin*,[i] a treatise written specifically on the Touareg revolutionary, Muhammad al-Jaylani, on how to found and maintain a nation. 'The concern of the *shari'a* to promote

i   MS in author's possession.

community life is well known. Due to this the jurists have ruled that it is lawful to transfer a foundling from the desert to the village and from the latter to the town but not the opposite. There is no doubt man is urban by nature. Human perfection is not reached save through urbanization and civilization.'[i] Bello said further that it was on the basis of this *shari'a* principle that, when Allah gave him victory and removed the people of infidelity and corruption, he embarked on building cities, establishing the Islamic institutions and founding centres and capitals. But the human perfection, which urbanization is intended to achieve, cannot be reached merely by building cities and commercial centres. Urbanization must go hand-in-hand with the development of knowledge and the building of human society strictly upon justice.

To emphasize especially the later imperative for a successful urbanization policy, Muhammad Bello insisted that taxation – one of the easiest excuses for oppression and economic deprivation – must fulfil certain criteria first. There must be a genuine need for taxes. If the state is sufficiently affluent, then unless it is bent on injustice, it should not impose taxes on the people. Proceeds from taxes must be spent in a just manner 'in the sense that no one is favoured above another, they are not wasted, nor given to one who does not deserve to be given them or more than he really requires.' Taxes must be imposed only on those who have the means to pay: 'whoever has little or nothing, there shall be no tax on him'. In addition, taxation must be subject to continuous review. When the economy improves, taxation must cease. In short, the Caliph's conception is that development of the kind that can lead to human perfection is not possible unless it is nourished by two things: education and justice.

### Foreign Policy

The philosophy of the Sokoto Caliphate's foreign policy is that the world is divided into two: *dar al-Islam* where faith in Allah and justice remains supreme, and *dar al-Kufr* which is characterized by wrong faith and injustice. Ideally all the people and states in *dar*

i   Norris, *The Tuaregs: Their Islamic Legacy and is Diffusion in the Sahel*, Aris and Phillips, 1975.

*al-Islam* should live in harmony since they constitute one universal community. As for *dar al-Kufr*, the Islamic state should do its best to invite it to Islam or to enter into a treaty of peace and non-aggression; but if these are refused the Islamic state is permitted to adopt a belligerent attitude towards it. If *dar-al-Kufr* accepts Islam, it becomes an equal and sister state. Where it accepts a treaty of peace, the Islamic state is obliged to abide strictly by the terms of the treaty. In *Ahkam al-Aman*,[i] Muhammad Bello reminded his governors and ministers that all agreements with non-Muslim entities must be faithfully observed and that violation of treaties is 'one of the greatest sins', whose consequences are likely to lead to the collapse of a state. He added that, according to the Prophet 鈴, there are three things in which the *shari'a* does not make concessions to Muslims: obedience to parents, observance of treaties and agreements, and discharging of trusts. In all three cases, it is immaterial whether the other party is Muslim or non-Muslim.

Muhammad Bello's foreign policy was, however, more complex than the letter of the law envisaged.[ii] The Caliphate found itself in many instances surrounded by enemies. Borno, its most powerful Muslim neighbour to the east, was not only hostile but aggressive. In the west was the pagan empire of Oyo, whose sole preoccupation was to pull down the Caliphate. Even the Caliphate of Masina maintained an ambivalent relationship. Muhammad Bello, in these circumstances, had to chart a somewhat ingenious foreign policy capable of weathering the storm of the volatile regional policies. It is worth noting that so far as non-Muslim states were concerned, Muhammad Bello maintained two approaches. He tried to integrate the smaller ones, by negotiation or sword, into the Caliphate. For the

---

i   The full title is *Tanbih al-Ikhwan ala Ahkam al-Aman*. MS in author's possession.
ii  This section is based largely on the following sources: Yaro Gella, *The Foreign Policy of the Caliphate of Muhammad Bello (1817-1847) Towards the States of Bormo, Adar, Ahir and the West*, Ph.D., Ahmadu Bello University, 1986. John Lavers, 'The Diplomatic Relations of the Sokoto Caliphate: Some Thoughts and a Plea'; Diibo Hamani, 'Adar, the Tuareg and Sokoto: Relations of Sokoto with the Hausa and Tuareg during the Nineteenth Century'; and C. C. Stewart, 'Diplomatic Relations in Early Nineteenth Century West Africa', in *Studies in the History of the Sokoto Caliphate*.

larger ones he attempted internal destabilization as he did with the Oyo kingdom.

The contention between the Sokoto Caliphate and Borno may well be that the revolutionary process in Borno in the wake of the collapse of Saifawa dynasty did not quite meet Muhammad Bello's high standards. He probably felt that Borno had failed Islam by going only half way. Borno ought to have employed what he termed 'the Qur'an and the Sword' to its logical conclusion. The failure of the Sokoto revolutionaries to integrate this vast imperial Islamic power into the Caliphate may have conditioned Bello's attitude towards the one man who had frustrated the Sokoto's aspirations, Muhammad al-Kanemi, who had also sought to destroy the Sokoto Caliphate. So Bello was faced with the frustrating challenge of dealing with a Muslim state bent on destroying his own power.

Bello employed diplomatic and military weapons against al-Kanemi. His military might thwarted all of al-Kanemi's attempts to crush the Caliphate by force. On the diplomatic front, Bello opened new fronts, establishing links with Borno's powerful friends – Morocco and Tripoli. Morocco, in a major shift in its relations with *Bilad al-Sudan*, endorsed the Sokoto revolution unreservedly and threw its weight behind it. Tripoli responded to Muhammad Bello's moves with an overflowing praise for the Caliph and promised 'complete friendship' and the pursuit of common interests. In short, Bello had snatched away from Borno the love of her neighbours.

Borno's other neighbours to the south, Bagirmi and Waday, were hostile to her and more or less friendly with Sokoto. Bello also created two new emirates in addition to Fombina on its eastern frontiers to serve as a revolutionary counterforce against Borno. It was clear that what Muhammad Bello had done was to isolate Borno diplomatically, subjecting her, as Yaro Gella says, 'to an international diplomatic quarantine'. Al-Kanemi, clearly alarmed, sued for peace. 'We profess the same religion', he wrote to Bello, 'and it is not fitting that our subjects should make war on each other.' He suggested a demarcation of the boundaries between the two powers. Bello generally ignored al-Kanemi's pleas: if there must be peace, he may have thought, it must be on his own terms, not on al-Kanemi's.

With the Caliphate of Masina, the situation was completely different. The Masina Caliphate came into existence as a result of a revolution, not only similar to that of Shehu Usman Dan Fodio, but inspired by him. Ahmad Labbo was a disciple of the Shehu's and was invested with an authority by his master to undertake the *jihad*. After the death of Shehu Usman, Ahmad Labbo withdrew his allegiance to the Sokoto Caliphate and assumed total control of Masina as a caliph in his own right. In a reply to Bello, who had asked Labbo to return to the fold, Labbo confronted Sokoto with its own argument. Shehu Abdullahi had, in his *Diya al-Hukkam*, justified the existence of two imams in a territory, which is so large as to render it ungovernable in some parts.

Labbo, after referring to the authoritative remarks of Abdullahi, said to Bello: 'Then look upon this with a just eye. Did your jurisdiction reach us since the death of our Shaikh, the late Uthman, up to the present time? If you agree that your jurisdiction reached us then you might as well say that places like Khurasan and Andalusia have been attached to you'. Labbo asked Bello to view his withdrawal of allegiance as a 'favour of Allah', claiming that his action was not done 'out of boasting or pride and ungratefulness of self-interest (on my part), but out of affection for you .. . and the conviction that you are the leader by entitlement and I am a follower.' Bello accepted Labbo's arguments as valid but misapplied but he was constrained from taking drastic action against Masina because of Labbo's impressive credentials as a *mujahid* par excellence and a state-builder. All he did was to attempt cultivating revolutionary groups around Masina, probably to keep Labbo busy.

It was, however, in the long-drawn political drama centred around Muhammad Jilani, the Tuareg revolutionary, that the main thrust of Bello's foreign policy came out clearly. In 1813 or thereabouts, Jilani raised the standard of *jihad*, with the aim of establishing an Islamic state. Within three or four years Jilani had established his supremacy over the Tuareg state of Adar and had his eye on the neighbouring state of Ahir. He then embarked on an ambitious programme of solid reform and human development. He declared the equality of all people and abolished all distinctions based on ascriptive rights. All men, he said, are slaves of God. Jilani relied in most part on the advice of Muhammad Bello who, in a series of letters and treatises, sought to provide the emerging revolutionary with a blueprint for creating a new social order based on equality of opportunity, justice and genuine human mobilization. Unfortunately, Jilani underrated the force marshalled against him, that of the Tuareg nobility who had most to lose. There is no doubt that he had a large section of the community deeply loyal to him. According to Djibo Hamani, his 'relentless struggle against the Tuareg nobility, against racial prejudice and inequalities of class,' helped to entrench that loyalty. 'Above all, however, Jilani was in too much of a hurry to transform his society. The forces of vested interests regrouped to effect his overthrow. After an heroic struggle, Jilani proceeded on *hijra* to Sokoto Caliphate, where Bello welcomed him as a defeated hero. But Sokoto could not forgive Ibra, the leader of the counter-revolutionary forces, for overthrowing a legitimate Islamic government. As far as Bello was concerned, the struggle was not over: the counter-revolutionaries must be destroyed at all cost. The opportunity came in 1837.

The Jilani episode shows that, in the thinking of Bello, Islam is the religion of Allah and has an inherent right to establish itself anywhere on earth. The Islamic revolution, of which he was the undisputed leader, must permeate everywhere, whether in Hausaland, in Borno, Yorubaland, Niger Bend or among the Tuaregs: it shall defer to no boundaries, and accept no barriers. After the defeat of Jilani Muhammad Bello launched a diplomatic offensive to win the Tuaregs to the side of Islam by cultivating new leaders and employing to the maximum advantage his own moral authority as the Imam. Where military option failed, sufism came to his aid. 'By the end of the reign of Muhammad Bello,' wrote Yaro Gella, 'the Sokoto Caliphate had become an important factor in the lives of the Tuaregs. The authority of the Caliph had become accepted by a larger section of the Tuareg leadership, to the extent that the rulers of Ahir and Adar, as well as the various clan leaders, needed their appointments to be sanctioned by Sokoto in order to be accepted by their societies as legitimate. The influential position which Bello secured for the Sokoto Caliphate enabled the Caliph to act as a judge and a mediator for the Tuaregs.'

On the whole, then, Muhammad Bello's foreign policy had the following effects: it undermined the non-Muslim states and incorporated others into the Sokoto Caliphate; it kept the hostile Muslim state of Borno at bay and isolated it diplomatically; it 'exported' the Islamic revolution in all directions and created satellite states and polities throughout west Africa; and, above all, the conditions this aggressive policy generated imposed on the Sokoto Caliphate not only the obligation to maintain political dominance over the region as a whole but also to achieve economic self-sufficiency so that the momentum of the revolution might be maintained.

Chapter Nine

# The Imam

The Sokoto Caliphate was an ideological state, whose roots dug deep into Islamic spiritual values. It was these values that served as the binding force, bringing the people together as one social community. They defined the role of each individual, his responsibilities and obligations. And in periods of crisis, it is these values that were invariably invoked, so as to awaken the conscience of the people and increase their commitment to the purposes of the state.

Caliph Muhammad Bello took personal responsibility for raising the moral tone of society by writing books and issuing various messages aimed at reiterating and strengthening the ideology of his people. He himself had grown over the years in political as well as spiritual status. As a caliph, he was easily the most powerful ruler in Bilad al-Sudan and, as an Imam, he towered above others in knowledge and in moral stature. He held the sword firmly and, at the same time, his pen was incisive. We shall attempt to have a glimpse of the Caliph's pen at work, nourishing minds, expressing concern over moral issues, appealing to Muslims to live up to expectations, emphasizing the Islamic nature of the state.

### Commitment to Allah

We shall start by examining the content of three of the messages, or *rasa'il*, Muhammad Bello sent to his people. Although they were no doubt issued at different times, they nevertheless show a remarkable consistency. Two of them have the same title, *Risalat al-Amir al-Muminin ila Jama'at al-Muslimin*, the third and longest is titled *Risalat lil Amrad Shafiyya*. One of them exhorts the people to observe fifteen matters; another, nine; while the third speaks of seven matters which, if observed, constitute the doors of goodness or *abwab al-khair*.[i]

i    The *Risala,* containing fifteen matters, has been translated into English by

In the introduction to *Risalat Shafiyya*, the Caliph urged the people to 'be conscious of Allah'. In the context of Caliph's thought, consciousness of Allah – *taqwa* – involves two things: first, guarding against the temptations of this world, and second, striving to secure the abode of the Hereafter. The latter imposes the duty on the people to 'turn towards Allah' unreservedly, which, in turn, imposes the duty on them to turn their backs on the aimless materialism of the world. Relying on the Qur'anic verse, *'So do not then the life of this world delude you, and do not let the Deluder delude you about Allah'*(31:33), the Caliph explained how unwise it would be for any Muslim to place his reliance on this world. The world, he said, is the abode of fate, trials and tribulations. What is lawfully acquired from it and herded as possessions must be accounted for in the Hereafter, and what is unlawfully acquired inevitably invites punishment – so that either way, the world does not offer anyone much comfort. In addition, such is the low esteem accorded the world by the Creator that he never cast even as much as one glance at it after he had created it. The world then, the Caliph asserted, 'is an abode of him who has no abode; only a person devoid of understanding accumulates for its sake, and only a person devoid of intelligence settles himself in it'.

Consciousness of Allah or *taqwa* is perhaps seen by Muhammad Bello as the essence of a successful Islamic life and as the chief of all values. Next to it is the practice of *tawba*, or in another context, *istighfar*. *Tawba* is an act of repentance, of turning towards Allah to solicit forgiveness and mercy. In the words of the Caliph: *'Tawba* involves a conscious act of self-reproach and a change of heart regarding what one has committed of sins. This must be followed by complete and irrevocable abandonment of the offending conducts and the adoption of a positive attitude to henceforth avoid all those activities which may lead to disobedience of Allah and the commission of sins.' As an act of supreme importance – being essentially an attitude which shapes a Muslim's way of life and not just an isolated or occasional act – *tawba* 'should take precedence over all other undertakings'. It is seen as an act of worship which

Auwahu Yadudu; the one with seven matters is MS and the third is privately published by Alhaji Abdu Magayaik, Salona.

is necessitated by man's inherent and inevitable moral weakness which occasions his tumbling into sin time and again. This weakness is only rectified by an act of return to Allah, the source of all strength.

*Istighfar* is an act of begging for forgiveness in respect of sins one has committed. It is an acknowledgement on the part of a Muslim that he has failed to live up to expectation in given circumstances and therefore entreats his Lord to forgive and overlook. It is an aspect of *tawba*, less comprehensive but equally vital in the process of self-examination and combating the evil within. Here the Caliph comforted his people with the Qur'anic verse: *'Anyone who does evil or wrongs himself and then asks Allah's forgiveness, will find Allah Ever-Forgiving, Most Merciful.'* (4:110) Further, they would never perish as a historical force, as an *umma*, as long as they sought Allah's forgiveness. *Istighfar* in this context of society and polity acts as a safety valve, as an *aman*, which saves the *umma* from being completely destroyed.

Does *tawba*, one may ask, consist only of prayers for pardon, without any social or political dimension? The Caliph, who was always more inclined to practice than theory, was quick to point out the other aspects of *tawba* in a comprehensive work entitled *Budur al-Musfira*.[i] In it he sought, through the medium of hadith, to establish the philosophy of *tawba*, emphasizing three points in particular. First, inherent human weakness makes the commission of sins inevitable. Thus, in the words of the Prophet 🌸: 'By Him in whose hand my soul is, if you had not sinned God would have removed you and brought a people who sin, then ask God's pardon and are forgiven.' Second, if sinning is so inexorably bound to human nature, it is best to convince man to do more good deeds than evil ones, or at least to follow a sin with a good action, rather than harp on the impossible – not to commit evil at all. Third, man's real assurances come from Allah's infinite readiness to forgive, a saving grace which man should seize zealously. The human heart is, as it were, ever under the influences of the opposing forces of good and evil, and even though man on his own cannot resist evil successfully, he is nevertheless aided to victory if he decides to resist.

i   MS in author's possession.

Now *Budur al-Musfira* was written towards the end of the first ten years of Muhammad Bello's rule, when the Muslims were just emerging from political upheavals and rebellions. They had gone through a period of great hardship which is reflected in the work. One can discern the Caliph's attempt, albeit subtle, to employ *tawba* to re-orientate the human personality and offer it a complete set of priorities. In line with the philosophy that good deeds obliterate evil ones, the Caliph provided a set of good deeds which can wipe clean the human state. On top of his list is devotion to knowledge, for even the sleep of a scholar is worship. Then, of course, participation in *jihad* or *ribat*. So also the diligent and conscientious practice of Islam. Cleanliness and purging oneself of all physical and bodily impurities is also a kind of *tawba*. Then one of the greatest of all forms of *tawba*, the search for bread, for there are sins which cannot be obliterated by *salat*, fasting or hajj, the Prophet 🕌 said, they can only be obliterated by a person's exertion to earn his livelihood. Finally, the Caliph assured the people that the tribulations they had gone through were in themselves a means of obtaining the pardon of their Lord, and rising higher still in the scale of things, for *musibat al-dunya*, as he called the sufferings and hardships, would ensure that a person meet his Lord 'with no sins at all in his record'.

By emphasizing the importance of *tawba* and *istighfar* as a duty on the individual, the Caliph was probably trying to drive home three basic principles. Firstly, that the individual, as a microcosm of the state, matters profoundly in influencing the destiny of the nation: it is the condition of the individual human conscience and the direction in which it is employed that ultimately determines the fate of society and state as a whole. Secondly, in the quest for an upright and law-abiding society, priority must be given to enhancing the relationship between man and his Lord. The Caliph appealed directly to people's consciences to induce them to voluntary submission to Allah and discourage them from offending against the sacred law. Conscience, when sufficiently sharpened and aroused, acts to police society and maintain proper order. Finally, morality plays a crucial role in deciding the course of history. People prosper and attain contentment only when they commit themselves unconditionally and unreservedly to Allah's laws: and these laws are built almost entirely on moral foundations. The issue here is that, since human destiny rests squarely in the hands of Allah, it is His retribution that should be feared and it is His pleasure that should be sought.

Muhammad Bello also spoke of some of the fundamental moral responsibilities which lie on the shoulders of every member of society. The most important of these is the need for a person to maintain *ikhlas*, or purity of motive, in all his undertakings, since motive 'determines the value of all conduct, and a person attains that which he desires'. Then there is the responsibility to 'stand firmly by the commandments of Allah' in all spheres of life, especially in matters relating to the institution of family. Proceeding from the principle established by the Prophet 🌸 that every member of society, from the caliph to the ordinary servant, is a leader in his own right and therefore answerable for the responsibility which he bears, Muhammad Bello stressed the need for Muslims to ensure that all the members in their families were educated, oriented towards goodness and morally disciplined. He deplored the laxity which was being shown by parents to the education of their children, lamenting that 'matters have reached a stage where there appears to be two types of religion, one for the youth and another for the grown-ups'.

The Caliph also urged Muslims to take adequate care of their wives, to clothe, maintain and provide suitable homes for them, and above all to let them receive guidance in Islam. Another responsibility was the quest for knowledge, which, as the Caliph stressed, is the best form of worship and the main pillar of Islam. Whereas knowledge elevates a person, he implied, ignorance leads to his destruction. Finally, the Caliph emphasized the need for individual Muslims to observe the *salat* with diligence and steadfastness. This entails, among other things, that the *subh* prayer is observed in its proper time; that people take the trouble to walk to the mosque; and finally, that *salat* is performed in congregation. Perhaps the Caliph was aiming at the spiritual and social integration of the nation through *salat*.

Muhammad Bello was also equally concerned to achieve the political integration of the Caliphate. Hence his passionate and persistent call on his people to obey their leaders and remain loyal to the Islamic government. He stated that Allah had commanded Muslims to be loyal to their leaders and, significantly too, that the Prophet 🌼 had in his farewell pilgrimage speech made it known that prayer, fasting, *zakat*, hajj, together with obedience to Islamic government, constitute one single, inseparable and integrated set of obligations which assures Muslims of the ultimate felicity. A hasty reading of the Caliph's speeches and writings on this subject might suggest that he was advocating blind obedience to authority, for he does appear to be urging Muslims to tolerate their rulers, pious or otherwise, and maintain calculated and deliberate patience in dealing with them. Yet this obedience has severe restrictions and pre-conditions, especially one that emphasizes that orders and policies may be obeyed only when they are 'in line with the truth'.

Obedience is thus subordinated to compliance with the sacred law, so that when government oversteps its legal limits, it is not to be obeyed. A Muslim is asked to tolerate a bad government as long as that government is basically loyal to the *shari'a*. 'If the ruler should insult you,' Muhammad Bello quoted Umar as saying, 'be patient; should he manhandle you, be patient; should he take your property, be patient. But if he should seek to lure you away from your religion then say to him: I will rather obey my Lord, and not a creature like myself.' Moreover obedience to government is conditional upon the pressing need of the *umma* to remain united. In this context Muslims may tolerate a government not so much for its performance as to maintain the cohesion of the nation in the face of enemies. In addition, a government that does not apply the *shari'a* but adopts an alien system of law, and which does not see itself as responsible for preserving the institutions and values of Islam, is not in any way entitled to obedience since it is outrightly illegitimate. A bad government which Muslims are asked to tolerate is one which, in spite of all its failures, maintains security, carries out *jihad*, upholds the *shari'a*, provides facilities and support for hajj and under which a Muslim can worship in perfect security.

The Caliph also dealt with the issue of maintaining the momentum of the Islamic revolution, and safeguarding the ascendency of the

Sokoto Caliphate. This is the province of *jihad* and *amr bil ma'ruf.*
The latter involves society's critical examination of itself in the light
of its basic ideological commitments. The Caliph urged his people
to be relentless in their opposition to those who wanted to reverse
the achievement of the revolution – 'those who say one thing and do
another thing'. He also urged the *'ulama* to stand up to their duties
and speak the truth to government. It is only through this vigorous
process of self-criticism and self-examination that the social order
can be maintained.

*Jihad* is essentially a war against the enemy without, but it also
has the effect of strengthening Islam within. In one of the *Rasa'il*,
the Caliph espoused the merits of *jihad*: it raises the individual
*mujahid* to a high rank in the sight of Allah; it is a test of one's faith; it
stands in order of merit next only to faith in Allah itself. In political,
social and spiritual terms, *jihad* is an immeasurable asset: it invites
Allah's forgiveness; assures one of the ultimate abode; and, in this
world, 'victory soon to come'. Lastly, the undertaking of *jihad* by
the Islamic state is the best guarantee of its continued ascendency
over other communities and states, and its insurance against
decline and collapse. Considered from all angles, therefore, the
Caliph maintained that *jihad* was a most sensible and rewarding
undertaking. This fact explains Muhammad Bello's concern over
what he saw a waning enthusiasm for *jihad*, a development which
spelt disaster for the state.

### Family Obligations

Next we turn our attention to Muhammad Bello's discourse on some
of the basic social issues of the day. It should be appreciated that
the turbulence that greeted his assumption of office had serious,
though not lasting, effects on society. There were rebellions where
Muslims fought Muslims; there were tensions even within the
members of the *Jama'a*; and worst of all, there were power tussles
among kith and kin. Although these are natural reflexes of any
state emerging from a revolution, the adverse consequences of such
developments can only be overlooked at the cost of the state itself.
So quite naturally the Caliph endeavoured by precept and example
to heal the wounds before they became uncontrollable. Three of his

works: *Fawa'id Mujmila, Tanbih Ahl al-Uqul* and *Jala as-Summam*[i] indicate the means he took to heal society.

In *Fawa'id*, the Caliph's purpose was clearly aimed at giving a new impetus to the family, to establishing more firmly the authority of parents over their children, and parents' obligations to children. The Caliph, in thus seeking to support and strengthen the family institution, was acknowledging its role in the shaping of society. 'The Hour will not come,' he quoted the Prophet 🖫 as saying, 'before a man disobeys his parents only to obey his associates.' A society that does not rely on definite and permanent family ties is sure to collapse under pressure. He reiterated the fact that Allah has made obedience to parents 'parallel' to obedience to Himself, even before obedience to the state. The Caliph quoted this passage from the Qur'an: *'Your Lord has decreed that you should worship none but Him, and that you should show kindness to your parents. Whether one or both of them reach old age with you. do not say "Ugh!" to them out of irritation and do not be harsh with them, but speak to them with gentleness and generosity. Respond to them, out of mercy, with due humility and say: "Lord, show mercy to them as they did in looking after me when I was small."'* (17:23-4)

He suggested that devotion to parents entails at least five responsibilities: to refrain from being contemptuous of them; to guard against offending them, by deed or word; to address them reverentially; to show mercy and tenderness to them, serving and caring for them; and finally, praying for them. The family institution, he reasoned, owes more to the mother than the father and it is at the same time much wider than the immediate family circle. The mother bears three fundamental responsibilities: pregnancy, delivery and upbringing. Each of these involves considerable pain and hardship. For that reason scholars are unanimous that, on the basis of the hadith of Abu Hurayra, the mother deserves seventy-five percent of one's devotion, and the father only twenty-five percent. The mother is the one that really gives a part of herself to the child, she invests her whole being, and stakes her very life, to bring forth the child. The father's role is in most cases symbolic.

i  All the three works are in manuscript, in author's possession.

The family, as conceived by the Caliph, is an extended one, embracing a wide network of relations. Individuals, as part of their devotion to parents, must necessarily discharge certain obligations to this extended family. These include: strengthening ties with the members of the larger family; guiding them to the right path; sheltering their imbeciles; honouring their scholars and the upright amongst them; sharing one's possessions with their poor; and urging the rest of the family members to do the same. A family is seen here as a self-supporting, interdependent and self-caring social unit.

**Obligation to Society**

The Caliph showed considerable concern about the kind of information that circulated within the Caliphate. Islam does not prevent people from speaking their minds, even if it involves criticism of the government; nor does it attempt to block the flow of information; nor does it impede the cultivation of ideas. What Islam permitted him, as imam, was to counsel people regarding speech and to urge them to maintain self-discipline in what they said, and to purify the atmosphere of free speech.

In *Tanbih Ahli al-Uqul*, a work directed at the general public, Muhammad Bello urged them to cultivate the habit of maintaining prolonged silence, partly because Allah has demanded it and partly because it 'is among the characteristics of the people of faith'. The *Tanbih* is developed around the theme contained in this Qur'anic verse: '*There is no good in much of their secret talk, except in the case of those who enjoin sadaqa, or what is right, or putting things right between people. If anyone does that, seeking the pleasure of Allah, We will give him an immense reward.*' (4:113) So whoever was going to speak must consider not only the implications but also its overall purpose for society, otherwise it would be best to hold his peace. Silence, it is implied in *Tanbih*, is a supreme virtue in its own right. The Prophet ﷺ advised Muslims either to speak what is right or hold their peace; he warned that the tongue is the one thing most likely to bring one to Hell and that whoever maintains silence secures his own peace. Furthermore, as the channel through which a man communicates to the outside world, the tongue is the barometer by which his character is measured. 'A servant of Allah cannot be upright until his heart is straight, and his heart cannot be straight until his tongue is so,' says the hadith. And when silence is combined with character in a person, then he will be pre-eminent among men.

The Caliph then urged people to use their freedom of speech for constructive and beneficial purposes such as urging fellow citizens to be charitable, cementing social relations and effecting reconciliation. He referred to the hadith which describes as *tijara* – trade or investment – the practice of reconciling people. It is an act which compares favourably with *jihad*, he implied. *Tanbih* does not consist only of urging and persuading; it cautions too. To those who did not share the values and goals of the Caliphate, the Caliph delivered a tough admonishment. He warned that those who tried to sow discord amongst the people, or divulge state security to the enemy, or cause injury to Muslims, or spread evil and scandal in society, would face the wrath of the Islamic state, apart from the risk of Allah's wrath which awaited them in the Hereafter. He reminded them that the option offered to the Prophet ﷺ to deal severely with hypocrites, scandal mongers, alarmists and those who overtly undermined the security of the state was also open to him and he would not hesitate to deal the severest blow to them.

In *Jala al-Summam* Bello specifically addressed the most vocal and powerful section of society. This was the elite, which in this context comprised the *'ulama*, influential elements, as well as the sons and daughters of men who had fought with the Shehu during the revolution. This generation seems to have caused considerable anxiety to Muhammad Bello who perceived in many of them a tendency to reap where they had not sown. He appealed to them to exercise restraint and a sense of responsibility in their criticisms of government as well as in their public utterances in general, to promote the general well-being of society, and above all not to rock the boat. Certain standards must be observed in counselling or *nasiha*. While giving truthful *nasiha* in a council appears to be right, in reality it can sometimes serve as a means of humiliation for those who are supposedly being counselled. Besides, the one being advised may be forced to tell lies in explicating himself. In the event, the purpose of *nasiha* – which is to bring benefit to all concerned and to establish mutual love – is defeated. If *nasiha* is given in private, it will have the effect of generating love amongst people, and bringing about good. To insist on making *nasiha* public is a sign of immodesty.

The Caliph inveighed against those who speak of others in terms which they detest, saying, 'Had he concerned himself with his own faults, he would not have had the allowance to look at the faults of others.' Islam has, additionally, strongly prohibited the intrusion into affairs which do not involve one or inquiring into the activities of others or harbouring suspicions about them. It is wrong for a person to inquire what his family has been doing in his absence. The Prophet 鸞 never surprised his family, but returned to them from journeys at stated times: 'he knew that every human being has got his own weaknesses'. Thus a wife is an individual person with a right to privacy, and to be treated with honour and integrity not as an object of suspicion. To reinforce his point the Caliph quoted the Prophet 鸞 as saying, 'Part of someone's being a good Muslim is his leaving alone that which does not concern him.'

A social disease that caught the attention of the Caliph was the desire on the part of the children of great men to inherit the honour of their parents without having to go through the hazards their parents had done. He particularly mentioned sons of rulers who imitated their fathers in living in a secluded atmosphere; sons of merchants who, while doing nothing to produce wealth themselves, would nevertheless spend it; sons of *'ulama* who, although bereft of knowledge, wanted to teach, give fatwas and be given preferential treatment. Others wished to be great saints or leaders overnight without working for it. These people were, in Caliph's opinion, oppressors. Greatness is earned, not inherited, he said. 'Rarely do children inherit the ranks [*maratib*] of their parents.'

### Women as the *Umma's* Conscience

In 1250/1834 Caliph Muhammad Bello issued a message to women under the title *An-Nasiha al-Wadia*,[i] in which he expressed anxiety over the force of materialism which appeared to be encroaching

i   MS in author's possession.

upon Muslim society, and he appealed to them to help defeat this potent force and stem the tide of social decay or *fitna*. On reflection, one concludes that the Caliph was using the forum for more comprehensive purposes: to emphasize the ideals which Muslim women should aim to achieve; to set for them the models they should endeavour to emulate; to impress upon them that there was practically no limit to the spiritual, moral, and especially intellectual, heights they could attain if they made the necessary efforts; and finally to remind them that their role in uplifting society, was crucial.

He started by expressing his concern about materialism, which is contrary to the Islamic way of life as it distracts attention from the Hereafter. He quoted the Qur'anic verse: *'Allah expands provision to anyone He wills and restricts it. They rejoice in the life of the this world. Yet the life of the this world, compared to the Next World, is only fleeting enjoyment.'* (13:26) He was disheartened that society was beginning to show tendencies of 'rejoicing' in the comforts of this life. In so far as women are seen by most men as symbolizing the ultimate in joy and comfort, women could play a key role in stemming the tide of social decay, or accelerating it. In fact, society as a whole is, in the ultimate sense, saved by the self-restraint and moral discipline which women display. To that extent, it is possible to say that society is upheld by the conscience of women. This is perhaps the way to look at the hadith which the Caliph quoted in the *Nasiha*. It expresses the Prophet's fear that Muslims might not yet succeed in confronting the corrosive effects of the temptations of comfort in the same way that they have successfully overcome the trials of hardship and deprivation, because men seek comfort through women who lack the ability to resist the moral pressures brought to bear upon them by a society which revels in ease. Comfort here denotes the immodest form of luxury in which, according to the hadith, women deck themselves in gold, wear the softest, choicest clothes, and as luxury takes its toll on society, they ruin the rich and put an unbearable burden on the poor. It is the state of affairs such as this – where the resources meant for the well-being of the state are diverted for pleasure – that the Prophet ﷺ feared most for his people, and Muhammad Bello feared most for his own people.

The Caliph reminded women of how, in the Prophet's years in Madina, when riches began to pour in and his wives requested to have more comfort for themselves, Allah rebuked them and gave them the choice to opt either for this world or the Hereafter. Their choice of the Hereafter entailed definite moral commitments on their part, as spelt out in these Qur'anic verses:

*'Do not be too soft-spoken in your speech lest someone with sickness in his heart becomes desirous. Speak correct and courteous words. Remain in your houses and do not display your beauty as it was previously displayed in the Time of Ignorance. Establish the prayer and pay zakat and obey Allah and His Messenger. Allah desires to remove all impurity from you, People of the House, and to purify you completely. And remember the Signs of Allah and the wise words which are recited in your rooms. Allah is All-Pervading, All-Aware.'* (33:32-4)

In *an-Nasiha* Muhammad Bello enumerated the qualities of some of the prominent women in Islam – more than thirty were mentioned – many of whom carved for themselves a permanent and noble place in history and many others have earned the acclaim and reverence of the Muslim *umma*. He started with the Prophet's wife, Aisha, stressing her abstemiousness. Then the Prophet's wife, Zaynab b. Jahsh whose qualities included exceptional devotion to Allah, truthfulness, goodness and fidelity to kith and kin, generosity and care for the poor. Then the Prophet's daughter, Fatima, whose personal discipline and elevated status the Caliph highlighted. After these came other women, four of whom deserve special mention.

The first is Rabia al-Adawiyya, a towering figure in the sufi world, and one who best epitomizes piety and sanctity, not only among women, but mankind as a whole. She is described in the *Nasiha* as pre-eminent among such women as devote themselves to Allah. She is depicted as a strong and independent personality, intelligent, self-confident and awe-inspiring. She was among the rare human beings who have attained 'perfect honour and complete asceticism'. She was so deeply shy of her Lord that she never raised her eyes to the skies. And in the hierarchy of saints, she stood on a par with the greatest of all saints, Abd al-Qadir al-Jaylani.

Then there was Fatima b. Abbas, a contemporary of Ibn Taymiyya. She is described as 'a sheikh, a jurisconsult, an intelligent teacher, a devotee, an ascetic, a sufi, a fighter in Allah's cause, and a savant'. She used to mount the *minbar* – the pulpit – to lecture congregations of women. She mastered jurisprudence in all its details and intricacies. Scholars of her time, including Ibn Taymiyya, could only marvel at the breadth of her knowledge, her intelligence and profound piety. Hers were seas of knowledge, which, because they were full, surged with agitation. There was also, in Sokoto Caliphate, Aisha b. Muhammad, a wife of Shehu Usman. She was an ascetic, righteous, obedient to Allah, given to much fasting, much occupied with the remembrance of Allah. She exerted herself in acquiring lawful earning and spent her resources in the cause of Allah. And finally, there was Hawa b. Adam, Muhammad Bello's mother. She was described as, among other things, righteous, obedient to Allah, a spender in the cause of Allah, one who ate only from her lawful earnings or from the sweat of her brow, a constant reader of the Qur'an, reverent and good to relatives.

Among other women, there were Umm al-Banin, who freed slaves and 'mounted on the horseback in the cause of Allah'; Ummiyya al-Mausiliyya who, according to a contemporary scholar of hers, had no equal; Umm Harun, a fighter in the cause of Allah, whose face shone like the moon; Abida b. Abu Kilab, a saint of the highest order who, according to her contemporaries, surpassed the scholars of her age, men and women, in intelligence; and Fatima al-Naysaburiyya, one of the elect, concerning whom the great saint Dhun Nun-al-Misri said, 'I have not seen one greater than her.' Yet others included Fakhriyya b. Uthman, who was 'unique in her time ... and accepted nothing but the highest ranks'; she was the 'second Rabia'; the first and last to be seen each day in al-Aqsa mosque, in Jerusalem; and Muadha b. Abdullahi, who ate only what was lawful, weaned her offspring with lawful milk and was overjoyed when her son was martyred in the cause of Allah. Caliph Muhammad Bello added to this by saying that there were in the company of Shehu Usman 'countless women' who were righteous, obedient to Allah, and given to the reading of the Qur'an – and whose deeds and qualities should be emulated.

Muhammad Bello, it can be said, wanted women in the Caliphate to emulate Fatima, the daughter of the Prophet 饗, who was unreservedly committed to *zuhd* or abstemiousness, even when her father was the Messenger of Allah and the head of state. The Caliph wanted women to be concerned with the well-being of society and the amelioration of the miseries of the underprivileged. He wanted them to be deeply devoted to Allah, to frequent the mosques, spend their nights in worship and their days in fasting, to orient their husbands to worship, and not pander to the latter's sexual appetite. He preferred women to be of strong character, exuding self-confidence and seeing themselves as individuals in their own right; women who could carve for themselves a place in society and walk towards Allah on their own. He wanted women to mount their saddles in *jihad* and also to orient their children towards the noble cause and endear them to martyrdom. He wanted the women of the Caliphate to go out in search of knowledge, not stopping until they had made themselves pre-eminent among scholars. He wanted them as sheikhs, jurists, and scholars, from whose feet men and women alike learn. He wanted them on the *minbar*, addressing gatherings of Muslims. He wanted women to seek their own livelihood, and to insist on being given only lawful and wholesome resources from their husbands. They should reject from their husbands, he implied, property looted from the public treasury, or seized from the poor, or acquired by swindling, fraud and trickery. Finally, the Caliph demanded that women be good to their relatives and ensure that social relations remain strong and harmonious.

**Unity of the Umma**

Disunity, and therefore the disintegration of the *umma* that goes along with it, can be brought about by a number of factors. The first, and perhaps the most important, is *al-munafasatun ala al-dunya*, the unrestrained drive for the enjoyment of this world. This occurred when Muslims became masters controlling vast regions of the earth. They would succumb to the temptations of the world, losing sight of their ultimate objectives, forgetting their obligation to the very cause which gave them the power and privilege which they were enjoying. The Prophet 饗, sensing the enticing power of the world, said to his Companions when reflecting on what might happen if they became masters of the world, 'Nay, you shall be filled with ambitions and mutual envy; you shall turn your back on each other and become enemies one to another, and, what is more, you shall descend on the poor and the dispossessed, and set them one against the other.' In a situation of such luxury, corruption, and rivalry, the centre of the *umma* would lose its hold, causing the whole structure to collapse.

When its goals are lost, the *umma* will revert to trivia, hence, *al-mira wal mizah* – disputes and amusement. Disputes occur among people only when their fundamental principles have been eroded, for there can be no disputes on society's dominant principles, nor on important and pressing social issues. Disputes and arguments are in themselves a mental luxury, an escape from the world of reality, a detraction from the objectives of the *umma*, and therefore, an exercise that is unworthy and dangerous to the integrity of the *umma*. On the political and social plane, the loss of goals in the *umma* creates the taste for amusement, which then becomes the character of the state. Life becomes trivial, politics becomes a game, religion becomes a pastime, a nonissue. In the event, said the Caliph, the hearts of Muslims are extinguished, Allah is forgotten, the ability to think on the weighty issues of Islam is lost, and so Muslims themselves feel low in the scheme of things, and lose their dignity and honour.

And can justice thrive on such a shaky moral foundation? No, for the decay of the political process, the evaporation of fundamental moral values, must necessarily create a brand of justice of its own – a system based on self-interest. Justice, in this context, becomes a matter of manipulation to serve questionable and dishonest ends and to protect corruption and evil. Social violence will be the inevitable result when justice is perverted. It also invites the wrath of Allah, who then withdraws His blessings from the society. Moreover, a corrupted political process also creates its own breed of leaders: a 'reverse leadership' where the worst takes the highest office, and the best the lowest. It gives rise, quite naturally, to a system of government which, because it operates on a reverse logic – putting leniency in place of firmness and firmness in place of leniency - is bound to carry a nation to extinction, as Muhammad Bello warned.

How then can the unity of the *umma* in the Caliphate be achieved? This depends on a number of factors. The foremost is the fostering of a climate of mutual love in society, a climate of social solidarity which ensures that good flows freely among the people, their economic well-being is secured, and their general condition reaches the highest that can be achieved. Next is the practice of *ihsan* in society. This entails, on the one hand, that the state should look after the economic well-being of its citizens - particularly the poor and the needy - and on the other hand, that the citizens do acts of kindness and goodness to one another. Muslims, by virtue of faith in Allah, have undertaken to provide everyone in distress a way of escape - that is, to uplift the conditions of the poor and redress any social imbalance that may exist in society. When this is done, and citizens freely do *ihsan* to one another, love flows among them, keeping misfortune at bay. They will remain a viable nation a long as *ihsan* is practised among them. A united people will never perish. Only a people in whom it is absent, who commit violence among themselves and expel some of their numbers from their homes, face the prospect of doom.

A further factor which enhances Muslim unity is *mushawara*, mutual consultation. Allah made it a binding duty on his Prophet to consult his Companions on matters of state. How much more, then, do less perfect people need it? Consultation in the case of the Prophet 🌸, was intended, among other things, to please the hearts of his Companions and, in general, to generate trust and confidence in the people. Individual people are obliged in Islam to consult the pious among them. Government, however, is in greater need of consultation, which it should seek from its people. Advice should generally be accepted, the consulted should do his homework well, and employ his reasoning faculties. Government should accept criticism in good faith, and not subject those who speak their mind to harassment.

Another factor which contributes to Muslim unity is that only those who are acknowledged to be good and competent should be given the responsibility to manage the affairs of the *umma*.

There can be no doubt that when Allah desires good for people, he entrusts their affairs to the best of them in terms of morality, merit and ability. He gives rulers capable lieutenants to help them govern, men of resolution in times of difficulty, men of insight to solve problems, energetic men for work, as well as saints to pray for the well-being of the nation. In the end you have a state which operates on a divine system, guided by men of insight, united behind common goals.

**The Epilogue to a Life**

As the Caliph continued to nurture his people, so were the enemies of Islam busy plotting against them. At the head of a confederation of forces was the Tuareg war Lord, Ibra, supported by the ruler of Katsina, Rauda, and the ruler of Gobir, Ali, and the forces from Zamfara, Nupe, and other states. The confederation overran the town of Katuru, not very far from Sokoto, the Caliph's seat of power in 1252/1836, killing all whom they could lay their hands on. Islam now faced its greatest threat since the establishment of the Sokoto Caliphate. On his part, and facing the greatest challenge of his rule, the Caliph began his campaign from the mosque. 'The news [of the sack of Katuru] reached the Commander of the Faithful, who came forth, addressed the people, urging them on the Holy War, quoting the chapter of the *Battle*, and that of *Immunity*. I read the verses and he expounded,' wrote Hajj Said. He took three months – Ramadan, Shawwal and Dhul Qa'ida – preparing and coordinating the Islamic forces from his *ribat* town of Wurno. He sent to the emirs, instructing them to prepare their own forces and join him in this ultimate struggle. By the beginning of Dhul Hijja, contingents from the emirates, many of them commanded in person by their respective emirs, had gathered in Sokoto, to be joined by the Caliph's contingent, to form what was undoubtedly the largest army the Caliphate had ever mustered.

Muhammad Bello set out from Wurno after the Friday prayer, joining the emirate forces at Lajinge, where all the Muslims swore to conquer or die. There would be no retreat, they all resolved. The Muslim army marched northwards, searching for the enemy. On the way, it was struck by a scourge which nearly destroyed it: thirst.

'[Bello] said each man should dig a hole into the hillside and water would be found,' wrote the Caliph's sister, Nana Asma.[i] 'Each man obediently followed these instructions, and each one found water. We witnessed an astounding thing when the water came.' The day of relief was also the eve of Id al-Kabir. The following day, Tuesday, the Muslim forces arrived at Gawakuke, to celebrate the Id fighting their most decisive battle ever. This is how Nana Asma described this momentous occasion:

> Very shortly afterwards Ibra arrived with his army, Tora in person with his warriors.
> Then Bello ordered the standards to be brought and unfurled. He told his men to gird themselves, for the Kafirai [unbelievers] would be ashamed.
> Then the Muslims prepared themselves and took up their weapons: the spears looked like fields of ripe corn-heads...
> With the standards flying, Bello mounted and rode at the head of his men: spears and swords flashed in the sunlight –
> Surrounding the matchless Caliph; they were numberless, like locusts.
> On his arrival, battle commenced. The bodies of the slain resembled reaped corn.

Among the enemy forces, over twenty thousand died, including the rulers of Katsina and Gobir, Ibra having managed to escape. 'Bello was usually generous in victory,' observes Johnston, 'but on this occasion he had no mercy and, while women and children were spared, about a thousand combatant prisoners were put to death. In its completeness, as well as in its sequel, Gawakuke was a Cromwellian victory.' The battle itself was Muhammad Bello's greatest, so also the victory. It was, to crown it all, his last major battle in the cause of Allah – his forty-seventh! In 1808, he had led the army that crushed Gobir forces, thus ushering in a new dispensation in *Bilad al-Sudan*, the Sokoto Caliphate. Now, after the passage of twenty-eight years, he led the army that dealt the death blow to the forces opposed to Islam, giving the Caliphate a new breath of life, and a secure future.

i   Jean Boyd's translation of Asma's poem on Muhammed Bello used bere.

Shortly after Gawakuke, the Caliph entered into a period of prolonged illness lasting eight months. As the inevitable hour drew nearer, he wrote a letter to his brothers and sisters, in which he said: 'If death occurs its effect is deep except on him whom Allah protects from its evil. Beware of disputes; all matters are in the hands of Allah. So consider what is necessary. Peace.' He also sent for his eldest son, Aliyu, and warned him not to bid for the Caliphate, but let the electoral college decide on the matter of succession. The *wazir*, Gidado Dan Laima, pressed the Caliph to nominate his successor, saying, 'In whose hands do you leave us?' The Caliph replied, 'I leave you in the hands of Allah.' On the following day, Thursday, 21 Rajab 1253/1837, the Caliph died, shortly after the asr prayer. *'Every self,'* says the noble Qur'an, *'will taste death. You will be paid your wages in full on the Day of Rising. Anyone who is distanced from the Fire and admitted to the Garden has triumphed. The life of this world is just the enjoyment of delusion.'* (3:185)

Thus died one of Islam's great men of all time. H. Johnson wrote the following about Caliph Muhammad Bello: 'He was exceptionally well-endowed with a wide variety of talents – a good brain, a strong personality and a sound and uncomplicated character... Bello, though devout, had none of Shehu's mysticism and never experienced Abdullahi's revulsion from the world and its ways. On the contrary, he obviously had a taste for power and enjoyed wielding it. Nevertheless, he never allowed it to cloud his vision or tarnish his standards. That for twenty years he was the most powerful man in the whole Sudan, and yet remained completely uncorrupted, must be counted among the greatest of all his achievements. As a man, he could sometimes be inflexible, as he was with Clapperton, and occasionally ruthless. These were but the defects of his virtues, however, for the hallmark of his character was magnanimity. In his career we encounter this magnanimity again and again – in the objectivity of his historical works, in his forbearance under Abdu Salami's provocation, in his reconciliation with Abdullahi, in his avoidance of bigotry, in the great sweep of his own achievements, and in the sense of personal humility before God which, in the moment of his greatest triumph at the taking of Alkalawa, no less than on his death-bed, though in a wholly different way, he proved himself to be one of the most remarkable men whom Africa has ever produced.'

# Chapter Ten

# A Sense of History

## Conception of History

It is time now to reflect on the fundamental issues arising from the study of the Sokoto Caliphate. And, as a mark of respect for Caliph Muhammad Bello, we will consider first his views on history – in other words, the vicissitudes of time – as expressed in *Infaq al-Maysur*[i] and *Al-Dhikra*.[ii] The former is a reference to the history of West Africa, and the most authoritative account of the *jihad* movement of Shehu Usman Dan Fodio. It also deals with the causes involved in the rise of nations. *Al-Dhikra*, on the other hand, is a work expressing anxieties about human failures, yet maintaining faith in man's inherent ability to stem the tide of decline and recreate his society anew. *Infaq* was written during the revolution and *Al-Dhikra* after it, so, when considered together, the two works present an almost total picture of Muhammad Bello's world-view and conception of history.

Nations, he implied, are built on knowledge and commitment to fundamental moral values. As such, the first cardinal rule in the transformation of society is that those who strive for a new order from the ruins of the existing one must themselves be a true embodiment of the best traditions of knowledge and piety. In addition each of these scholars must possess 'a noble and patient character' to enable him to deal with the people in an appropriate manner. When ignorant men lead an Islamic movement, nothing but disaster must be expected. 'You will meet many an ignorant man, full of evil deeds himself, who does not know half of what is commanded, much less the minimum knowledge we have prescribed. When the devil spurs him, his self-seeking will drive

---

i     Cairo edition. See also Arnett, *The Rise of the Sokoto Fulani*.
ii    MS in author's possession.

him to ambition and vainglory of rank, and the hunt for worldly possession.'

Then of course, there must be a community dedicated to change and a nobler society. The *Jama'a* remained the model of Islamic movement for Muhammad Bello. This movement, we venture to say, was a microcosm of mankind, containing all the elements of human strength as well as weakness. It embraced in its ranks people of immense knowledge as well as the ignorant, men of piety as well as the most uncouth, the rich and the poor, the strong and the weak – all manner of people, all levels of society, all stages of morality. 'The learned was increased in his learning and at the same time benefited the less learned; the strong was restrained by the greater strength of the community, which oriented his strength towards higher goals; the weak were protected and made strong through the community spirit. Similarly, men of piety received further inspiration, while the less pious were nurtured to moral maturity; the poor were supported by the rich and both strived, hand in hand and along with others, to create a just society. No one was despised, neither the poor for his poverty, the profligate for his moral failures, the rich for his riches, nor the weak for his weakness; they were all one, a single community.

In other words, a movement that does not contain in its ranks all these categories of people, but seeks only perfect people is not worthy of being called an Islamic movement. There are no perfect people but only the fundamentally weak who want to improve themselves. The function of the Islamic movement is precisely to provide the atmosphere where they can receive knowledge, social consciousness, and collective strength to create a new society for themselves, one that is dedicated to Islam. For it is only when the strong support the weak, and vice versa, that the entire community can create the necessary strength to uproot the forces dedicated to evil. In subsequent years, the formerly weak and immoral in the *Jama'a* rose to greatness and became rulers and statesmen and those who were ignorant became scholars, thanks to the broadness of vision and patience and perseverance of the leaders. These leaders reaped the fruits of an endeavour, which acknowledged human weakness and resolved to turn it into strength.

Yet there can be no real power for a people unless they commit themselves unconditionally to justice and the rule of law. This is a fact implied in *Infaq al-Maysur*. The *Jama'a*, even in the most hostile conditions of warfare, always proved its dedication to justice, and willingness to remain within the law. It also made sure that a system of legal and social justice was established in places it had liberated, and that the grievances of the oppressed were adequately relieved. The striving for a new society requires from Muslims nothing less than heroism. Consider for example the great trek, undertaken by the *mujahidun* of Sokoto during the revolution, covering hundreds of miles, where they fought not only political and military enemies but those of starvation, thirst and disease. The whole phenomenon of the *jihad* and the establishment of the Sokoto Caliphate represents one of those instances in history when the human spirit, nourished by extraordinary courage, resolution and perseverance, triumphed over the flesh. One can see clearly heroism at its best.

Finally, an Islamic political and social order can only come about when Muslims are prepared to invest all that they have – property, time, family and, above all, life – in promoting the cause of Islam. Muhammad Bello recalled how in one battle he stayed behind. The Shehu, on realising this, ordered him to set off immediately and join the rest of the Muslims. 'Thereupon,' said Muhammad Bello, 'I followed them by night and overtook them in camp at Kambaza.' The Shehu himself dedicated his life to this cause and he also surrendered his comfort and all that he held dear. Other *mujahidun* followed his example and raised their children as *mujahidun* as well and felt a sense of fulfilment when these were martyred in the cause of Islam. It was this spirit of total sacrifice for the cause that explains the phenomenon called the Sokoto Caliphate.

Yet all human achievements are bound to decline and perish, even those intended for the pursuit of the noblest of goals. So Muslim communities, like all others, are not immune from this painful inevitability. This is the subject of *Al-Dhikra*. One can sense the feeling of anguish, or perhaps helplessness, in Muhammad Bello, as he compares the fate which befell the Children of Israel to the fate which awaited his own people. No doubt his purpose was to warn the Caliphate against following the path of the Israelites. In general,

Muhammad Bello attributes decline to five factors.

The first is the craving for idols, after having rejected them – as the Israelites did shortly after they had been saved from Pharaoh, who had inflicted upon them untold hardships and suffering. Muhammad Bello referred to this Qur'anic verse: *'We conveyed the tribe of Israel across the sea and they came upon some people who were devoting themselves to some idols which they had. They said, 'Musa, give us a god just as these people have gods.'* (7:138) This is the height of ingratitude to Allah. When considered from a broader perspective however, it is possible to say that the craving for idols involves two fundamental attitudes: firstly, a desire on the part of those who have gone through a prolonged and gruesome struggle to take it easy, and enjoy the fruit of their labours; and secondly, an attraction for the ways of Pharaoh, who was not bound by moral values, and not therefore restrained in the conduct of government. He could imprison, exile or kill at will. In short, the object in such circumstances is to return to the old ways, the decadent ways, where expediency, rather than precepts or fundamental values, dictate the direction of government and the destiny of people.

Another factor is what Muhammad Bello called *tabdil*: a situation where the principles which had brought the people to eminence are abandoned one after the other. The principles, which he regarded as having universal validity, are set out in the Qur'an as follows in 6:151-153:

> *'Come and I will recite to you what your Lord has made haram for you: that you do not associate anything with Him; that you are good to your parents; that you do not kill your children because of poverty – We will provide for you and them; that you do not approach indecency – outward or inward; that you do not kill any person Allah has made inviolate – except with the legal right to do so. That is what He instructs you to do so that hopefully you will use your intellect. And that you do not go near the property of orphans before they reach maturity – except in a good way; that you give full measure and full weight with justice – We impose on no self any more than it can bear; you are equitable when you speak – even if a near relative*

*is concerned; and that you fulfil Allah's contract. That is what
He instructs you to do, that hopefully you will pay heed. This is
My Path and it is straight, so follow it.'*

People decline in direct proportion to the extent of their departure
from these universal principles. Muhammad Bello traced briefly
the rise of Islam and told how Muslims, faithful to those values,
continued to overrun civilization after civilization, including the
Roman Empire, only declining in subsequent centuries when
their fidelity to the principles began to wane. He lamented that
the same trend was beginning to appear in the Sokoto Caliphate,
as some people were reverting to the ways of unbelievers; others
were busy imposing illegal taxes on people and seizing their goods;
yet others were reverting to oppressing women and appropriating
their property. Others had 'reverted to night in vanities. They have
abandoned the study of the Qur'an, and learning and remembrance
of Allah. ... As far as commanding the good and forbidding the evil is
concerned, they would have none of it, but rather follow reprehensible
custom.' If there were no change of attitude, the Sokoto Caliphate
would repeat the tragic drama of the early Islamic era.

Another factor which can undermine the structure of a state is
what Muhammad Bello called *tanfis*, the drive for comfort and
ease, in a word, materialism. Here again, the Israelites are the
ready example. Instead of pursuing the purpose for which they
were liberated, which was the promotion of the cause of Islam,
they preferred to hanker after luxury without labouring for it.
Muhammad Bello suggested that the immediate casualties of the
drive for luxury are the *shari'a* and *amana*. When people are no
longer able to uphold the *shari'a* because of a decline in moral
standards, they will have no choice but to revert to a *jahili* system
of law where they will 'argue on behalf of the criminal and defend
him, in pursuit of nepotism.' The government whose real purpose
is 'to redress the grievance of the oppressed on behalf of Allah'
will then itself degenerate into an oppressive system. On the other
hand, *amana*, or trust, will cease to be, as Muslim rulers lose
their sense of justice and fairness, and abolish the rights of their
people, especially the non-Muslim citizens, whose property and

life they will then violate with impunity. And when minorities are oppressed, Muhammad Bello warned, the inevitable result is that the state will lose its legitimacy and political control.

Finally, the decay of morality is another factor in the decline of nation. In a world-view which sees morality as central to the shaping of human destiny, the prospect of moral degeneration within the *umma* is bound to cause great concern. Bello quoted the hadith which says that when moral decline can be measured by the prevalence of homosexuality, the end of the nation is at hand: 'Allah will withdraw His protective hands from them.' Similarly, when the *'ulama* pervert their role and associate with tyrants and compete against each other to acquire the dross of this world, they have set the stage for the overthrow of whatever order they seek to protect. In addition, when Muslims, overcome by decay, are no longer willing to undertake the *jihad* they will eventually lose their glory, power and independence. He feared that some of the symptoms of decline had already emerged, eroding the fabric of the Sokoto *umma*.

But does all this mean the beginning of the end? No, he said. For although decline is inevitable, the seeds of regeneration which exist in the *umma* almost immediately begin to grow. No amount of corruption and degeneration, Muhammad Bello maintained, can consume *all* Muslims. There must always remain a 'party of Allah' who will raise high the banner of Islam, fight in its cause, achieve victory and restore once again the glory of Islam. Fear and hope intertwine in *Al-Dhikra*: fear that the Caliphate, being essentially the product of man, would decline and collapse, and the hope that a new to restoring the glory of Islam would emerge from its ruins.

### The Vicissitudes of Time

The Caliphate left by Bello to his successors continued to display elements of strength and weakness, but it retained the essential character given to it by its founders. The greatest weakness was the retention of the institution of monarchy. This restricted the utilization of the full resources available to the Caliphate in the management of the state so severely that it was forced in several instances to endure being ruled by incompetent caliphs. In other words, monarchy did not give strength or stability to the Caliphate: it acted as a cancer, slowly eating away the vital energy and moral reserves of the state.

Similarly, on several other issues, the Caliphate performed far below expectation. Muhammad Bello's call for a comprehensive transformation of the law seems to have fallen on deaf ears. His farsighted policy of empirical approach was abandoned immediately after his death and the Caliphate relapsed once more into the past, taking shelter in the old books of law. In this respect, it lost the opportunity to bring about a legal revolution, which would have helped even more in transforming the outlook of the people and giving Islam renewed vitality. In addition, Shehu Usman's earlier call for the opening of new frontiers in knowledge and fresh ideas relevant to the issues of the day was not heeded with the courage, energy and determination it deserved. True, a new generation of scholars headed by Abd al-Qadir Mustafa, penetrated more deeply into philosophy and history than their predecessors, and medicine continued to have a pride of place in Sokoto scholarship, but the scope of intellectual and scientific endeavour was often dangerously low. Women did not respond adequately to Muhammad Bello's challenge to cultivate their intellect and participate fully in the development and regeneration of society, to aspire for the best and refuse to bow to the hedonism of men.

Another weakness of the Caliphate is to be found in the lack of leaders of a sufficiently high calibre. It does it no credit that only one Muhammad Bello was produced in a century. This failure betrays perhaps a fundamental weakness in the system of education or, alternatively, in the political structure. For Islam, which produced Usman, Abdullahi or Bello in the first instance, was quite capable of reproducing them whenever they were needed, if there were no inhibiting or intervening factors.

These weaknesses do not, however, detract from the fact that in many respects the Caliphate has provided worthy examples of statecraft or how best a polity can be preserved. For example, it maintained throughout a profound respect for upright scholars, whose advice it sought in important issues and to whom it turned for help in critical moments. Hajj Said wrote of Muhammad Bello: 'He spread knowledge amongst them [the people], and the learned of the land came to him from every direction. He regarded them with the eye of solicitude, looked on them with the eye of favour and was extremely kind to them. No learned man came to him from the east or west, north or south without his treating him generously, keeping him and refusing to part with him.' This remained an established convention in the Caliphate. Moreover, the state maintained faithfully its original commitment to women's education, and created the atmosphere, and security where necessary, in which women could receive knowledge.

Similarly, some of the caliphs showed examples of simplicity of life, self-discipline and love of justice worthy of emulation. According to Hajj Said, Caliph Abubakar Atiku said to his son on his death bed: 'Do not ask your mothers who are in my house for what I have left, for I have left nothing to be inherited, not even a needle.' Yet he ruled the wealthiest state in West Africa. 'He was pious, a lover of the virtuous, to whom he was a benefactor, a hater of wrongdoers against whom he was on guard, and with none of them he had any dealings... He did not fix his gaze on anyone's face out of respect for him.' Caliph Aliyu, in spite of the difficulties he faced during his administration, preserved the tradition of justice and piety. 'He did not', in the words of Hajj Said, 'leave off learning by night or day, excessively hated shedding blood and was on his guard against that. He only put to death him whom the law condemned, and he attained the highest degree of justice.'

In addition, the Caliphate showed conclusively that a viable nation can be created and defended without the need for a standing army. The Sokoto Caliphate grew into a regional power relying only on the strength of the conviction of its populace in Islam. All it did was to militarize the people, who then assumed responsibility in defending their state and ensuring the survival of their ideology. Without a standing army to consume its resources, the Caliphate was able to cater for the welfare of the people. In fact, Islamic civilization was originally established on the same pattern. It overcame well-entrenched powers, including the Roman and Persian empires, with fighters motivated only by their faith. Standing armies tend to degenerate into pseudo-mercenary forces, whose members fight only because they are paid, regardless of whether the cause for which they fight is just or otherwise.

On the whole, the strong points of the Caliphate can be said to far outweigh its weaknesses. For even though moral tensions created by human weaknesses could be felt throughout its history, the pulses of its strength were infinitely louder and more vigorous. The Caliphate's greatest strength lay firstly in its impressive commitment to upholding the *shari'a*, which in turn ensured its survival for a whole century; secondly, it lay in the staunch loyalty of the people to the institution of the caliph rather than to the individual holders of the office, a factor which in critical moments ensured the cohesion of the *umma*. Moreover, the Caliphate never lost sight of its ideals, especially those that emphasize that government must be run on the basis of consultation, or *shura*, and that the caliph must act within the *shari'a* if he was to be obeyed.

Yusuf's revolt of 1893, just ten years before the Caliphate fell to the forces of British imperialism, illustrates this fact quite graphically. When Emir Muhammad Bello died, the Caliph unilaterally appointed Tukur as his successor, without due consultation with the *ahli al-shura* in Kano, or even of his own people. The motive for this extraordinary action, which obviously was contrary to norms of the Caliphate, is unknown. His action sparked off a bloody revolt, headed by the contender Yusuf, who was the more acceptable candidate to the people of Kano. The Caliph, Abd ar-Rahman, tried in vain to mobilize the support of other emirs to crush the revolt, the emirs showing their disapproval by finding excuses for not fighting against Yusuf. One of them was said to have told the Caliph that there was no way he could fight fellow Muslims. The revolt gathered momentum, as Tukur's forces suffered defeat after defeat. Meanwhile Yusuf died, and his brother Ali took over the overall command. Eventually, he gained control over Kano city, causing Tukur to flee and his supporters to scatter in all directions. Tukur was later killed in an encounter with Ali's forces. Ali, now in power, sent a message to the Caliph, asking for pardon and to be accepted back into the fold. The Caliph obliged, and notified all the emirs that he had pardoned Emir Aliyu of Kano. Thus the crisis was resolved.[i]

i    For details see Said Halil, Revolution and Reaction: *The Fulami Jihad in Kano*

Prof. Abdullahi Smith's comments on this episode are pertinent: 'This is often cited [by colonial scholars] as an example of the general abandonment of effective allegiance to *Sarkin Musulmi* [or Caliph] which is said to characterise the period after 1881. In fact it appears to be sensational vindication of the ideal of government accepted by Shehu Usman in the face of an attempt to corrupt it by an inefficient Caliph.' Prof. Last pointed out that the dispute was fundamentally over succession, not over the legitimacy of the Caliphate.

In fact at no time in its history was the Caliphate's legitimacy ever challenged and, on the eve of the British invasion, it was not essentially a state in absolute decline. Prof. Adeleye observes that often 'the fall of a state can be rightly ascribed to disintegration and decline of various kinds within it. It is, however, clear that the Sokoto Caliphate in 1900 exhibited no such features in any marked form. Its machinery of government, far from having become rusty, was in good working order.' Adeleye adds: 'Rather than look for elements of decay to explain the fall, the historian must direct his attention to the fact that the Caliphate was caught in the strong current of a historical movement [the European imperial expansion in Africa] the source of which was outside its awareness, not to speak of its control.' Prof, Last advances a similar proposition in *The Sokoto Caliphate*:

> Clearly, the reforms did not cover all the Community; music and gambling, for example, continued despite disapproval. But so long as the *shari'a* was upheld, and the practice of the Caliphs and the court was Islamic, the framework was maintained for a society in which a man could not only be a good Muslim but could also call others to the Faith. It was for this that the Shaikh had fought the *jihad*; and for the pattern of this society he had looked to the classical Islamic texts in order to reproduce, as far as possible, an Islamic state... Throughout the century, then, the ideals, and to a large extent the practice, of Sokoto did not change. This was achieved

*and its Aftermath 1807-1919*. Ph.D. dissertation, Universiry of Michigan, 1978; R.A. Adeleye, *Power and Diplomacy in Northern Nigeria, 1804-1906*. Longman, 1977; and Murray Last, *The Sokoto Caliphate*.

because the Caliph and his court upheld the traditions of the Shaikh, and the Caliphate itself remained strong.

## And Behold, Darkness Fell

The whole saga of British occupation of the Caliphate requires an independent study from the Islamic viewpoint but, unfortunately, it is clearly outside the scope of the present work. However, for our purpose here, it is sufficient to say the occupation was carried out through a combination of fraud, treachery and massacre.

The application of the *shari'a* had safeguarded the sovereignty and integrity of the Caliphate in crucial situations, particularly the provisions that non-Muslim powers may not be given rights of ownership to any part of the territory of Islam, and that *aman* – the right to reside in the Islamic state for commercial or diplomatic purposes – may be granted to non-Muslims only on the condition that they will be governed by the *shari'a*. When Britain asked for ownership of land for the Royal Niger Company and requested that its citizens residing in the Caliphate be permitted to be governed by British laws rather than the *shari'a*, the Caliph refused. The *shari'a* proved to be the single most important obstacle to imperialism, perhaps explaining the universal opposition to it by those who have come to dread its potency. In addition, as the British themselves conceded, the moral authority of the caliph in Sokoto, more than his military might, posed a formidable obstacle to the designs of the Empire. It was clear that as long as Muslims applied the *shari'a* and were ruled by a caliph, imperialism would be kept at bay.

So Britain resorted to forging treaties of its own. In 1890 for example, a British trade delegation in Wurno could not see the Caliph after waiting for ten days. Meanwhile, some of its members had behaved improperly to Muslim women. The Caliph ordered the delegation to leave Wurno within twenty-four hours, although they were permitted to move on to Gwandu. Yet, despite this expulsion and the Caliph's unmistakable displeasure towards them, the delegation claimed that it had been able to secure treaties from Gwandu and Sokoto granting the Royal Niger Company some form of political concessions, which, above all, conflicted with the *shari'a.*[i] The treaties were, as Adeleye remarks, clearly forgeries. But it was precisely on the basis of such spurious documents that Britain declared its claim to the Caliphate and justified its wars of aggression. Even a committed imperialist like Hugh Johnston had to admit that the legal ground on which the British claimed the right to invade Sokoto 'was astonishingly tendentious'.[ii] The original decision to occupy the Caliphate had already been taken at the Berlin Conference of 1884 and, therefore, all the legal, political or historical reasons manufactured later to justify and rationalize the invasion must be regarded as fundamentally spurious. The Caliphate, disgusted by British treachery, broke off all relations with the Royal Niger Company. Caliph Abd al-Rahman wrote the following letter to Lugard:

> From us to you. Know that I do not consent to any of your people dwelling among us. I myself shall never be reconciled to you, nor shall I permit any further dealings with you. Henceforth there shall be no exchanges between us save those between Muslims and Unbelievers – Holy War as the Almighty has enjoined on us. There is neither authority nor power save in God on high.

It was a message, as Johnson aptly observes, containing a defiant grandeur of its own.

On March 15, 1903, Sokoto, the caliphal capital, fell to British troops. Fifty Muslims died heroically trying to keep the Caliphate's flag aloft. Caliph Muhammad Attahiru, who commanded the Muslim forces in person, thereupon embarked on the *hijra*, heading eastwards. All along his route the Caliph was joined by thousands upon thousands of Muslims of all classes. In some cities practically all able-bodied people, poor and rich, high and low, left

i   Adeleye, *Power amd Diplomacy in Northern Nigeria.*
ii  Says Johnston: 'In 1902 Lugard sought the advice of his Chief Justice on the validity of the treaties. He was advised that, under the third meeting, the Sultan had surrendered his independence and that, having done so, he had surrendered his power to repudiate the treaty, which was therefore still valid and binding. As it was very doubtful whether (Caliph) Abdu had even signed the treaty, which in any case made no mention of sovereignty or its surrender, this advice appears today to be astonishingly tendentious.' *The Fulani Empire of Sokoto*, p. 241.

their homes and property to answer the Caliph's call. The scale of movement of people was, as Adeleye remarks, unprecedented in the African encounter with imperialism. The colonial officer reported: 'Attahiru's following is immense, his people are said to take from sunrise to mid-day passing.' And: 'The *Sarkin Muslumi* has now many thousands of people with him. The whole population from Kano to the Gongola have joined him.' Reports continued to indicate the alarming proportion the *hijra* was taking, stating that to allow the Caliph to stay in one place for even one week would mean the entire population joining him *en masse*.

The British at last came to the realization that *hijra* was proving to be an even more potent threat to their occupation of the Caliphate than the *jihad*. So they decided to pursue the Caliph with the aim of liquidating him, conceding that Attahiru in exile was even more dangerous than Attahiru at home. Hence the Battle of Burmi, some six hundred miles from Sokoto on 27 July 1903. It was to be the last battle between the Caliphate and Britain. 'It was also the best organised,' writes Adeleye:

> The defenders of Burmi fought with determination and a ferocity which can only be ascribed to the zeal of Muslims fighting in *jihad*. In the face of heavy losses on their side and heavy firing from the British the defenders held out in their trenches where many of them were shot or bayonetted. Some advanced to meet the storming party of the British at the risk of certain death... Superior arms and ammunitions, rather than superior morale or even military strategy, explains the British victory.

The Caliph, who had been praying in the mosque, at last emerged. 'He was on foot, unarmed,' says Johnston, 'and his intention was not to fight but to go out and meet his fate... . Death came to him with merciful swiftness, for when he was within a stone's throw of the southern wall he was shot through the head. Two of his sons died by his side and ninety of his followers, showing the same devotion as the bodyguards of Hayatu and the Emir Zubeiru, chose to perish with him rather than save themselves in flight.'

## A Ray of Light in the Darkness

Meanwhile in Sokoto, the Muslims, under the *wazir* Muhammad Buhari, gathered together at Marnona to decide on a course of action. The *wazir* had no choice but to accept British rule, bitter and frustrating though it was. He also sought advice from the leading scholars in the Caliphate. And here again, as in all other crises and issues, the Caliphate took recourse to its roots and its imam: the *shari'a* and Shehu Usman Dan Fodio respectively. The result of consultations and deliberations was epitomized in the *Risala*,[i] or proclamation, which the *wazir* issued to the people at large.

The decision had been taken to abandon the idea of *hijra* 'owing to the scarcity of water along the roads, or the total lack of it along some of them, as well as the severity of heat and the presence of the Christians camped along all the routes'. Caliph Attahiru had earlier sent a message to Sokoto asking the people not to undertake the *hijra* any more, because the British had mounted blockades everywhere and were killing Muslims indiscriminately. The *wazir* stated that the writings of Shehu Usman had been consulted to find out precisely what attitude Muslims should take towards the Christian conquerors. The Shehu had said that it was forbidden in *shari'a* for Muslims to befriend and love unbelievers because they are unbelievers and because of their hatred for Islam and the Prophet ﷺ. The same applies to having relations with them 'as a means of acquiring the wealth in their hands'. But when Muslims are overpowered by unbelievers and are too weak to repel their aggression then it is permissible to have relations with them, 'with the tongue but not with the heart', until such a time as Muslims become strong again and can fight back. The *wazir* then wrote to the 'Chief of the Christians', Lugard, asking for assurances that the practice of Islam would not be impeded.

'I rode out and went to Sokoto,' the *wazir* revealed, 'fearing that they would oppose our religion, sway us from Islam and order us to adopt their religion. When I discussed with them, I heard from them a talk which did not bear on the prohibition of prayer, which

---

i    See generally, Adeleye, 'The dilemma of the *wazir*: the place of the *Risala al-Wazir ila Ahl al-Ilm wal-Tadabbur* in the history of the conquest of the Sokoto Caliphare,' *Journal of the Historical Society of Nigeria*, Vol. 14, No. 2, June, 1968.

is the greatest of the acts of worship, nor on the prohibition of the Ramadan fast, payment of *zakat* and going on pilgrimage to the Holy House.': 'However,' the *wazir* added, 'they were showing off their subjugation of Muslims and gloried in their conquest of them and in the greatness of their own power. They were ordering [the Muslims] to carry heavy things and to build houses here and there.'

But how did the *'ulama*, who symbolized the spirit of the *umma*, interpret the British occupation of the Caliphate? Ahmad Said, whose reply to the *wazir* is contained in the *Risala*, articulated their views: 'We have a precedent in what the unbelievers did with the Caliph of the Messenger of God in Baghdad. They burnt it (Baghdad), destroyed it, desecrated the graves of the saints, tore the community apart and killed the Caliph.... We have a precedent and a consolation in the Qarmatian unbeliever whom God granted the power (by means of his army), over Mecca on the Day of Sacrifice. Muslims were killed until the Holy Mosque was filled up with their corpses. ... Even the black Stone he took away with him. As God restored normalcy for the Muslims by the return of the Stone and the Khilafa [Caliphate] to them, so also do we hope that God will resolve this matter for us and grant us amelioration by His power and His grace... We show regard to them [the Colonial power] with the tongue and have intercourse with them in affairs of the world but never will we love them in our hearts and adopt their religion... But friendship with them in the sense of helping them in what the *shari'a* does not permit, such as fighting Muslims, destroying Mosques and raiding Muslims, is unbelief... The Islam of our land, and its being an Islamic country, are manifest and undoubted. Therefore, let us busy ourselves with planning the preservation of this Islam in our land until every village returns to its place and its mosque... Thus it may be that God will strengthen His religion by making them, through His power, go away from us... We hope that God will make us healthy and settle our affair for us as he did for our forefathers when He tested them and they were patient and repentant.'

Just ten years after the collapse of the Caliphate, in 1914, the British created the country called Nigeria, which incorporated the better part of the Caliphate. But barely forty-five years thereafter, the

British found that their rule had become untenable, having neither roots in the hearts of the people nor legitimacy. In 1960 they pulled down their flag and left, Once one of the most awesome powers in the world, the British Empire has now reverted to its original size as a tiny island in the Atlantic Ocean.

But Islam has survived. Its roots were too deep, too strong, for it to be obliterated from *Bilad al-Sudan.* This enigmatic spiritual power called Islam, this indelible print of Allah's mercy, this profound mover of human destiny, may yet provide a new impetus for the people of west Africa, for the community of the Shehu, and for Muslims at large to rise once more to glory and self-fulfilment. *'That is how Allah depicts the true and the false. As for the scum, it is quickly swept away. But as for that which is of use to people, it remains behind in the ground.'* (13:19)

# Glossary

adala: moral uprightness
ahl al-ikhtiyar: a form of privy council
ahl al-sunna: people of the Sunna, orthodox Muslims
aman: safe-conduct
amana: trust
Amir al-Muminin: Commander of the Faithful, the Caliph
amir: governor
amr bil ma'ruf: commanding what is right
asr: the afternoon prayer
bay'ah: pledge of allegiance
bayt-al-mal: state treasury
bughat: rebels
dar al- harb: domain of war
dar al-Islam: domain of Islam
dar al-Kufr: domain of disbelief
dhikr: invocation, remembrance of Allah
din: religion
du'a: supplication to Allah
fay': state owned spoils of war
fitna: civil strife
ghasb: extortion
ghusl: ritual purification of the whole body
hadd: prescribed punishment
hara'im: protected place
harim: harem
hijra: emigration
hima: land set aside for religious purposes
hisba: market inspection
hudud: legal limits, prescribed punishments
ihsan: kindness, excellent behaviour

**ijma'**: legal consensus
**ijtihad**: independent legal reasoning
**ilm al-kalam**: theology
**imara**: governorship
**isha**: the night prayer
**istighfar**: seeking forgiveness
**istihsan**: juristic preference for the good
**jahili**: ignorant, belonging to a time before Islam
**jama'a**: community, particularly the one formed by Shehu Usman
**jihad**: struggle, fighting in the path of Allah
**jizya**: annual tax paid by non-Muslims living under Muslim rule
**khalifa**: caliph
**kharaj**: land tax
**kufr**: unbelief
**mashwara**: consultation
**maslaha**: welfare, best interests
**muharibun**: robbers
**muhtasib**: upholder of public standards
**mujaddid**: renewer of Islam
**mujahid**: fighter of *jihad*
**mujtahid**: someone qualified to make independent legal judgements
**murid**: follower of a shaykh
**nasiha**: counsel
**nawafil**: voluntary acts of worship
**qadi**: judge
**qiyam al-layl**: standing at night in prayer
**radd al-mazalim**:
**rak'at**: one cycle of the prayer; each prayer consists of a number of *rak'at*s
**Rawda**: burial place of the Prophet ﷺ in Madina
**riba**: usurious commercial practices
**ribat**: frontier outpost
**Sahih**: sound, often referring to the hadith collections of Bukhari and Muslim
**salat al-Janaza**: funeral prayer
**salat al-duha**: a voluntary prayer during the morning
**salat al-Istikhara**: prayer seeking guidance

**salat al-Istisqa:** rain prayer
**salat al-Jumu'a:** the Friday midday congregational prayer
**salat al-Khawf:** the fear prayer
**salat al-Kusuf:** eclipse prayer
**salat:** ritual prayer
**shari'a:** Islamic law
**shura:** consultation, consultative body
**siyasa:** politics
**subh:** the dawn prayer
**sunna:** practice of the Prophet ﷺ
**Sura al-Fatiha:** the opening chapter of the Qur'an
**ta'lim:** teaching
**ta'zir(at):** offence(s) with no prescribed punishment
**tafsir:** Qur'anic commentary
**tahajjud:** prayer during the night
**tajdid:** renewal (of Islam)
**talaba:** student(s)
**taqwa:** active fear of Allah
**tarawih:** night prayers in Ramadan
**tarbiyya:** education, particularly religious education
**tawba:** repentance
**tawhid:** doctrine of Divine Unity
**tijara:** trade
**'ulama:** religious scholars
**umma:** the Muslim community
**'urf:** customary practice
**wali al-mazalim:** ombudsman, protector of the wronged
**wali al-radd:** appeal judge
**wazir:** chief administrator, advisor
**wizara:** ministry
**wudu:** ritual purification
**zakat:** obligatory poor due
**zuhr:** the midday prayer
**zulm:** injustice, oppression

www.ingramcontent.com/pod-product-compliance
Lightning Source LLC
Chambersburg PA
CBHW021228090426
42740CB00006B/428